nineteen seventy-nine

rhona cameron

nineteen seventy-nine

A Big Year in a Small Town

EBURY
PRESS

First published in Great Britain in 2003

10 9 8 7 6 5 4 3 2 1

Text © Rhona Cameron 2003

First published by
Ebury Press
Random House, 20 Vauxhall Bridge Road, London SW1V 2SA

Random House Australia (Pty) Limited
20 Alfred Street, Milsons Point, Sydney, New South Wales 2061, Australia

Random House New Zealand Limited
18 Poland Road, Glenfield, Auckland 10, New Zealand

Random House South Africa (Pty) Limited
Endulini, 5A Jubilee Road, Parktown 2193, South Africa

The Random House Group Limited Reg. No. 954009

www.randomhouse.co.uk

A CIP catalogue record for this book is available from the British Library.

Cover photo © Rhona Cameron 2003

Song lyrics reproduced by kind permission of EMI publishing.

'I'M NOT IN LOVE' Words and Music by Eric Stewart and Graham Gouldman
© 1975, Reproduced by permission of EMI Music Publishing Ltd, London WC2H 0QY

'THREE TIMES A LADY' Words and Music by Lionel Richie
© 1978, Jobete Music Co Inc/ Libren Music, USA
Reproduced by permission of Jobete Music Co Inc/
EMI Music Publishing Ltd, London WC2H 0QY.

Cover Design by Antigone Konstantinidou
Text design and typesetting by seagulls

ISBN 009189428X

For my mum and dad

GRATIANO

Let me play the fool:

With mirth and laughter let old wrinkles come,

And let my liver rather heat with wine,

Than my heart cool with mortifying groans.

Why should a man, whose blood is warm within,

Sit like his grandsire cut in alabaster?

Sleep when he wakes, and creep into the jaundice

By being peevish?

The Merchant of Venice, Act I, Scene I

acknowledgements

Firstly, thanks to my editor, Jake, for his huge leap of faith. And for making me a marvellous compilation tape.

To Jerry, my manager, the funniest man in the world, whom I love with all my heart. To Sarah and Julie Dalkin. To everyone at Ebury.

To my Auntie Ella and Uncle Joe for always saying that they're there if I need them.

To S. Lucas of Musselburgh, for making the best ice cream and the best homemade soup known to humankind.

To my English teacher, Alison, for taking extra time to encourage my talents.

To the memory of my art teacher, Ian Patterson, whom I let down so badly.

To Joyce, for being there.

To Grace, for holding my hand.

Thanks to Barbara, for her love and friendship, and my dear Naomi, who's like me round the knees.

To my Auntie Rona, for being such a tower of strength to Mum and me when it mattered.

To my dear mum, for her love, her strength, her positivity, and her entrepreneurial spirit, which took us to Venice and Rome in the years that followed, to enable me to see great works of art and beauty.

But most of all, Mum, thanks for your coconut sponge!

And a very special thanks to Sue, for always being there for me, whose support, help and encouragement got me through this.

Thanks to Pickle the dog for being such a little ray of sunshine, and cheering me up.

And thank God for football!

And Jerry, the CD …

prologue

When I was seven years old, my parents and I moved house. Up until then, we lived in a ground-floor flat in Grindley Street in Edinburgh, opposite the Lyceum Theatre. My grandmother lived opposite, in a flat with my grandfather and her brother. She played a hugely important part in my upbringing, almost on a daily basis. It was through her I learnt about older people, the generation that lived through the war. My parents moved to Grindley Street shortly after they were married, on the day of my father's 30th birthday. My dad's family had lived in the street for many years, and my parents had met through being members of the same church, St Columbus Episcopalian Church, by Edinburgh Castle.

It was through the church that my parents arranged the private adoption of me, a few years after the death at birth of their baby. I was born in an unmarried mothers' home in Dundee, in September 1965, and two months later taken to Edinburgh to live with William and Jean Campbell. They named me Rhona, after my mum's Welsh cousin, Rona Mann, who became my godmother (sadly she died in childbirth when I was six), and my mum's best friend Rona McIntyre. My dad worked locally as a mechanic, and my mum was a secretary. On my sixth birthday, I got a dog called Hector, who I named after *Hector's House*. He was a West Highland terrier, and arrived in a cardboard box. He was the final addition to the family.

In 1972, we fell victim to a spate of burglaries that left my mother distraught and our home vandalised. I had also taken to meandering up and down the street (it was safe in those days) singing 'I Was Born Under A Wandering Star'. One day, I disappeared, and was discovered hours later in the gutter under a car, concussed from falling off my tricycle and banging my head on the bumper.

My parents decided it was time to leave Edinburgh and move out to the country.

We bought a brand new Wimpey house, not even built yet, on a new estate in a picturesque fishing and mining town seven miles outside Edinburgh called Musselburgh. Musselburgh is a small town, where most men are called Jim, John, or Davey. There is one local secondary school, Musselburgh Grammar (although it hasn't been a grammar school since the war), which I attended from 1977 (the day after Elvis died) until 1983. Catholics went to a different secondary school a four-mile bus journey away. There were a handful of primary schools, half a dozen places of worship, and countless pubs.

Musselburgh is a place steeped in its traditions and its ties to the fisher folk. Each summer events would take place, like the

Fisherman's Walk, an old celebration where the town people walk along with banners and pipe bands play. Everyone dressed in traditional fisher-folk attire, celebrating their history. Musselburgh is also famous for its golf (boasting the first golf course in the world), its horseracing and its rugby.

It was at the edge of the rugby pitch where we lived for four months in our caravan while our house was being built. We moved there in the middle of a builders' strike. I knocked myself unconscious again, while swinging on a towel rail in the site toilets, and was hospitalised for the night. After this, we were allowed to use the bathroom facilities in our new house, but still forced to live in the caravan, which was parked in the driveway for a while. We were one of the first families on our housing estate. I remember playing and exploring in the shells of the other houses, which were to become homes for many of the characters in this book.

Musselburgh is a beautiful place, and I was lucky enough to play outdoors my entire childhood. It had a long beach, a harbour, woods, golden hayfields that overlooked our estate, and plenty of places to explore and imagine all sorts of mysterious things were occurring.

I was always a creative child with a wild imagination. I liked to draw, and write, and read, and play sport. Nothing else at school interested me. I won various essay prizes, my first at the age of eleven when I wrote 'The Day I Got My Hair Cut', about a dog's view of the world. Always an outsider looking in, I felt comforted by making things up.

When we moved into our new house, my mother told me in the nicest way possible about my adoption. This stunned and shocked me, and confirmed an oddness about myself I had always felt.

At thirteen I acquired an American pen pal through my old primary school teacher Lawrence, a huge, vibrant influence on my life. For my birthday that year, in 1978, Pam, my pen pal in Boston, sent me a diary. On the cover was a young woman in a long flowing dress, with one high-heeled sandal on and the other kicked off, which I took to mean she was so engrossed in the writing of her diary she didn't notice.

Next to her is written 'Dear Diary …' in old-fashioned letters. It was my first diary, and what's more it had a lock on it.

The first thing I did was to write in the sleeve:

Private and Confidential. What is written in this diary is the whole truth and the way I feel on occasions in life.

On the next page, my pen pal had placed a sticker of a setting sun, with 'There's a miracle inside you!' written in curly letters. I wrote 'Too right, mate!' next to it.

On the first page I wrote:

Take Every Day As It Comes.

And next to it I began the first official diary entry of my life. I did not write the diary continually. There were weeks, even months, when I didn't write it at all. I think I mainly turned to it when I was lonely, or angry – feelings which increased from the age of eleven onwards. My last entry was August 1981 at the age of fifteen and a half. I had started drinking around this time and perhaps used that as an escape instead.

When I left home at eighteen, I took this diary and all my other notebooks with me. Despite the unstructured and drunken way I lived as a young adult, I managed to keep them safe in a box. Call it a mid-life crisis if you like, but at the end of last summer I began looking at the diary again, fascinated at the way I had, or sometimes hadn't, evolved.

I decided that 1979 was a pivotal year in my life. Up until then I had marked out my life like this:

Born, adopted 1965

Moved to Musselburgh 1972

Elvis died 1977

Then 1979, the year that changed my life for ever

I remember an awful lot. More than most people. I could even tell you what we all wore to school. I always watched people, and obsessed about what it would be like to be them and not me. I felt so different, because I was adopted, because I thought I might be gay, because I was an only child with older parents. Just different. There is nothing like life in a small town to highlight differences.

Last Christmas Eve, I went to a local pub in Musselburgh – something I have never done at such a time – with an old school friend who was also in town for Christmas. In the pub were many boys I had gone to school with. I told one that I remembered sitting next to him in class when we were eleven. He had a vague recollection of it. I also told him I remembered how our pioneering teacher, just back from the States, introduced us to enamelling. This he couldn't remember. Then I went on to describe the piece of metal he enamelled. I knew everything about it. The fact it was square, that it had a white H in the middle because he supported Heart of Midlothian, and how he had to settle for a red background because he couldn't make maroon. This disturbed him.

'That's a bit sad, isn't it?' he joked as he made his way to the bar.

Yes, I thought, it is. And that, I guess, is me. A bit sad with a great memory for bizarre detail.

I have put my diary entries in the book exactly as they appeared in the diary itself. I have, for reasons of privacy, changed all the names of the characters in this book. Though all the events are true, I may have, for structural reasons, changed the time frame on occasions. Something that happened in June may have had to move to July, for example, but almost everything is reported as it happened.

I stopped drinking in order to write the book, and that added to me feeling as young as I did in the book, while writing it. I also made various trips back to my mum's in Musselburgh to work on it, as well as a visit to school. None of it seemed long ago. I've never let go of it.

one
january

nine minutes to twelve on New Year's Eve 1978 and I'm leaning against the radiator in my bedroom with my head out of the window. For dramatic effect, I'm taking in exaggeratedly bracing gulps of East Lothian air. I'm watching the stars, mentally preparing myself for a new year and a new start. I'm going to be strong, and I'm going to be better. I am totally focused on turning over a new leaf. It is my last chance to redeem myself.

I am thirteen.

Aside from the stars, clear in a navy-blue sky, all I can see is the snow. Good, clean, crisp and criss-crossed from perpetual sledging. In 1979, snow was still liable to fall right through the winter. And thank God it did. For three dark months of the year it was just about all we had. There was no cinema. The boys had relentlessly turned up for

every film and thrown bottles at the screen until it was too tattered
to see anything projected on it. There was no dancing. The youth
disco that Chick Rankin had set up to combat glue sniffing was
closed, due to excessive fighting between second-generation mods
and rockers – and generally more glue sniffing.

You could get a drink at the Miners Arms, provided you had big
tits and wore blusher. But for those drinkers without adequate breasts
and make-up skills, the only other option was to drink cider and pop
aspirin under the Roman Bridge. However, the vicious Scottish frosts
could put paid to that behaviour by as early as mid-October.

Sledging was quite welcome for me because it took sex off the
agenda. As a child, all sexual activity took place outside. So the arrival
of snow meant that, happily, sex could be replaced by winter sports.
Snowball fights and hazardous icy gauntlets on the well-polished teachers' walkway that led from the school car park – all that was just fine by
me. It gave me a break from the usual. For come summer or winter,
I hated the whole sex thing. For me it was nothing to do with lust,
desire, physical drive or romance. Or experimentation (unless I was
experimenting with misery). It was all about pressure and fitting in –
part bargaining, part fear of losing whoever was interested in me at the
time, part living in pointless hope that it might lead to a boy holding
my hand, or wanting to take me to the school Christmas disco, where
we'd romantically kiss beneath the mistletoe held over our heads.

But all the fingering was in vain. By the age of twelve, I was officially a slag, a cow, and a whore. I couldn't fucking win. This was my
lot and it was all my fault. I gave it all up to them too early, because
that's what they wanted – and in my naïve logic I thought if I did
what they wanted they would like me for it. But instead they hated

me. They preferred the girls that gave them nothing: the silent, beautiful, boring girls, who wouldn't let them touch them for another four years. They waited patiently and respectfully, doing all the mistletoe, hand-holding, Valentine stuff with them until they finally gave way. Meanwhile, they passed the time with me.

And while I longed for the things the boys would never give me, I had other longings too – a desire, and the painful, hopeless pursuit of it, that dominated my life. This was the only thing on my mind tonight. No longer would I be obsessed with girls.

DATE: 31 December   *DAY: Sunday*
The below statement is a solemn promise. I am entering this in my diary at 11.51pm. Nine minutes before 1979. I want to forget the past and live in the present and the future. I no longer am the past Rhona Campbell because I am hopefully going to leave her at twelve o'clock. I dread school but I am going to try and forget Alison Calder as she hates me. I am going to be more refined, calm, cool, obedient and all the other things that make a respectable human being. Amen.

So, I was going to turn over a new leaf and become a reborn daughter and pupil. There'd be more tidying of my room, more diligence at school, more application to the chores, more churchgoing, more going anywhere and doing anything that would make me happy, healthy and respectful. Respectful. It was a word of immense importance to my father and one that I never really understood. But now I would learn it. I was set. Fewer tantrums. Fewer breakages. And an end to all compulsions.

And Alison Calder. Yes, I was going to straighten up and become a good girl in a sexual sense too. So no more fixating on Farrah Fawcett-Majors.

The way I saw it, being obsessed with girls was a bit like a disease, and the cure was surely to try and fancy boys. And with this new calm, cool, refined personality I was about to acquire in the next eleven minutes, they'd most likely start fancying me back. I couldn't wait for my new life. I would appear less desperate, more restrained, aloof – enigmatic even. At the very least alluringly mysterious. All I had to do was make some major personality adjustments and basically become not at all like myself. And besides, girls would like me more that way.

Delighted with my new resolve, and proud of the fact that I now possessed the self-knowledge to improve my life, both practically and romantically, I headed downstairs to see in the New Year with my parents – and Hector the dog.

Drinking wasn't a big thing in our family, but at New Year one of the traditions of first footing involves accepting a drink from the bottle of every neighbour who calls, and reciprocating by offering them some of your own, so, for the first time since last Hogmanay, the booze cupboard was open.

Standing in the middle of the lounge, our various glasses filled with our various drinks, we look at the television, and wait for the Alexander Brothers to tell us it's 1979 and that they hope it's going to be a happy one. They do and we cheer, clink glasses, and say all the best to one another. My mum goes off to phone my gran, and my dad and I joke about the Alexander Brothers.

Looking around at our lounge, I can see that it suffers from an absence of smoked glass, which at the time I felt represented style, sophistication and modern-day living. Jamie Ritchie's lounge was riddled with it: around the stereo, on the sliding doors that separated the kitchen from the lounge, and (the ultimate in pure class) round the mini-bar area in the corner. The smoked glass that surrounded the Ritchies' mini-bar was what I aspired to. No chance of that in our house. I'd pleaded with my mum on many occasions, but she thought of the glass as ugly! (And was puzzled as to why I was so interested in home furnishings at the age of thirteen.)

The three of us are not saying much. Mum and Dad, fixed on the TV. Me all caught up with my resolutions. My strict new protocol. I will have to concentrate at all times.

I am allowed some Advocaat and my father sips from his can of Tennent's, which bears a picture of a half-naked woman with her name printed above it. We didn't often drink wine in our family, because that was quite trendy. Wine was just something you got in church. But for about a year, we had had in our lives a bizarre box of really shit red wine that lived in my mum's wardrobe. Uncle Alec had acquired it under circumstances which were never revealed to me, but which caused much grown-up hilarity whenever the box appeared. Tonight was maybe its third or fourth appearance, and the only thing that stopped you from retching as its contents reached your nose was the addition of copious amounts of lemonade. By the time the box was half empty – five years later – it could only be drunk with ten parts lemonade to one of wine. It never occurred to anyone that it might be a good thing to just pour it down the sink.

So here we are – part-time drinkers huddled together, shit

Scottish New Year's Eve celebrations on TV – in that kind of family group and doing those family things that an adolescent finds so comforting and familiar.

And then, of course, there's a knock at the door. It's the first of the first footers. It's Jamie Ritchie and a bunch of his mates.

The Wolf Gang. And the Wolf Boy King.

Suddenly, I am beyond embarrassed and bordering on ashamed.

As Jamie steps in, the house suddenly seems tinier. My parents morph from being comforting to looking entirely ludicrous. Even the dog takes on a new persona, as if he might start shagging someone's leg at any moment. And Jamie Ritchie stands in my hallway, which is too small for any number greater than two, with a can under each arm, his jacket sleeves rolled up over his bare olive arms and a smirk that lets me know he has my number down totally.

f or Jamie Ritchie is the boy. The boy I believe I should try to fancy. The boy who I want to fancy me. The boy I maybe do fancy a little. And hate myself for doing so. The boy who occasionally behaves as if he could fancy me. The boy who torments me, the boy who abuses me and humiliates me. The boy who protects me from the others.

In short, the boy I want to be.

k ing Jamie Ritchie. Always living life two years ahead of the rest of us. So sexually prolific. So tough. He had started at Campie Primary School a year after me, although he was the same age, and immediately became a big presence. He was terrific at football and basketball. He was the hardest fighter and the greatest lover (or at least he gave that impression). He had the best sledge and was naturally a brilliant sledger. He had a Chopper bike on which he could do wheelies, all the way down the street. He had cow-bar handles on a spare bike. He had a great body. Tight. Muscled. He had cut-off denim jeans. He'd either just stepped out of *West Side Story* or walked off the set of *Grease*. He had a leather jacket, just like The Fonz's. He had messy unstructured seventies-style hair. Even his parents were good-looking. They were the only people I knew who went abroad for holidays – Benidorm every year. His mum looked half-Spanish or something, and his father was very Scottish, and somehow they seemed to be younger than everyone else's parents. Even from the age of eleven all the girls just wanted him. He truly was a very beautiful boy.

But he was an absolute fucking cunt. A nutcase. He made my life hell. Yet I would have done anything he asked of me.

jamie offers my father a can of lager, called Linda. My father says he's OK, halfway through a Sheena. My mother offers up a huge slab of 'black bun', rich Scottish fruitcake traditionally only eaten on New Year's Eve. This just confirms my belief that I will never be cool, unlike Jamie. Out with the boys, at thirteen.

At this point, I want to disown my dog, my parents, the black bun, our fucking house and everything in it.

'How you doin', Mr Campbell, alright aye?'

I'm mortified as the exchange begins.

'Yes, not bad, thanks, erm …' Dad, being a typical dad, loses track of who anyone is, and looks at me for help.

'Jamie,' I mumble, sipping more stupid, childish dessert-like Advocaat.

'How's your mum and dad doing, Jamie?' Mum asks. Dad looks puzzled.

'Nancy and Jamie.' Mum helps Dad out on the names front.

'No bad, thanks,' says Jamie, completely unaffected by the pointless, moronic fucking dialogue that just can't go on. I sense meantime my mum has perked up. Maybe she fancies Jamie. She may as well. Everyone always does.

amie was an object of envy for me from day one. He quickly established himself as a leader even at the age of nine. He founded The Wolf Gang, all Rangers fans, all dressed in blue tops, riding around on their Choppers doing this stupid howl thing with a laugh at the end of it. As 'Wolf Leader', in the summer Jamie carried around in his shorts a totemic, miniature wooden Viking axe, which his Orange-Lodge-attending father had made for him. And on a daily basis he used it to beat the shit out of Andrew McCarthy on the grounds that he (McCarthy) had an Irish dad and supported Celtic.

He would often beat the shit out of me too. Not so often with his fists as with his vicious tongue – although on more than one occasion I had been on the end of his traditional challenge to mortal combat after school on the fields by the Westholme Housing Estate.

'You die. Tomorrow. Half-three. At the Westies.'

In Musselburgh, if you were challenged to a fight by someone in such a way, not to turn up was unheard of. It would be like a Premiership football club just refusing to play a fixture. Not only would the other team win by default, but the humiliation would be devastating. And of course the spectators would be vociferous in their outrage. Which is what would happen after school at the Westies. News would travel that a challenge had been issued and you had no choice but to show up. When school finished a mob would be waiting outside to physically take you there. There was just no reasoning with them. Fighting was usually a same-sex activity, but the rules were bent slightly for me. I think it was at this point it started to dawn on me that perhaps I wasn't really being treated like a girl, for one afternoon, at the age of ten, and for no apparent reason, Jamie Ritchie challenged me to my first fight.

Terrified at the thought of receiving a permanent scar on my iris, like Graham Baird, Jamie's last conquest, I tried during the course of that afternoon to distract him with mindless and largely arse-licking conversation.

'So that garage door. The purple one. Is that yours, Jamie?' I simpered.

'Aye, what if it is? You still die.'

'Do you like The Bay City Rollers, then, Jamie?'

'They're a'right. And you still die at half-three at the Westies.'

And so there I stood, hemmed in by a crowd of Wolves, and those who just wanted to see my nose bleed. The crowd moved me forward. The crowd moved him forward. I was so dead. There was no way I could take Jamie. Nobody in Musselburgh could. Except Stuart Menzies, a Grade A lunatic of the highest order, who was now in secondary school. Seconds before battle commenced, while Jamie was pushing me off balance slightly with his shoulder from the pressure of his side of the crowd and I was imagining both irises scarred for ever, a miracle occurred. Ms Millar, an attractive dark-haired teacher who wore a lot of suede, spotted the crowd from the back gates and shouted for us to disband.

'Who is fighting?' she shouted.

Silence. Nobody would dare grass to a teacher. That was something you really wouldn't crawl back from. Though I did want to speak. I wanted to grass. In a Wilson from *Dad's Army*-type way.

'You see, Ms Millar, I really have no interest in fighting and it would be terribly nice if we could all just go home.'

Ms Millar moved us on. The crowd split into almost perfect quarters, and dispersed.

It was King Jamie's tongue, though, that did most of the damage. I hadn't known him more than a month when I'd turned up at school and naïvely told everyone that I'd just found out I was adopted. Later in the day, our class assignment was to read out a diary of what had happened to us at the weekend. Mine included the information that I had been to stay with my cousins. When I returned to my seat, Jamie leaned across and, just loud enough for most of the room to hear, said, 'I didn't know bastards had cousins.'

And at the same time as inflicting all manner of physical and mental acts of bullying against me, I would allow Jamie Ritchie to touch my tits and kiss me whenever he fancied. And whatever else he fancied. And whoever else he allowed to fancy me.

On a Thursday night, youth club night, something I would look forward to because we'd play spirits and I'd get to hold hands with Marion Foster, he would request a fingering down the railway. He would bring his Wolf Gang along and I would be there, five or six boys all waiting in a line to do what they wanted. The golden embankments were floodlit from the rugby pitch at the edge of the youth club, so the queue would be formed lying down – that way we wouldn't draw any adult attention to ourselves. I wanted them to promise not to tell anyone but it was far too late for that. Jamie was already calling me Mrs Cow. To him this was another way of calling me a slag, but it also happened to be the name of my gran's neighbour, which was confusing. My status had been confirmed on a class outing to another secondary school. As we'd all walked from the gates, an older boy I'd never seen before shouted, 'Mrs Cow.' Future looks bright, I remember thinking.

I am eleven or maybe twelve, sitting in my house. There's a knock at the door. It is Kev Moffat, a quiet, fairly sensitive boy – but also Jamie's chief henchman and, as such, top of the list for Thursday night fingering privileges. He has a summons for me.

'Jamie wants to see you in the gang hut.'

Of course, I drop whatever I am doing – essentially a whole bunch of nothing – and head down to the gang hut. It is one of many huts I will visit over the years. Always an old car seat. A scrap of carpet. A sheet of corrugated iron for a roof. And a few pieces of pornography.

Kev and I don't exchange words on the way. He just escorts me to the spot on the railway. I've been here a million times before, but usually in a group. Eventually I come upon the Wolf Boy King, lounging against a tree, his Chopper leaning on the corrugated iron 'den'. He challenges me.

'Look – d'ye wanna huv sex or nuh?'

Kevin leaves us to it. Whatever 'it' is. And I sense 'it' is IT.

'Huh!'

'D'ye want to huv it or nuh?' As if he's just offered me one of the least interesting Liquorice Allsorts in the box.

'Well, em, I don't think so.' I think about church, pregnancy, girls, adoption. How much I love the Guides.

'Ye havnae got yer period yet, huv ye?' His voice becomes softer in an attempt to be persuasive.

'Nuh.'

'Well, then, ye cannae get pregnant, cun ye?'

'Nuh.'

And that's it. I agree. By that last singular No. Miserable, guilty, and half in a trance, I finally agree to 'spread the legs'.

'Take yer clothes off,' he orders. 'I'll be back in a minute.'

Where is he going? What is there to do?

I lie on the sloped ground, naked, and wait for him to return. Bits of gravel and the detritus of a hundred 'Wolf Gang' gatherings are sticking to my arse.

He is gone for a while. For maybe ten minutes, he leaves me there contemplating the rocks under my bottom.

He returns. I watch him take off his T-shirt. His breath smells of cigarettes and Polos. His hair smells of railway grass. His mouth is small and his kissing is warm and boring.

For about two minutes he lies on top of me. He doesn't hold me, he doesn't touch me and he certainly doesn't penetrate me. There is no movement of any kind. I lie under him, not touching him, not moving, and vaguely wondering how long this sex business is supposed to take. After a couple of minutes of lying on top of me, he suddenly says, 'Right, that'll dae.' And leaves.

I go home and carry on doing nothing.

I wasn't always summoned. I often went to the hut of my own accord. I would hang around the headquarters trying to follow the intricate and arbitrary rules that Jamie had dictated. You had to stick to them without question or you weren't allowed the privilege of sitting on one of the old car seats.

Of course I always failed to keep up with the ever-changing code and inevitably did something wrong. I might be punished by having my top stripped off, being tied to a tree, or getting whipped with a big branch that Jamie had whittled with his penknife – the one with 'Benidorm' carved on the handle. Which I suppose is something some women might have liked.

Or we could be mucking about just outside Musselburgh, a bit further down the coast, when some of the gang would decide it would be a good idea to strip off my top, drag me over the shale on Portobello beach, then throw me in the sea.

But I would always go back for more. If we were quite some way from home and it was getting late, Jamie would sometimes give me a lift back on his Chopper. The glory! Just to be able to be on the back of Jamie Ritchie's bike was enough to wipe the slate clean for all the horrors he had previously inflicted. Of course he would never say in front of everyone else, 'A'right Rhona, I'll give you a lift home.' Rather, I would start off walking while he cycled away at walking speed, then once everyone else was out of sight he'd do this thing with his eyes. Like a half wink, and then a casual nod of his head to the back of the bike.

I remember one famous day I was so excited. I was on the back of Jamie Ritchie's bike. It was boiling, the sky was blue and the air was very clear. He had on only a pair of cut-down Lee jeans and a pair of trainers. His naked back was so brown and so muscular. He had a mini transistor radio taped to his crossbar and we set off to Roxy Music singing 'Dance Away The Heartache', with my hands on his hips, Jamie moving up and down with the pedalling. For a happy fifteen minutes I felt what it must be like to be Carol Cowan, the most popular girl in my year. All the boys loved her, in particular Jamie.

He dropped me off at my house and came in for a while. I still have pictures of us there. For the first time in my life it was almost like being his girlfriend, Jamie twinkling at the camera, his hand on my leg, or arm around my shoulder. And me so happy to be wallowing in the affection which he only ever showed me when we were alone.

and now we're alone again on New Year's Eve. He's done the nod and the wink thing to me and we're out round the back of the house, him swigging from his can, me trying to be sophisticated with my five-year-old table wine and Bon Accord lemonade. I hadn't seen much of him lately. He'd become so legendarily sexually active that he'd had no time to torment me. There were rumours of condoms as bookmarks in his returned library books. Big conferences with his parents and the teachers.

We snog and he is gone. I have no idea where: perhaps he has other girls dotted around Musselburgh he has to go and humiliate.

King Jamie Ritchie. With all that he had going for him, I have to say he was always a lousy kisser.

DATE: 1 January   DAY: *Monday*

This year Christmas has been very dull. Before, when I was friends with Alison, I was the happiest person in town and I wanted to be with everyone and have fun. I had lots of friends and everything was fine but then Alison wouldn't listen to me so I had to turn to other friends. At least that's what I called them. They spread it about and Alison got called names as well, but I took the most. Finally I knew it would happen the day after school we met and she said, 'Don't go in a huff, but I don't want anything to do with you.' And I asked her if she hated me and she said 'yes'. After that I begged her to come back but she said 'no'. I drank and drank and grew grumpy and bad tempered and sad. And now I just want to be on my own, so you see last year was hell.

DATE: 2 January   DAY: *Tuesday*

Today I decided to go to see Alison, but instead I played all day on Gibson's sledge and he always seemed to favour me in what he said. I could imagine Valerie turned green. I fancy Gibson. Later my mum came down to ask if I wanted

21

to throw a party, so I said yes. Colin, Michael, Valerie,
Alan, Karen, Gibson and Alistair came and it turned out to
be a success.

On New Year's Day, I went down to the self-assembly shed at the bottom of the garden. There I performed the same ritual that I did every morning of my life. First I would hoist a badly made Union Jack on a piece of string, then play 'Taps' on my mouth organ, then beat a military tattoo on a perforated old drum Uncle Hebbie had brought back from the First World War. He had taught me to play it only a little bit, but I thought it very important to incorporate both harmonica and percussion in my opening and closing ceremonies. Finally there would then be a lengthy salute and a minute or two of silence for the Queen. Only then was I able to go about the important business of *a)* maintaining my Fact Files, *b)* staring out of the window, *c)* talking to myself, *d)* playing *Elvis in Concert* on a battery-driven Hitachi tape recorder and *e)* masturbating.

I didn't just masturbate in the shed. I did it anywhere and everywhere. I was an obsessive masturbator, like a boy in that respect – at least, I suppose. I did it in the back of the car on trips out to see relatives, in between classes at school, in front of the TV when my parents were out of the room. But most of all, I did it in the shed on my broken swivelling office chair, underneath the shelf of Secret Seven books surrounded by posters of Lee Majors, Starsky and Hutch, John Travolta, Bruce Lee and Roger Moore.

I never had any particular masturbatory fantasies to accompany my compulsion. There were no images in my head. And I certainly never fantasised about girls ever. Which was odd. Because for the rest of the time I was wholly and compulsively obsessed with them to the point where it became almost an illness.

Of course, it was important I kept all the girls I knew under surveillance and maintained dossiers on them all. Or 'Fact Files', as I labelled them.

FACT FILE 1

SUBJECT:	ALISON CALDER
AGE:	13
HAIR:	BLONDE
EYES:	BLUE
FAMILY:	FATHER – HAULAGE CONTRACTOR. 2 LORRIES
	MOTHER – HOUSEWIFE
CAR:	SILVER MERCEDES
REGISTRATION:	INL 5RS
ACTIVITIES:	GIRL GUIDES
	BASKETBALL
	RUNNING TIP OF TONGUE PROVOCATIVELY
	OVER BRACES
ADDRESS:	23 NEWCRATHIAN ROAD
PHONE NO:	645 2513
MOVES:	MONDAY. 3.45PM. MOTHER PICKED HER UP
	AND TOOK HER HOME
	5PM. MOTHER DROVE HER TO GIRL GUIDES
	7PM. MOTHER TOOK HER HOME
	8PM. WAS IN KITCHEN MAKING TOAST
	9PM. MAY HAVE BEEN IN HER BEDROOM
	P.T.O.

Lanky, gangling, gawky Alison Calder with her cheesecloth shirts, her long blonde hair and blue eyes. Why was I so fixated on her? She was entirely lacking in personality. She wasn't an obvious beauty. Not like Carol Cowan, who clearly resembled a young Natalie Wood. But I thought Alison was beautiful for a long time. I wasn't even put off by the fact she had a mouth more full of brace than teeth, and a permanent slightly startled look.

Because her dad was quite rich with his two-truck haulage business and property investments, there was a unique air of wealth about Alison Calder. Matching pencils and rubbers in her pencil case, expensive hairdressing and jewellery that looked like it may have been real silver. The whole family – there were two younger sisters – had that sheen of the well fed and the well groomed. They rode around in a silver Mercedes. And they looked like the car had been built for them.

I'd met Alison when I started secondary school at the age of twelve. Immediately, I decided she would be my friend. I wormed my way in – and within hours was smitten enough to be running after her mother's car trying to follow her home. Futile. She lived miles away. I did finally track it down, a big, white, strange house at Newcraithian Road, over the old railway bridge. My periods started while I was crossing that bridge after a night of stalking Alison. At the time, I was convinced it was some sort of retribution from above.

That entire winter was taken up with keeping Alison Calder under surveillance. I very quickly learnt her moves. She was totally reliant on her mother's transport, and I used to ride down to wherever she was going in order to arrive a little while before they did. It would start with leaving school. Every day she'd get picked up in the same place at the same time in the silver Mercedes, and I would get on my bike and pedal like hell to try and get ahead so I could catch a glimpse, even if it was only for a second or two at traffic lights.

On Mondays she went to Girl Guides, a different night from me, so I would go down on my bike and stand outside shivering, trying to peer through the frosted windows of the hall. Shortly before I knew she was to be picked up I would cycle as fast as I could – often in a blizzard – back over the Roman Bridge to the other end of town and wait for her there.

There was a bowling green to the left of their house, and a small clubhouse which overlooked Alison's bedroom. I would clamber up the side of this hut and lie on the slanting, snow-packed roof with my parents' racing binoculars, spying on her for hours at a time. When the bowling season started and I had to stop, I was really pissed off.

The snow was perfect spying-on-Alison weather. The landscape was quiet and soft, and this made it easy for me to track her every move. Moves which were fairly limited, given how cold it was. She would mostly stay in.

As futile exercises go it was right up there as possibly the most pointless of them all. One night, I wasted hours and hours, shivering with the cold, sweating with the fear and anticipation, binoculars practically frozen to the sockets of my eyes. And for very little reward. I saw the car arrive. Alison got out and went into the house. That was it. (I considered myself lucky if I managed to glimpse a vague Alison-shaped silhouette through the heavy brocade curtains. Once in about 30 times I would see her cross the landing window for a second.)

Then, suddenly, someone left the house and drove off in the silver Mercedes. As the car turned around in the vast drive, the headlights lit up the bowling club roof. I shat myself, because I could easily be seen and there was no valid reason on God's earth why I should be so far from home at night, on the roof of the bowling club, with a pair of binoculars. It was definitely not something that could be carried off with a casual wave and a 'Hi, how are you doing?'

So, holding the binoculars slightly aloft so that they wouldn't get wet, I slid down the roof on my stomach until I was out of sight, praying that my frozen feet would find the guttering which would halt my sliding progress and prevent me from ending up in a heap on the pathway below.

I was never caught. In all the time I was stalking Alison, I never once got found out. I must have been very good at it.

Even though she was oblivious to the surveillance, Alison Calder knew I was obsessed with her – but she put up with it like the rest of them. She'd come to the house when I asked her to, and after I'd sat and stared at her nervously for ten minutes she'd say, 'Why do you want me here?' I would carry on staring and wait for some sort of inspiration or intervention from someone. God knows who. Elvis maybe. This was my history with girls. My 'girl friends'. Although I could never really be any of their friends because I wasn't girlie, I didn't chat about boys, I didn't fix my hair and take advice on foundation techniques and when I thought you weren't looking I stared at you weirdly. But I must have been entertaining and alluring to some degree, because these girls – and there were quite a few – seemed happy to come whenever I asked them over.

With Alison I had tried to take things a step further, firstly telling her how I felt and then by making some sort of pass at her. In other words, I touched her leg. She had got all panicky and scurried off. I remember thinking, Well, what the fuck do you keep coming around for, then? My diary for December 1978 deals with the aftermath of this moment.

DATE: 22 December   *DAY: Friday*

This was a memorable day. It was the last day of term. I woke up with a head like a steel box. I walked to school and decided to skive it by going a walk in the graveyard. It was a cold foggy morning and the graveyard quiet and undisturbed suited the somewhat gruesome weather. I walked around the graveyard for 1 hour. I followed the steps that Alison and I had walked 1 year ago. A tear ran down my face. When I went back to English the class neglected me so I walked around the corridors. Later at 11.30 a.m. it was the school service with that wimpish minister who didn't find the slightest thing funny. His microphone took a relapse and he sounded like Sid Vicious singing 'The Body Of Saint Mary's'. Then it came to the choir and Alison was in it and she was still the same as she had been for 9 months. I decided to tell her my long and sad speech after school.

It was strange seeing all the school and the staff together.

Seeing people I used to speak to.

I started to cry but wiped my eyes and joined in the songs. Afterwards I asked Louise where Alison was. And she had gone to the Burgh to get a lift home. I walked more slowly and Mrs Calder passed me in her car. I just quickly hid behind a gate to avoid embarrassment. At 2 o'clock I went to Louise's house to play games. I tried to get as much information about Fiona as I could but all I got is where she stays and her love life up the woods, in a tent with two boys. I came home thinking about Alison. And thinking about how much I would miss her at Christmas.

Nothing ever happened between me and Alison, except in my imagination, until I sprang this clumsy speech in which I tried to proclaim my love.

It was the last day of term before the Christmas break. Alison was relieved, no doubt, that she would have a rest from me. I, on the other hand, was devastated at the thought of two weeks' separation.

She's walking up the back road behind my housing estate, towards her house. I follow her from school, to the start of the back road where she parts with her friend Louise who lives on the other side of Musselburgh. Then I step in.

'Alison!' I shout after her and half run. She ignores me, and from behind I can see that she hasn't even reacted.

Now I'm a few steps in front of her, having to half walk backwards to stay ahead of her as she quickens her pace.

'Alison, please let me talk to you.'

'What do you want?' She's exasperated already, I can tell. She's gone all red, and is now walking with her eyes to the ground.

'I just need to talk to you, like I said. Please.' I hate the sick moronic words that are coming out of my mouth, and although they are entirely of my own making, I can't stop them.

'WHAT?!'

Oh my God. Alison Calder shouted at me. Nevertheless, I continue.

'I've tried to tell you. I think … I … I … love you. I just want to spend time with you. I've felt like this since I first saw you. I've been trying to tell you.'

'LEAVE ME ALONE!!!' She grabs her bag tighter and walks even faster. This causes me to become more manic. I have to trot backwards.

'I want nothing to do with you.' She is turning around every few seconds, desperately hoping her mum will pull up in her silver Mercedes.

'Alison, please, I love you. I can't go on without you.'

'I MEAN IT. STOP IT. I DON'T WANT TO GET A NAME.'

'Don't you love me?'

'NO.'

'D'ye still like me even?'

'NO!'

In my head, in my mad stalker head, we had been conducting some sort of intense relationship throughout 1978. Just before Christmas it was over. I would finally have to accept her reply was a no. Now we were divorced. One of us would have to pack our things and leave. I dedicated the playing of Elvis's 'Separate Ways' to her and the end of us.

at the beginning of 1979 I was trying to get over Alison and turn over a new leaf. To start having normal healthy obsessions with normal healthy boys like Jamie Ritchie, and cut out the abnormal unhealthy obsessions with blue-eyed, blonde-haired girls.

Evidently the new leaf remained upturned on its new side for nine days.

DATE: 9 January   *DAY: Tuesday*

Today nothing exciting happened at school, but I decided to get Alison up the road, but of course I would have to invite myself. I ran after her but she walked on. I tried to say I was sorry again, and that I wanted her to be my friend, but of course she said 'no'. I still walked with her up to her house and I wouldn't let her pass. Finally after a long argument she said 'no' and I went home sad and depressed.

I did leave off Alison for a while after that, if only a short while. The spring and summer of 1979 would see me plummeting to new depths of melodramatic, psycho-nutjob (a word used a lot on *Grange Hill* at this time) behaviour. In the meantime, I made occasional visits into the world of liking boys – while shifting my abnormal affections to Fiona. Or Lisa. Or Valerie. Or Karen. Whoever.

In 1979, I stepped up my fantasy life by playing Rhona Campbell, Mafia Getaway Driver On The Run. Throughout the preceding year, I had developed a number of alter egos, but Rhona Campbell, Mafia Getaway Driver On The Run was my most constant companion.

It would always start as I was doing the washing up, the steam billowing around the Venetian blinds, the washing-up liquid suds piled high in the bowl. The suds looked creamy. Maybe like ice cream. The mashed potato scoops (because in Scotland you have mashed potato every night of your life) would put me in mind of ice-cream scoops … ice-cream scoops (rippling harp music) …

Our kitchen dissolves to …

Scene: A small Italian café. A woman is serving ice cream. Two men appear.

ME: Hi. What do you want?

HOOD 1:   We want you to come and work for us again.

ME: Look, I can't talk right now. I don't want to get into any trouble. My bosses are in the other room there *(my parents, watching TV)*. You know I'm on proba-tion here, you son of a bitch *(massive Starsky and Hutch influence)*. I know it's not much, but it's a job. I'm not in any trouble. I'm clean and I have a roof over my head. It might look like nothing to you, but it's a fresh start for me. So I can't come back and drive for you. I won't go back to that life.

HOOD 2:   You have no choice. You owe us. You gotta do one more run. You're the best, and we need you.

ME: Get out of here, goddammit. Leave me alone. Don't ever come back. I told you. No. *(Under my breath)* Sonofabitch.

(At this point, I lower my voice and turn around to make sure my employers can't hear the conversation.)

HOOD 1:   Jeez. You really got it good, don't you? You're worth so much more than this. Selling ice cream in some two-bit joint.

ME: Yeah, I know, but I'm not going back inside for anyone. Besides, they treat me good here. Here, I got no past.

HOOD 2: We been patient with you so far, but you don't wise up and we're gonna have to play a little rough.

ME: You don't scare me.

HOOD 1: Yeah? What about that sweet little old couple out back, Mr and Mrs Campbellini? How they gonna look once they been at the bottom of the river for a coupla days, fish chewing on their asses?

ME: OK, you bastards. Come back here tomorrow night. I'll think about it. But you lay one finger on the Campbellinis and I'll waste the both of you.

MRS CAMPBELLINI *(off camera)*:
      Rhona! Who are you talking to?

ME: No one, Mum. Just singing.

MRS CAMPBELLINI:
      OK. Don't forget to wipe the draining board.

Creosoting the fence, I was a fence painter on the run. Polishing the silver, I was an odd-job man on the run. Cleaning the car, I was a mechanic on the run. My parts of the dialogue I always spoke out loud, leaving gaps for the other characters to speak their lines. The action was always set in New York, and my parents were always the new employers who I didn't want to find out about my past. Of course, there was a girl as well. Someone who broke my heart, some other reason why I could never go back.

You could say that this was a normal part of a young child's playing patterns. But I was thirteen, nearly fourteen years of age. I was supposed to be growing up. In fact, even I had noticed that I appeared to be getting older. I was getting pubic hair. I was depressed about it. I kept cutting it off. I didn't want it. I didn't want to grow up.

It was more than just play. At any point in the day, where there was the slightest chance that real life could be shaken off, I'd be out of there. Into my little Italian café or desert highway truck stop. Hiding with my Mafia guys. Cut-throat and ruthless they may have been, but they seemed much safer than any reality I had going on around me.

And while I was alternately making up film scripts in my head and sneaking around after girls, I had a third obsession going on. Sport. Specifically, swimming. From the age of six, three times a week at 6.30 to 8.30 a.m. on Saturdays – I would get up and pile into a car with three other kids to go to the pool. Not just those days either. There were sometimes time trials in the evenings and on Sundays, and of course there were competitions throughout the year.

We swam for Tranent Amateur Junior Swimming Club, which was about ten miles from Musselburgh, and we were the most

Scottish-named bunch of swimmers in creation. There was me, plus Douglas Cameron, William McKean and Heather Stewart. Heather was our club champion, and unfortunately we both swam butterfly and breaststroke, so I was always going to come second, despite my intensely competitive streak. Coming second week in and week out did not sit well with me.

I did win trophies and medals despite lurking in Heather's shadow. I had a natural aptitude for it. Swimming and winning. I was also totally fearless in water. At seven I had swum a length of the Commonwealth Pool in Edinburgh without armbands and got my first certificate. When my parents had asked me what it was I wanted to do – Dancing lessons? The piano? – I had chosen to swim because that's where I felt good and that's where I knew I could win stuff.

When I was nine I was entered into a competition and I came third. Afterwards, my mum found me in the changing rooms crying because I'd been beaten. 'Rhona,' she said, 'you did really well to come third.' I remained inconsolable. 'They beat me,' I kept howling. 'They beat me.' The other swimmers were nineteen years old.

The training was relentless. Early winter mornings were the worst. 6.30am before school. Walking down to the bus stop at the Brunton Hall, freezing, fucking freezing Hibernian frosts, taking your breath away. Then a hot car, heating on full, trying to defrost the window. Five of us, all with straw hair from a life of chlorine. Half asleep again just as you reached the baths. No one spoke once we got changed; you just got into the water, eyes stinging, body on automatic pilot. Mind elsewhere. And you swam. For an hour. Various strokes, various speeds. Never stopping. Two sounds only, alternating between them. Exhaling in the water, face down. Inhaling the air outside, with the coach shouting and our bodies chopping through the pool. The feet in front. The fear of the hands touching your feet behind. You couldn't slow down enough to let that happen. That way you would be overtaken. Maybe you wouldn't make the team.

I only ever watched three swimmers in that pool, but I watched them very closely. I envied Douglas Cameron the most. He was the fastest boy, with the best looks and the best body. The swimmer-boy I wanted to be. Tiny trunks barely covering his pubic hair, neat little bum from butterfly. Gorgeous broad shoulders, strong arms. Steel-blue eyes, jet-black textured hair. Cheekbones of perfection. Still managing to look good in a rubber Speedo hat and goggles. I could swim like him, I thought, as he passed me in the next lane, the fast lane. My eyes fixed on his trunks at every opportunity. If only I didn't have these fucking massive tits.

Imagine what it would be like to be Douglas, with his chest designed for swimming. A light, free chest. How comforting it would be to be a boy. How everything would fall into place. How studious and focused I'd become. How happy I would be. I'd go out with a gentle, beautiful girl, like Susanne Flynn or Alison Calder. Or the very aloof and quietly spoken Melissa Gilbert, who had a pony. I'd walk my girlfriend to school, I'd conduct an old-fashioned courtship. I'd wear a large wristwatch with a bracelet, not the silly little girl's Timex my parents had given me.

Sometimes after swimming, in the showers when the others had left, I'd roll my costume down to my waist and tuck it in to make it look like trunks. I'd hold my tits apart, to see what I'd look like with a boy chest. It didn't make me feel sexual, just relaxed and comforted.

As if the swimming wasn't enough, I would play hockey every

week as well. On a Saturday morning – when I noticed most kids like to sleep – I would be up at seven to get picked up for swimming. I'd train for two hours, then cycle down to play a hockey match.

But that was for different reasons. Hockey was all girls. And for me that was heaven.

t he sledging, the trying to like boys, my Mafia guys, the swimming and the hockey all coincided in the January of 1979 to some good effect. There is one last brief diary entry for that month.

> *DATE: 21 January*   *DAY: Sunday*
> *Today was a fantastic day. I had great fun and I forgot about Alison.*

Perhaps I could keep my 'solemn promise' after all. Maybe I was a new Rhona Campbell. Maybe.

two
february

I arranged to meet Amanda Knight and Lindsay McIntyre at the Brunton Hall at 7.00 p.m. to go to the Valentines disco. I told Dad it was strictly fifteen years and under and that it would be well catered for and quiet. It turned out to be the most rowdy lot of shit I had ever been to. When we all met they dragged me into the toilets, which was occupied by eight sixteen-year-old big-chested girls combing their hair, some smoking and others having a good slosh of McEwan's Export until they were sick. All they spoke about was what happened when they went out with the boys. The conversation and behaviour was not of my line – not that I'm an angel, but I felt so clean and sacred compared to them. I decided to lose Amanda and Lindsay upstairs and find someone else to talk to. I bumped into Elizabeth Riley and she seemed to be stoned but she was only putting it on. How could anyone be on two bottles of cider that they bought at the Co-op? So I went up the back table beside Susan, Susan G., Audrey, Fiona, Lorraine came later, Catherine, Lisa. And then it all came back to me when I banged into Fiona Nesbit. She used to be a short, fat, long-haired creep but now she was somewhat beautiful. For a moment I didn't remember her but it all came back. I tried to chat her up and succeeded. The hours dragged on until I retired to the gruesome smell of chips at the chip shop. Then after I had filled my guts I went back to the disco. I found Fiona really quite interesting and I didn't want to leave, so after I had snogged a few boys I went back to talking to Fiona. I heard rumours about her. People saying she was cheap. By now I could strangle whoever said that. The music was a second version to Concorde taking off. You couldn't hear yourself shout.

Finally it all finished, I got Fiona downstairs and said I would see her later in the week, and she agreed. All the time I couldn't forget Alison. I did miss her. Well, my dad picked me up and we went home. I felt rather giddy.

Who the fuck was Fiona Nesbit? I have absolutely no memory of her whatsoever, other than a vague notion of some bright blue eyes and light brown hair. I was miserable at that damned disco. And every other disco I ever went to at the Brunton Hall. Attached to the building was a tall tower, making it one of the highest points in Musselburgh. I often thought about climbing the steps to the top, looking down and jumping off to land with a splat at the feet of the people below. They all knew me and had contributed in their various ways to my being miserable.

I know that flirting with suicide is a not uncommon symptom of teenage angst. I am well aware that the line 'I'll be dead and they'll all be sorry' is pretty much part of the standard-issue script for the tortured adolescent. But I think I was a little closer to the edge of that tower than most kids.

It was a very grim time for me. From the age of nine I had been regularly sitting in the bath and pretending to shave my face with my dad's old-fashioned safety razor. That was a favourite of mine. That and pretending to save a small child from drowning.

Scene: Harbour, just an average day in Musselburgh during the school holidays. At the edge of the pier stands a group of schoolchildren. Mostly girls, except for one boy – Jamie Ritchie. There is a tall girl with blonde hair and blue eyes. Her name is Alison. She is playing there with her baby sister, who is very young and small. I'm standing with the crowd, when suddenly there's a scream from one of the girls. It's Alison. She's pointing to the water. In it, struggling, is her baby sister – clearly drowning. There are no grown-ups.

ALISON *(shouting)*: Jamie! Someone help, my sister can't swim.

JAMIE:　　I can't, either, I've always been frightened of the water. I've only just stopped using armbands.

ME: Waste no more time, time is of the essence. You! *(I point to Jamie)* Go and get the life-saving rubber ring from over there, and you *(pointing to Susanne Flynn, an attractive girl with blonde hair and blue eyes)* go to the harbour master and alert him.

(I was fond of formal speak in an emergency: they were always doing it in the Secret Seven books.)

I remove my top, but keep on my junior bra and cut-down Levis. I remove my Adidas trainers, but keep on my sport socks, because it makes me more boyish, and dive into the murky water. I'm underneath the water for what seems like minutes. I can't find her. The water is too dark with fuel and dog shite.

I'm aware time is running out for the kid. My lungs can't bear it. I have to come up for air. By now the water is choppy, not aiding my rescue. I gasp at the surface for more air. I can hear Alison screaming.

ALISON: Please save her, Rhona!

I am pleased she uses my name.

ME: I'm going back down.

This time I'm successful, but only because I train every day in a swimming club and have developed abnormally large lungs. No one else could have done it. I'm willing to risk my life, I don't mind.

Somewhere near the bottom, I can see Alison's baby sister. Eyes open, they are blue like Alison's.

I scoop her up in one strong arm sweep and use my free arm to breaststroke us to the surface. I appear.

I save the kid. Through the water I can see the face of Alison Calder, crying, hands covering her mouth, so relieved that I've reached the kid.

ME: She's still unconscious!

I drag her to the edge in the life-saving position. Jamie throws me the safety ring, but he's too slow. I don't need it by now. Alison notices how slow Jamie is, and even through her tears manages to shake her head at him.

I take us both to the harbour ladder in the life-saving position. With the tiny kid over my broad shoulder, I pull us up the rusty old ladder on to the pier. Jamie has gone into shock and is doing nothing. I look very good when I'm covered in water. It makes my eyes sparkle, my eyelashes more pronounced, and it shows off my tan. I know Alison thinks this.

By now a crowd has gathered at the scene, but the emergency forces are a long way off and I have to make do with my own skills. I put her in the recovery position. Some water trickles out of her mouth. This is a good sign.

ALISON: Oh my God, is she dead?

ME: Stay back. She needs air.

I perform mouth to mouth, but it's not working. Alison cries more. I fear the worst. I'm exhausted as it is, but I must remain calm and think on my feet. I don't want to say anything, but I think she's beyond saving. I must protect Alison from this information. When suddenly I have an idea ...

I realise we are standing underneath the harbour warning light ... No, I couldn't, it's too shocking, too dangerous. A life may be lost, but to risk my own as well?

But the look on Alison's face says it all.

She reaches out to touch my hand.

ALISON: Please, is there anything you can do?

ME: There is one thing, but ...

ALISON: Then do it.

And with those words from her I do.

I roll up my sweatshirt around my hand, and get Jamie to let me on his shoulders, which he struggles with, and I smash the glass covering around the harbour safety light, revealing the exposed electrical socket. I pull it out. It's on a long wire and I drag it down on to the ground beside the kid.

I hold hands with the unconscious kid, and with the other hand I push my fingers into the live socket.

ME: HERE GOES!

As I push into the socket, a massive electrical current passes through me, my hand, my body and into Alison Calder's little sister.

She comes back to life.

No one including me can believe I have the strength to withstand that. But it works. The crowd cheer. I put on my sweatshirt and ruffle the kid's hair. I'm about to walk away, not wanting any fuss made over me – just glad the kid made it.

ALISON: Rhona! Wait, please.

I stop in my tracks and turn around smiling, from the side of my mouth (which I always thought suited me).

ALISON: Rhona, oh, Rhona, Rhona. How can I thank you
          enough?

ME: You don't have to, it was nothing. Anyhow, it's about
              time I made myself useful.

ALISON: I love you, Rhona. I'm sorry if I ever …

I cover her lips with my hand.

ME: Love means never having to say you're sorry.

I get my bike and walk away, for once too tired to pedal.

I was resigned to the fact that it would take a huge act of outstanding bravery to make people in my home town like me. Sometimes when down at the harbour I almost felt tempted to nudge a small child over the edge into the water, only to save them seconds later. Then, elevated to the rank of hero, I'd be able to live a normal and happy life.

But for now, my child-saving fantasies were restricted to the bathroom. I spent a great deal of time engaged in real bathing, fake shaving and imaginary resuscitating – and scrubbing the white tiles around the bath with a nail brush. This, of course, was in my alternate identity of Rhona, Bathroom Cleaner On The Run.

Around the age of eleven or twelve, I began to unscrew Dad's safety razor and remove the blades, in order to have a pretend shave. Of course, much of the time I was also engaged in one of my Mafia fantasies in which I had needed to alter my appearance so that I could continue to work incognito in the Campbellinis' Ice-Cream Parlour.

Always a hypochondriac, I was excited by the idea of injury. And

I loved the props. I had built up quite a collection of walking sticks, acquired from my many infirm relatives. Eye patches were good. And then there was my absolute favourite – slings. Just like in the cowboy films. Men looked so handsome in a sling; it was surely a way to attract beautiful girls. In my opinion the greatest sling-wearer of all time has to be Warren Beatty in *Bonnie and Clyde*. And he had no trouble getting women. Men looked so good all scarred and band-aged in movies.

That February, though, several factors had combined to send me closer to the edge of a razor blade. On the first of the month, Sid Vicious had died of a heroin overdose in New York. Sid was the undisputed world heavyweight champion of self-mutilation. In every picture you saw of him, he was sneering and spattered with blood from self-inflicted wounds to his arms, chest and face. One of the most memorable images was that of Sid, bare-chested, playing on stage with the word 'Hate' so recently carved into his torso that you could see the blood dripping on to his guitar.

I was nowhere near cool enough to like the Sex Pistols, and found their music unappealing anyhow. But I did take a brief interest in a disturbed young middle-class punk who dated my cousin Gillian for a while. He lived close by her, miles away at the other side of Edinburgh. There was much talk about how undesirable he was for Gillian. They spoke of his journey into petty crime after his parents' divorce, and how it left him 'removed'. My cousin, under the influ-ence of her parents, quickly ended the relationship. Hearing about this oddball interested me immediately. I arranged to have him visit me. And I choose the word 'arranged' carefully, because that's how I saw it at the time. I was a great psychologist, or Sherlock Holmes, or a social worker – and with the boy under my watchful eye, I could help him. But first I had to gain insight.

Our meeting took place at my house and we sat in the caravan at the bottom of the garden, the folding table that doubled as a bed between us. His head was bowed slightly under the weight of a massive padlock hanging round his neck and he nervously gripped the oversized sleeves of his mohair jumper. His skin wasn't great and his tight jeans tapered into cheap baseball boots. He was fifteen, two years older than me.

For our first session, I had chosen a tan denim safari suit from the Kays catalogue – a replica, I liked to think, of the one worn by Lee Majors in *The Six Million Dollar Man*. I toyed with a pen that also doubled up as a fake plastic cigar. In between puffs, I asked him about his post office crime. He had stolen some money from a counter and was facing possible borstal. He said very little, but seemed full of hate. I found him gentle and misunderstood. He had piercing blue eyes, which helped, of course. I thought him far too interesting for my cousin. Perhaps he could be my new project. If I didn't fancy boys I could at least study them and maybe help the injured ones.

He asked me if I liked punk. I told him I liked Elvis, Tony Bennett and Showaddywaddy. He'd brought some tapes, and we played them on my Hitachi tape recorder, which was now running on batteries for caravan purposes. This had the effect of slowing down the music, and we listened to the Dead Kennedys labouring their way through a version of 'Holiday In Cambodia'. This, and my general lack of appreciation for the music he'd based his life on, made him agitated and bad tempered. He left. In the end, there was nothing I could do for him.

I changed back into my tracksuit. My tastes had let me down again. Musically, I had been too dependent for far too long on the old records my mother brought home when she did some promotion work with the local radio station – presumably ones they were never going to play again. Barry Manilow and Glen Campbell provided the soundtrack to my Mafia fantasies. Among my peers, my beloved Elvis, of course, didn't even register on the Coolometer. Even when I was occasionally grabbed by a contemporary song, it was highly unlikely to be a guitar-driven howl of outrage. 'Reunited' by Peaches & Herb was a big hit in 1979. And I was glad. 'London Calling' by The Clash was also big, but I didn't even notice.

The only thing that enchanted me about Sid Vicious was that he was, briefly, a man who cut himself up and then killed himself. I was also quite impressed with the half-dozen or so mini-punks at my school, who gritted their teeth and scratched 'SID RIP' down their arms with metal compasses. I was less impressed when they all turned up next day with pink sticking plaster over their 'wounds'.

Then, all of a sudden, I got interested in politics.

I'll run that again.

All of a sudden I got *obsessed* with politics.

In 1979 Britain elected its first ever woman Prime Minister. Mrs Margaret Thatcher ruled this country for fifteen years and changed Britain's history in countless ways. She waged war – at home on the miners and abroad on the Argies. She divided the nation. But I couldn't give a shit. Her very existence passed me by completely at this time.

My political interest had begun a few months earlier, when I had learned that the leader of the most insignificant party in the country, the Liberals, had been forced to resign over allegations of a 'homosexual' affair with a 'male model' called Norman Scott. Strictly speaking, of course, Jeremy Thorpe was in trouble because he'd been linked to a farcical plot to kill his former lover which had culminated in the shooting of Scott's dog. I think I may have tuned most of that stuff out.

Almost all I tuned into was the word 'homosexual'. Over and over again. On the radio and on the TV and in the papers. And this was very odd, because I swear I had never even heard the word until the winter of 1978/9. Then suddenly even my parents were using it while discussing current affairs over the tea table. Hitherto there had been one single reference to the entire subject of homosexuality in our house. We had all been watching tennis on TV and I had criticised a player for being a 'lazy sod'. My father hit the roof, and then me.

'Never, ever, use that word in this house again!' he raged. 'You have no idea what a "sod" is or what "sodomy" means.'

And now here was the word 'homosexuality' being bandied about as if it were a perfectly legitimate activity. And deep down, I knew that I was also a homosexual. Just like Jeremy Thorpe and Norman Scott were supposed to be. And here they were being treated as outcasts, objects of derision and all-round weirdoes. They were so obviously my kind of people.

I followed that case with incredible interest: every media report was scrutinised and analysed for clues which might tell me how a 'homosexual' lived, what they did and how they dressed.

Thorpe, I quickly became disillusioned with – he denied his sexuality throughout – but Scott proved to be a much more attractive role model. Always perfectly dressed, quick to give a soundbite, and obviously somewhat deranged and debauched. I knew I loved him when I saw this quote:

> *'Homosexuality was an illness, a disease, and I had been infected by Jeremy Thorpe. If he had not seduced me I may have had a different life … with a conventional family, a wife and children. I would not have been put through hell.'*

Someone else knew! Someone else was struggling to give up their obsessions and cure themselves by trying to fancy the opposite sex. And because of it, that someone else was also going through hell.

Just as my fervour for the facts about Scott was hitting its peak, I then learned what appeared to me to be the single most important aspect of the story. In 1974, when Scott's obsession with Thorpe was at its highest, in an attempt to convince people that he 'meant business', he had taken a razor blade and on to his arm etched the word 'INCURABLE'.

The allure of Sid, Scott and Suicide was all proving too much for me. Instead of merely discarding my dad's razor blades as I played at shaving, I began to apply them to my flesh. Just nicks and slight slashes, under my watchstrap at first, so I could keep them hidden.

I would lock the bathroom door. Then get out the razors. Sitting down on the dirty-washing box, watching the veins in my wrists as I pressed the blade in. I would apply enough pressure so that it would make a mark but not pierce the skin. I would think intensely about what it would be like to actually do it. To cut myself fatally, and bleed to death. How long would it take? Would there be a lot of mess? Would it be better for everyone else if I did it in the bath, so they didn't need to clean up as much? What would the teachers tell the classes? Would there be a special tribute to me at school assembly? If so, what would it be? Perhaps they would have a Rhona Campbell swimming trophy. Would everyone at school miss me and have lots of regrets?

Staring intensely at myself in the mirror while pressing down on my wrists further, I would produce a tiny scratch or cut. Then I would lose concentration and interest once I'd reached a certain point. Or I'd become aware that my mother might think I'd been in the bathroom for a long time and hadn't flushed the toilet. So I would put back the blades in the razor and place it in the cabinet. I'd put a small plaster on my wound, conceal it underneath my watch-strap, and go about my business.

my dad was from a long line of Scottish men who believed in corporal punishment. Severe misbehaviour always led to my pants being pulled down and being put over his knee and spanked until my arse was covered in raised pink welts and handprints. I thought for many years that I had exaggerated the details of this until a year before my gran lost her speech to a stroke. She had something on her mind she wanted to tell me. I was shocked when my gran, who had always been incredibly strict with my mum expressed great regret at not intervening in my dad's hitting of me. 'It was too much,' she told me. She felt she should have done something. This was amazing coming from a woman who told me repeatedly that I had an evil black man lying at the bottom of my spine in the form of a devil (which would explain my tantrums), who had to be hit out of me for my own good.

The threat of my dad's temper got far worse in 1979. He was increasingly moody, withdrawn and constantly tired from shift work. He showed little interest these days in golf, formerly his great passion, or attending any social gatherings with my mother. Instead he chose to walk the dog, in order to smoke in secret, or to spend hours alone in the garage with the door closed. But during this difficult time for him, he always took me swimming, shifts permitting. And he always picked me up from discos. I carried in my purse a piece of paper with a timetable of his shifts on it (abbreviated for quickness to L.O.N.E. – late, off, night, early). My poor old dad, the Lone security man. To avoid wear and tear on the timetable, I had it protected with a sheet of tightly wrapped cling film (which we were always being told at school WAS NOT AN ADEQUATE FORM OF CONTRACEPTION).

On one particular night Dad was waiting for me in the foyer of the Brunton Hall in his trademark sheepskin coat and pork-pie hat. He was by far the tallest dad of all time, standing an amazing 6' 4". Unlike some, I was delighted to have my dad pick me up, although I knew you were meant to feel mortified. But the sight of him standing there, with his Sean Connery-type panache, was such a relief in contrast with the rough ugliness of Musselburgh teenage life. And the dross upstairs.

Reversing the car out of the car park, he got shooting pains in his back, which had been bad since he'd damaged it working as a mechanic. Sometimes, and this was one of those times, it was so agonising that I had to help him by turning the wheel while he operated the pedals. By the time we got home, the pain was so bad that he took a couple of paracetamol and went straight to bed. This wheel-turning thing was becoming increasingly common at the scene of my pick-ups.

The next day I was counting my Valentine cards. This didn't take long, as I had exactly none. They could go into some sort of imaginary memento box with all the cards I'd never received in previous years. I dreaded Valentine's Day.

What had gone around was definitely not coming around. That year I had sent out dozens of cards – to a couple of the powerful, bullying boys, but mainly to my girls. Every year, I sent heaps of the things to a boy in my class called Tom Falkner, who was very tough but shy with girls. He hated me. If someone hated me – and often people did from the word go, although I couldn't understand why – I would immediately become very insecure. I couldn't just dismiss it. I wanted them to like me and I would put all my energies into ingratiating myself with them. Tom Falkner, like a lot of boys, found me annoying and repulsive, although I wasn't ugly; I was quite cute-looking, but odd and androgynous and unconventional. I baffled the shit out of that boy. The ruder and more antagonistic he was towards me, the more I would come right back at him with notes and messages of endearment.

The other person I bombarded that year was, of course, Alison Calder. And although I would let on to the boys when I sent them cards, I kept quiet with the girls. In Alison's case, I sent several, sequentially, with extracts of the lyric of Lennon and McCartney's 'For No One'. I often wonder if she actually received them in the correct order.

Valentines was a miserable day. The day when, if you were already an outcast, you really felt cast out. An annual awards ceremony for judging the most fanciable. They might as well have just got some fucking experts into the school to put us into groups and conduct a series of scientific tests to measure how popular we were. S.A.P.S. The Standard Approved Popularity Scale. 'Rhona Campbell, we were so excited to discover that you deviate so radically from the Average Popularity Curve that we are going to suggest exhibiting you in a travelling freak show.'

Meanwhile, a classful of attractive and popular girls were waving their spoils in the air and rubbing my nose in the dirt. Going to school on Valentine's Day was a punishment, like double maths, or extra geography. Subjects without a soul. Worse, some of the golden-haired bitches were sent chocolates too. The blonde bitches, too good at the enemy subjects, no interest in PE and shit at writing stories.

My pain was eased slightly the following year when I did get one card. And for a couple of years after that. They came from Alistair Ferguson, a lovely boy who was my boyfriend for a long time (two years), even though I never had sex with him. The first time I saw him he was emptying laundry out of one of those plastic 'Ali Baba' wash baskets so that he could mix coleslaw in it at Valerie Armstrong's Uncle Alan's house.

Valerie was one of my best friends for a long time. She was a quiet, mousy kind of character, but fun, and tomboyish. She was also the first person I ever discussed masturbation with. When I say 'discussed', there was nothing really explicit in the conversations. We called it 'making the feeling' and exchanged some information on how often we had 'made the feeling that week' and where we had done it.

She and I used to babysit her cousin, little Mari, for her Auntie Amanda and Uncle Alan Brown, who were staying at Valerie's grandfather's pig farm. We used to work there at the weekends, because we were both going for our Farmer's Badge at Girl Guides. Alan fancied himself as something of an entrepreneur. He also fancied himself as something of a playboy. In fact, he just plain fancied himself, with his porn-star moustache, hairy chest, gold cross and *Chariots of Fire* perpetually booming out of his expensive speakers, because he thought it was classy. Alan was from a poor family, and Amanda was fairly moneyed. Alan did everything he could to be respectable. He wore a long camel coat and smoked big fat cigars. I'm not sure if I found him respectable, although there was certainly something dangerously exotic about him.

He was a tough and frequently bad-tempered Italian Glaswegian, with – or so he told us – a black belt in karate (just like Elvis). One of the things I liked best about him was that he had an air rifle, which he carried around in the boot of his big brown Volvo. When I began working for him the next year, in his doughnut van at the markets, on the way home he'd hand me the unloaded gun and crank up *Chariots of Fire* really loud. I'd wind down my window and, driving through the long winding country roads, 'shoot' people as we passed them as a joke. The gun looked and sounded realistic enough to have pedestrians diving for cover in a blind panic. We would laugh together at the misfortunes of our victims as we drove along, but in my head we were the Mafia getaway drivers. It gave me no end of a buzz. I recognised that although he was an adult on the outside, he was a juvenile delinquent at heart. I also reckon that whatever fantasies he had with his gun and his Vangelis accompaniment weren't a million miles from my own ice-cream and Glen Campbell soundtrack dreams.

Alan's main income came from managing a disco, but there was always some other money-making sideline going on because he was determined to buy baby Mari a private education. Consequently, he always needed gullible teenagers to exploit. Which is where Valerie and I came in handy.

As his empire grew we became involved in all aspects of the expansion, culminating in our taking on key roles in his chain of newsagents. Valerie worked at one of them every Saturday and I worked at the other one. I was always happy to take on whatever work Alan Brown had going because it gave me the financial independence to buy magazines and records as well as the things that my mother would never let me have. Like Wrangler jeans. Which I needed badly, mainly because they made me look a little more boyish, then later on because they made me look a little more like Shakin' Stevens. (Alright, I know what you're thinking – technically, Shakey wore Levi's, but the Wranglers fitted over my hips better.)

Early on in his corporate development, Alan branched out into the catering business. So every Sunday I would get up at 5 a.m. and make my way down to the East Fortune Markets, which was quite a way out of town. There I would stand in a tiny caravan in the freezing cold, dishing up baked potatoes and doughnuts to horrid poor people on the lookout for cheap maroon leatherette jackets. Which could be embarrassing, because a lot of people from my school would be down there deriving amusement from seeing the four of us – me, Valerie, Alistair and Alan – all squished into this ridiculously small space, falling over each other to serve doughnuts and potatoes.

It was very tough work. Outdoors from way before dawn, my arms plunged into cold water to wash the spuds, then switching to non-stop doughnut frying, I would be both freezing and exhausted at the end of the day. On top of this, I was also compulsively over-eating, popping doughnuts for the whole day until I was often phys-ically sick. I steered clear of the potatoes, though. And their fillings. Especially the coleslaw.

Every Saturday night Alistair and Alan would chop up carrots, cabbages and onions, dump the dirty laundry on the floor and pour gallons of salad cream into the Ali Baba basket along with the vegeta-bles. Then, with sleeves rolled up to their shoulders, they would plunge their arms in up to the elbows and mix it all by hand. The coleslaw would be dumped into Tupperware containers and the basket refilled with soiled underwear.

Alistair had been hired by Uncle Alan on the same basis as we had – cheap child labour – but the boy had drive and ambition, as well as his mum and little brother to take care of. By the time he was sixteen, he was virtually running the whole show as a full partner in Uncle Alan's various enterprises.

He was a very tall, serious young man, with bad skin and ginger hair. An absolute gentleman. There was a lot of pain locked up in him, though. His father had left him, his mum and his wee brother when he was very young. For a while afterwards Alistair used to stand on a street corner every Thursday evening and wait for his dad, who would take him out for an hour. One night when he was about four-teen, Alistair arrived at the corner and waited for a couple of hours, but his dad never showed up. Or any other Thursday after that. In fact, they never saw each other again. Alistair, though, would ritually trudge down there every week for the next five years. Just in case.

Alistair was in the year above me at school. He left at sixteen to support his mother and younger brother, getting a job at Macdonald and Muir, the local whisky firm. He drank a lot, was a casual smoker and almost always wore a collar and tie. He liked to wear an old army coat and threatened eventually to join the Foreign Legion or join up for the Falklands (either would do) if I didn't get engaged to him. He told me this one night inside his white Escort (with black vinyl roof), outside my house. I noted the whole thing with fascination. I felt completely awkward; he felt desperate. His threat was very romantic but totally wasted on me. And I felt sad for this good, lovely boy who'd fallen in love with a girl, who'd fallen in love with many girls, and would again and again.

Those awkward teenage goodbyes in the car, at the end of an evening which nearly always included a Chinese meal (from which I'd never deviate from chicken and pineapple) were very tense for us both. I would never do anything other than kiss Alistair, and I'd only allow that at the end of the evening as a thank you. I slept in a bed with him twice, but never let him touch me. He never tried, out of respect for my wishes. I know everyone makes such a song and dance about poor sexually frustrated adolescent boys, desperate to get laid. And as a teenager, the greatest crime one could possibly commit against mankind was to be a 'prick teaser', but how do you think I felt? I wanted to shag girls from the age of nine.

Alistair was so polite, so shy. He was permanently red in the face, and touched his mouth a lot when he spoke. I was fascinated one time to observe him unawares at a disco with his two best friends, dancing together, in a deliberate comic way, to The Ramones' 'Baby I Love You'. It was so completely out of character for him. That's when I realised how much I inhibited his behaviour, and therefore how much he felt for me (this was before the Foreign Legion threat). It was something I had only ever experienced the other way round; I was used to being the inhibitee, not the inhibiter. That's love, I thought, at the age of fifteen – not wanting to look like the slightest bit of a dick in front of them.

You could tell that he was suppressing a lot of bad stuff. He was devoted to The Clash and in his leisure time adopted their rebel posturing, costume and attitudes: combat trousers, ripped T-shirts and black armbands were his uniform, sneering at authority. He was a very hard worker, and well thought of at Macdonald and Muir, but tension poured out of him, and the soundtrack to his life was all clanging guitars and angry shouting about dreadful injustices.

He was never anything but sweet and kind to me. After a long day flogging soiled coleslaw from the really naff baked potato/doughnut van, I would get five pounds. But Alistair always had a sheaf of notes in his pocket. He'd peel maybe a tenner off the top, give it to me and tell me to go and buy myself something nice off the market. Then he started buying me gifts himself – flowers and chocolates and perfume. He was the first person ever to make me compilation tapes, and to this day I consider that to be the most romantic and sentimental gesture of all time. Alistair must have spent days on his because he didn't simply record a bunch of songs – rather he would record little excerpts of tunes that had lyrics he felt were applicable to us. He'd fill a whole tape with ten-second 'songbursts', as he called them.

Within a short space of time, he started to ask me out on dates. And I started to go on them. And they were proper dates. Trips to the cinema. Chinese meals. Country pubs (following application of blusher, and the pushing out of my by now ample chest). And all the while he continued to behave like a perfect gentleman. I knew he was a virgin, very obviously in love with me and really, really in dire need of getting laid, but never once did he put any pressure on me to have sex with him. He just poured kindness and affection in my direction on a daily basis. I, of course, soaked it all up as fast as he could provide it. He'd maybe get a kiss on a special occasion when I'd had a drink or two, but he never touched me and there was a tacit understanding that he should never even try to do so.

The most perfect thing of all about Alistair Ferguson was that he was completely cool with my girl obsessions. In fact, he was beyond cool, and in time was happy to become complicit in helping me pursue them. As soon as he had turned seventeen, passed his driving test and bought the white Ford Escort, I had quickly commandeered it – along with Alistair as chauffeur – to drive around all the girls' houses I was stalking at the time.

After a lovely Chinese meal or a visit to the cinema, I would say, 'Can you just run me up to Josephine's now?' And off we'd go, without any conditions or complaints or even comment from Alistair. He loved me so much and so unconditionally that he would indulge me by parking up outside the home of some blonde-haired, blue-eyed object of fixation. Then he would sit patiently for hours while I scanned the place with my binoculars, waiting for that millisecond in which I might catch a glimpse that would feed my need for another day or so. He even became really adept at using the car to block the progress of any other vehicle I spotted with one of my stalkees in it.

'Quick! Look!' I'd shriek. 'There's Alison in her mother's car going the other way.'

Without a word, Alistair would swing his car around, head off in the opposite direction, and discreetly follow the silver Mercedes back to the big white house at Newcraighall.

For two years, Alistair followed my every whim, without much reward as far as I could see. But on my seventeenth birthday I really fucked it up. My mum had been in hospital for three months with a bout of severe psoriasis. I was fending for myself. I had recently lost my virginity to my next-door neighbour. I hadn't told Alistair. I was also going out with another boy called Callum. I didn't tell Alistair about Callum, or Callum about Alistair. Or either of them about David. Plus, I was still in love with Nicola Russell, who wouldn't see me any more – and I was going out with my first lesbian lover Josephine and trying to keep her under wraps too.

All of this came to a terrible head at my birthday party. Everyone took magic mushrooms. The central heating failed. Hundreds of gate-crashers piled into the tiny house. My stereo got smashed. The next-door neighbour turned up. Two boys I knew threatened to beat him up because they knew he had shagged me. I was drunk. Everyone else was tripping. I was depressed. I locked myself in the bathroom, took out my dad's safety razor, unscrewed the blade and slashed both my wrists the best I could. I did it, I think, to see if anyone really cared and to try and detract from my chaotic personal life. And although the cuts were minor, a few people cared enough to sit through the night with me, telling me how much they loved me (which was great). A few more people cared enough to come around the next morning to help me address practical issues like torn lace bed covers, vomit in the fridge and footprints up the living-room wall. While they all made well-intentioned but poorly executed attempts to address the mayhem, I cowered in a corner, cold, hungover and aching for another crack at the razorblades. Eventually I recovered enough to put on a long-sleeved jumper that hid my bandages, get in my mother's car and drive it – illegally – back up to the hospital to visit my mum.

A couple of days later I told Alistair what I had done, and he was beyond distraught.

'If I had been there,' he said, 'nothing would have happened to you. I could have taken care of you.'

We didn't see each other after that. I don't think he could face me. Maybe he believed he had failed to love me properly. Perhaps he realised that two damaged people could never really make a whole undamaged person between them. The Valentine cards carried on for a couple of years, though.

but before Alistair, back in the February of 1979 there was a new girl in my class to obsess over – Susan Tyler, a big, fairly non-descript girl with short brown hair from a hard part of town. I just woke up one morning and fancied her. So I sent her a Valentine card, which she brought to me at school and proudly displayed. I suppose in hindsight she was just sharing her joy, but my mad stalker head kicked in and I became convinced that she knew I had sent it. This was the beginning of another of my entirely imaginary relationships.

FACT FILE 2

SUBJECT: SUSAN TYLER

AGE: 14 AND A HALF

HAIR: BLONDE

EYES:	BLUE
JACKET:	HACKING, WITH SCARF
FAMILY:	FATHER – UNEMPLOYED
	MOTHER – BAKERY SHOP ASSISTANT
CAR:	NONE. ONE BICYCLE
REGISTRATION:	N/A
ACTIVITIES:	TALKING TO FRIENDS
	SATURDAY JOB IN BAKERY
	EATING LEFT-OVER BUNS
ADDRESS:	76 HALL STREET
PHONE NO:	665 6625
MOVES:	3.45 BUS TO ESTATE
	4.10 SITS ON STEP
	4.30 HAS TEA
	5.00 WATCHES TV
	6.00 DOES NOT APPEAR TO DO
	HOMEWORK!!!!!!!

I invited Susan to my house under the pretence of pursuing a normal teenage friendship. Which, as usual, involved her sitting uncomfortably on the edge of my bed while I did my weird staring routine and gathered the courage to tell her how I felt about her. Which in the end I managed to do.

Except that this time – unlike Alison or Isla – she went fucking ballistic. I was stunned and not a little scared by the fact that this girl was so clearly hostile to the point of fury. I may have been in a constant state of heightened ambivalence about the way I felt about fancying girls, but I was astounded to learn that it was possible to feel disgust at the prospect. Susan's rage was so primal, so instant and instinctive that I almost felt sorry for her, reaching out a hand to try to calm her down or comfort her. Before my fingers had even reached her shoulder, she was gone. I had this awful feeling that she would tell the whole school.

Added to this was the dread that the next time I would see her would be in the home economics class the following day. Home economics was really a posh term for 'cooking'. There may also have been an element of tea-towel washing involved, but it was primarily directed at ensuring that we grew up to be efficient and compliant little housewives. In those days there was no option for us to take any other practical classes. The boys did the boys' classes, i.e. woodwork and metalwork, and the girls did the girls' classes, i.e. cooking and tea-towel laundering.

I always had mixed feelings about home economics. On the one hand it was an all-girl group, which was pretty exciting. I really enjoyed life much more when there were no boys around. Girls seemed to act differently and I felt more powerful. I could make more jokes for a start. It always seemed to me that one of the big downsides of introducing testosterone into any social group – even if it was only in adolescent doses – was that we all had to shut up and listen to the boys' jokes. Jokes were important in establishing the alpha male. I wanted to be an alpha male, but in the established order of things neither boys nor girls would tolerate any attempts I might make to compete. Consequently an all-girl group gave me a golden opportunity to become the class jester.

On the other hand, while I was very good at cooking, the baking of cakes to please men seemed like a betrayal of my lifestyle.

It would have been easier if we'd got to make pasta. After all, I was an Italian man half the time and, in that context, cooking is very sexy. But there was nothing Italian or sexy about being on C floor. Holding a fucking Tala measuring jug and making egg mornay. C for cooking.

And C for cunt of a teacher.

For most of all, the thing that made home economics an ordeal was that the teacher clearly despised me. I don't really know why. Although I guess that if a teacher quantifies the success of her classes by how many good little wifey homemakers she produces, she wasn't going to look so favourably on an impudent little dyke in the making.

One of the ways her disapproval manifested itself was in giving my culinary efforts the lowest marks in the class. I never had a whole lot of skills, but I could write quite well and I could make people laugh. And I could cook. If the money was better for cooking than it was for making people laugh, I may even have considered it as an alternative career. After all, I already had experience in the catering trade as a baked potato and doughnut chef. So I knew full well that the only reason Mrs Fairclough humiliated me week in week out was because she was a twisted old fucker.

It pissed me off. And I was consumed each week with a sense of injustice and the basic need to redress the balance. Eventually I came up with a plan. I hatched it with another girl, Louise McKay, who was a very poor cook. At the end of the lesson we swapped dishes. *Et voila*. Just like that. Louise got the highest marks in the class, while my efforts were predictably trashed.

Triumphant and full of righteous indignation, I stepped into the centre of the class and delivered my speech.

'OK, listen, everyone. As I am sure you are aware, both Louise and I made macaroni cheese today – and as you are all probably also aware, Louise's macaroni cheese was judged to be the finest macaroni cheese ever made at this school and awarded a massive nine out of ten. My macaroni cheese on the other hand was – and I quote – "flavourless, lacking in texture and lacking in balance between cheese and tomato puree". So it was quite deservedly awarded a very low two out of ten. Which, as you may or may not be aware, is my average mark in home economics for this entire term. Two out of ten for everything except my chocolate brownies, which were awarded one out of ten. I am obviously a very, very, very bad cook. Except that, as an experiment, after I cooked my macaroni cheese today, I swapped it with Louise's macaroni cheese. So in actual fact, the macaroni cheese I really made is "the finest macaroni cheese ever made in this school" and Louise's macaroni cheese is really macaroni cheese which is "flavourless and lacking in texture and balance". And I would just like an explanation as to why. And I would also like my macaroni cheese to be awarded the marks it deserves.'

Nobody likes a smart arse – especially when they're articulate, justified and a bit weird. Mrs Fairclough liked me even less for that outburst. Instead of apologising and reversing the marks – as I had naïvely expected – she pointed out that home economics was as much about attitude and courteous behaviour as it was about cooking. The low marks remained, I was put on report, and her vindictive marking system was maintained for the rest of my time in her class.

The day after I'd made my play for Susan Tyler, I went up to home economics and stood in my little kitchen area with a sense of miserable foreboding. And yes. The worst that could happen had happened. Susan stood weeping on the opposite side of the room, occasionally glancing at me, and then burying her face in her hands as if I was too frightening to behold. The rest of the class were clustered around, some of them glowering at me as if I'd raped her and then made her shag the dog.

Although Mrs Fairclough wasn't privy to the details, she quite clearly realised – and relished the thought – that Rhona the outcast had just recently moved totally beyond the pale. I was in the midst of getting a lecture on ladylike behaviour when a message arrived from the head teacher's office. Mrs Fairclough read it out as loudly and clearly as she could manage while maintaining a smug expression which was in grave danger of becoming a grin.

'Rhona Campbell, will you please go to see Mrs Thomson for guidance immediately.'

A guidance teacher was assigned to each of us at the beginning of the year and we were supposed to approach them whenever we felt upset, or ill, or our parents had died. In reality, though, they were there to dispense another line of discipline. My guidance teacher was Mrs Thomson and we had been seeing a fair bit of each other lately, what with one thing and another. She didn't seem to be too worried about my various misdemeanours, though, and I was more than happy to sit with her because she was quite voluptuous. She was in her mid-30s, and I found something in her that was both maternal and yet slightly sexual.

You have to remember that at this point in my school career (until the blessed Miss Carlisle came along) the teachers were often ugly and weird. One smelt constantly of drink, and had been rumoured to have been sacked for pissing in a wastepaper basket. In front of his whole class. So anyone with a bit of lipstick and a pair of tits was going to be interesting. And Mrs Thomson did have the most magnificent cleavage.

Travelling up from the cleavage was another story, as her breasts merged into the most extraordinarily thick neck with unusually great folds of skin flapping loose around it. I would flick my eyes quickly from one to another while she was talking. Breasts. Lovely. Neck. Ugly. Tits. Mmmmmm. Neck. Urgghh.

Mrs Thomson was extremely agitated and tense from the moment I walked in the room. Her larynx was wobbling slightly, and the more I said that annoyed her, the more tense and uptight she got, so that the loose skin on her neck started to flap proportionally. For the whole interview she shifted restlessly in her seat and failed to meet my eye.

'We have had a complaint,' she told the door I had just walked through, 'from Susan Tyler that you are harassing her.'

'How am I harassing her?' (Tits = Tasty. Neck = Nasty.)

(To the wastepaper basket beside her desk) 'Rhona, you can't go around telling girls that you feel that way about them. It's not right or proper.'

'Well, to be fair, I didn't really harass her. She came to my house yesterday and I just told her I fancy her.'

'Well, you can't do that sort of thing,' she told someone about a foot and a half taller than me, standing to my left.

'But I'm not doing anything different from anyone else. Boys do it all the time.' (Hooray for your breasts. Booooooo for your neck.)

There was a picture of the Duke of Edinburgh on the wall, and Mrs Thomson told him, 'You cannot do what boys do! You're a girl. Girls don't tell other girls things like that. Now, you are going to have to promise that it will never happen again, because if it goes any further, I will have to bring your parents up to the school for a talk.'

So I promised, and went back to home economics where Susan Tyler and her friends made their feelings clear by refusing to speak to me. They also ensured that no one would be my cooking partner. For the rest of that year I did home economics in isolation, continually humiliated, of course, by Mrs Fairclough's refusal to ever give me more than three out of ten.

Advertisement in *Musselburgh News*, February 1979

EAST FORTUNE SUNDAY MARKET
OPEN SUNDAY FROM 10–4

Come and see for yourself the wonderful goods at this superior market. We have a large number of stalls increasing weekly and we are sure you will find what you are looking for. We have clean Tarmac to walk on and parking is FREE! Shopkeepers are most welcome.

three
march

DATE: 23 February   **DAY: Friday**

I was in a good mood today. I found myself very attracted towards Miss Carlisle and tonight I stayed in all by myself and done a self-portrait to sad music. I got on with Isla today. As I did with everyone strangely, but I feel I must stop being cheeky especially at school. (To Miss Carlisle.) And I really should write my diary more often if I'm going to be famous. p.s. I told Miss Carlisle that two months ago.

DATE: 25 February   **DAY: Sunday**

I done nothing much except ~~creat create~~ make something out of wood but I stopped when I hit my thumb with the chizel. Like every day it was incredibly boring. I now realise how much I miss Miss Carlisle.

DATE: 26 February   *DAY: Monday*

Today I didn't feel all that well and I had a headache. I never spoke to Miss Carlisle all day. I only caught a glimpse of her and I do need her. I really like her. And I think she knows. Someone spat in my face and called me a _____ . I came home and went to bed ill. I love Joan C!!!!!!

DATE: 27 February   *DAY: Tuesday*

Auntie Rhona came for tea and I watched Grange Hill. I had a usual boring day at school. I swore at Miss Carlisle, trying to be her. Everyone laughed but she didn't. Then neither did I when she slammed the books down.

DATE: 3 March   *DAY: Saturday*

I've really gotten over Miss Carlisle. But when I'm bored e.g. today, I think about her. I done nothing all day, I went up the town to see Gran then Susan, Kenny, Kev and I played badminton. I was in a creative thoughtful mood today. You know what, I think I'm growing up!

DATE: 4 March   *DAY: Sunday*

This morning I was in a bad mood cause I had to do the garden. My uncle came and Auntie Kay again. We all started arguing and I cried and felt like running away. I can't wait to get back to school to see Miss Carlisle. I done the garden fence all day then after tea Valerie and I went to Luca's. It was great. I like boys a bit now. But I can't wait to see Miss Carlisle.

DATE: 5 March   *DAY: Monday*

Right now school only means one thing to me – Miss Carlisle. God it was great to see her, we hardly spoke but she gave me a row for phoning her and now I feel that I can never face her again. God I really love her – she's really attractive to me. At night I just watched TV and went to bed.

DATE: 6 March   *DAY: Tuesday*

Today was rather boring. It's a biology test tomorrow, so I was quite busy. I don't think I'll pass it, but it's own my fault for I should have paid attention. I saw Miss Carlisle, but we never spoke.

DATE: 7 March   *DAY: Wednesday*

Today I was worried about my mum cause she's not been well lately, and I thought about her all day. At school I got on with Miss Carlisle today. God she's fantastic. And I acted natural in her company.

DATE: 9 March   *DAY: Friday*

I was supposed to go to a party, but Alan Brown asked me to babysit, so I didn't know what to choose. Miss Carlisle rushed off after school and I won't see her for 3 days. I can't stand it cause I know I'm in love.

DATE: 10 March   *DAY: Saturday*

Last night I never slept because of my headache. Valerie stayed with me all day. She brought along a train set that didn't work.

I seemed to talk about Miss Carlisle a lot. I think I could be ill because of her as well. I think my mum thinks it's all in the mind my illness but it isn't. We watched an Elvis film and then I went to bed.

DATE: 11 March   **DAY: Sunday**

Today I was getting very depressed about my loneliness and boredom and I wished that Valerie was here. I sat and spoke to myself as if Miss Carlisle was there (God I Love her). I think about sex a lot. I've gone off my food.

DATE: 12 March   **DAY: Monday**

Dear Diary. Today I asked Ian Shaw out and he said no. I've decided my stage is a stage in adolescence, and I'll soon overcome it. Though I like Miss Carlisle and I think she knows. Valerie went out with Jamie. But I thought it was funny. I've been eating a lot of oranges.

Around about the middle of March was a school skiing trip to Italy. It was also my parents' silver wedding anniversary, and they had planned a family party at a hotel in Musselburgh. I'd never shown any interest in skiing before but, as places started to get booked up, I realised three things. One, that a good friend of mine, Charlene Divine, was going to go on it. Two, so was Alison Calder. And three, Miss Carlisle was running the pre-trip ski lessons, which would mean two nights skiing per week after school for three weeks at the dry ski slopes on the edge of Edinburgh. And so I started to beg, plead, and make more and more solemn promises until my parents caved in and my name was added to the list. It did mean I would miss the silver wedding celebrations, but my mum explained it was going to be a late-night, grown-up thing anyway and that we could all have a special meal when I came back. She also made her usual joke about me having to do the dishes until the end of our lives.

Miss Joan Carlisle. She was short with big tits and a big nose. I loved her nose. She was muscular and athletic, accentuated by the fact that she always wore tight clothes. I didn't realise until later in life, but she had a traditional Jewish look about her. A sort of Bette Midler/Barbra Streisand thing going on. At this time I was totally into three famous women: Tatum O'Neal, Jodie Foster and Barbra Streisand. Farrah Fawcett was my fourth, but my plastic pull-out wallet that I got free in a Christmas cracker only had room for three photos, so I had to narrow the field down. I kept this in my back pocket and carried it everywhere. The Streisand look would eventually come to be one that I consistently fell for.

Joan Carlisle also proved to be smart and funny. The Fact Files on her were enormous, and maintaining them was the most time-consuming work I had ever done.

FACT FILE 3

SUBJECT:	JOAN CARLISLE
AGE:	25
HAIR:	BLONDE
EYES:	BLUE
CAR (now):	BLUE DATSUN CHERRY ESTATE
(before):	TURQUOISE DATSUN CHERRY SALOON (SOLD DUE TO LEAKY OIL TANK)

REGISTRATION: PUS 338W (BLUE ONE)

YGE 330S (TURQUOISE ONE)

ACTIVITIES: BADMINTON

HOCKEY

SKIING

WATCHING MEN PLAY RUGBY

ADDRESS: FLAT 5, 24 REDBURN PARK ROAD,

MARCHMONT, EDINBURGH

PHONE NO: 668 3214

MOVES: <u>MONDAY</u>

8.15 LEAVES HOUSE

8.30 PASSES MY WINDOW IN CAR ON

THE BACK ROAD

8.35 ARRIVES AT SCHOOL

8.36 TOILET

WALKS DOWN CORRIDOR TO GO

TO CLASSROOM

HAS CIGARETTE IN STORE ROOM OFF

THE CLASSROOM

9.00 TEACHES BIOLOGY TO THIRD YEARS

(CONT. PAGES 1 TO 39)

The first time I laid eyes on Joan Carlisle was the first week of term, after the summer break of 1978.

I was sitting in the classroom, somewhere near the front, where I preferred to sit. I didn't misbehave as I was rarely bored at school. I was excited by the company of others around me and felt genuinely disappointed when the 3.45 bell went and we were sent home. I would stare out of the window a lot, dreaming about some romance with someone or another, longing for the love of a girl/woman.

When Miss Carlisle walks in. I know I fancy her straight away. She's young, around 27. Small, very fit-looking. Long, dirty-blonde hair. Huge blue eyes, lots of eyelash and mascara. She has the most interesting nose I have ever seen. I'm aware of her clothes. A fawn cashmere skirt and jumper. The skirt is tight, and clings to her arse. It looks like she plays a sport because her buttocks appear extremely pronounced and she has prominent calves. On her feet she wears heeled sandals with an ankle strap. I'd say she's my height (5' 2") but the heels have to be three inches. So nice to see a teacher in heels. Miss Carlisle has clearly made an effort.

The class is talking and largely ignoring her. I know this moment is crucial for her, as a new teacher must establish him or herself immediately, otherwise the class will take the piss from that moment onwards. I'm fascinated as to what she will do. She stands still behind her desk for a few moments and listens to us chatting. Then she walks out front and talks.

'All righty ...' I can tell by her accent she's Glaswegian. She must be funny, because Billy Connolly is Glaswegian. So are all the pantomime dames, and they are funny as well. 'Here's the score. I teach you, you learn. You come into my class and you play the game, and everything will be hunky dory.'

Hunky dory. Interesting.

'But if you don't ...' Suddenly, she did this hand gesture, pretending she had a gun. Her thumb was the trigger, her free hand cocking it back as she fired it. Without most of the class noticing she quickly clicked her gun hand fingers together, to create the sound effect of it firing. I am totally fucking hooked from that moment on. I mean, anyone who has the guts to make a pretend gun, and who isn't afraid to pretend to use it ….

I'm mesmerised by her performance. The others shut up, which is their version of mesmerised.

'Right then, I need a volunteer to clean the board,' she commands.

'Me, Miss!' I'm straining my right arm up high at this point.

She looks at me and cocks her head towards the blackboard. I use the blackboard cleaning as an opportunity to get closer to her, to see what she smells like.

I'm cleaning slower than is necessary, to give myself more time to take her in.

I'm cleaning blocks of writing out in downward strokes. She's moving around her desk behind me, passing out papers to the class. I can smell her perfume. It's light and floral, quite fresh. I can also smell some coffee and cigarettes. Must be from the staff room.

I finish, and place the duster on her desk. She is completely unaware of me examining her, smelling her. I go back to my seat. She doesn't thank me. She passes more papers out to the class, but because I wasn't at my desk when she issued the rest she visits my desk to give me my papers personally. This is even better because I get to look at her hands. She's quite tanned for a blonde person, which makes me think she goes abroad a lot, probably with a boyfriend. Her hands are dry from lots of chalk. She wears no rings, so she's not engaged. The middle fingers of her right hand are stained with nicotine. So she's a smoker; she must be nervous beneath her hard front. Nervous about what? She's young, cool, sun-tanned, fit.

I must know more, especially the name of her perfume. When I get back to my office I'm going to ask for an A.P.B. on her and find out more. They're always doing that on *Starsky and Hutch.*

But for now I am much more than mesmerised: I am in love, and it's only the first few days of term.

I became more obsessed with Joan Carlisle than anyone before or since. Within the first few weeks of being taught by her, after the end of one lesson I had sneaked back into the classroom and rifled through the personal belongings in her desk drawers. I acquired so much information. She was from Glasgow, her father was a doctor. She smoked Benson and Hedges. She was a winger at hockey. She lived up the town (this means Edinburgh, six miles away, 25 minutes by bus, which in those days was as far as you were allowed to go).

It took another day or so to establish where she lived, but as soon as I did I was straight up to Edinburgh, using visiting my gran as an excuse, who luckily lived not far from her. Suddenly I was standing nervously opposite her house with my binoculars. Terrified she'd find me. What would I say if I was caught? Standing there, miles from home, freezing in my school uniform? I practised what I would say, just in case …

'Oh, Miss, hiya. What are you doing here?'

Reply.

'Me? I'm visiting my gran. I've been doing that for years, long before I met you. She lives round the corner.'

Reply.

'I'd love to come up … I know you love me … I love you too.'

I managed to get her home telephone number, and if I was away on holiday or unable to attend my vigil, I would ring her and tell her how much I loved her and was missing her. Once, while on a package holiday in Spain with my mother, I spent all my money on calling her, crying about how I couldn't bear my time there without her.

I lavished many gifts upon her during our courtship. Mainly chocolate, because gift-buying was fairly limited as a teenager. The most lavish gift by far was one Christmas, a bottle of Rive Gauche, her preferred scent. I got someone else to ask her what perfume she wore, in preparation some months before this. It was one of the most expensive gifts I had ever bought. I babysat and took on extra market work to pay for it.

I was so hyped up about giving the gift to her. I planned the moment. It was to be at the end of school Friday, so she could use it at the weekend and think of me.

The bell goes at 3.45, as usual, and I dash all the way down from C floor to the science labs on A floor. I know she takes a while to pack up after class, especially on Fridays, and she often has a quick cigarette in the adjoining storeroom before she leaves. So I have five or ten minutes spare, but I get there in plenty of time so I can calm myself and appear nonchalant when I hand it to her. I take up my position, which I practise a few times, leaning on my elbow on the window ledge in the corridor. I try to be casual. The perfume is wrapped. I hide it behind my back with my left hand.

She comes out of her classroom, a pile of papers held in one arm, her handbag over the other shoulder. In her free hand she carries a small plant. Lucky plant, I think. She looks tense at the sight of me and exaggerates her hurry. Before I can say anything she pre-empts me.

'Look, Rhona, I'm in a rush.'

I can smell her last cigarette and some of her hair product. What can that be?

'Miss! Wait, I've got something.'

She doesn't stop, and begins to rummage in her bag for her car keys.

'Well, it'll have to be quick.'

We begin walking along the corridor, and she slows slightly as she feels around for the keys. I panic at all the things going on with her hands – the bag, the papers, the search for the keys. No hands free to accept the perfume. This isn't what I had in mind. Suddenly I feel so stupid, I want to cry. I hate myself for my love for her and my stupid addiction to trying to please her. I'm exhausted.

'What is it, Rhona?'

Too late now. I would have to give her it. Hurried would have to do.

'It's for you.' I show her the package.

'What is it?'

'It's a present, Miss.'

She goes bright red, and can't disguise the panic in her eyes.

'Oh, Rhona. You shouldn't keep doing this.'

Was that pity? I think it was. No wonder, I even pity myself. Will the pity make her love me? Make her take me home with her and look after me like the plant? Fucking bastard smug plant.

'It's nothing, Miss. Open it.'

She begins opening it, which forces her to reluctantly give me the bloody plant to hold. I cling on to it, pleased that the pot is still warm from her hands. I place my hand on the warm bit. The closest thing to her. Other teachers are passing us, some saying hello to her, others looking over at us. She finishes unravelling the package, and recognises the bottle.

'I can't take this, Rhona. How did you …?'

'You have to take it, Miss, it's your perfume. I want you to have it.'

She sighs a big sigh. This is when she should kiss me. Instead there is a long silence where I maintain my false grin in an attempt to continue looking relaxed. She looks down at the ground and bites her bottom lip, looks at her watch and rolls her eyes. She sighs again, then looks at me.

'You shouldn't do this kind of thing, Rhona. I mean it.'

I'm still struggling with the grin.

'What kind of thing?' (The dumbest thing I could possibly say.)

'It's very kind of you but … What am I going to do with you?'

Does she really want me to answer that? I shrug my shoulders, running out of grin. I now feel like crying.

'I'll accept it this time but not again, please.'

I'm stunned and embarrassed into complete silence.

'Now, I have to go. Have a good weekend.'

And with that she takes the plant from me, shoves the perfume and screwed up wrapping paper in her handbag, and leaves. I watch her walk much faster down the corridor than usual and disappear around the corner.

For a moment I think. If I run home now really fast, I could just catch her driving by from my bedroom window. But I am drained by the gift giving. It all feels utterly pointless.

learned her timetable by heart. At any given hour, I knew which class she was teaching and its finishing time, so that I could get a glimpse of her for a few moments as she passed by. I was always late for my other lessons, because I had been dallying in the wrong part of the school, waiting for her to appear. There were nine separate exits to the school, and she once said to me, 'Rhona, how come you always know exactly which one I will be leaving by?' It was a combination of quality research, mathematically precise planning and the intuition of a born stalker.

As soon as I could I signed up for all the subjects she taught: biology, anatomy, physiology and health. I was bound to fail, partly because I had no interest in those subjects but mainly because I was incapable of concentrating on anything other than her while she was in the room.

I loved her biology lab. I loved the plants, because she tended to them. I loved her writing on the blackboard. I loved all the things she had to do there: adding potions to other potions, lighting the Bunsen burners, dissecting rats, using dangerous sharp knives to peel back layers of a bull's eye. I loved her lab and the subject she taught in it because I could watch her hands do so many things.

The layout of the science labs was different from other classrooms. They were set up in a more casual way. The benches and stools scattered around the place gave it a far less formal feel than the traditional rows of individual desks and plastic chairs. It felt like a wine bar. My classmates were merely padding, background noise. Like *Casablanca*, this was my bar and Joan just happened to walk into it.

I was in the bottom three in the class. I did no homework. Instead I decorated my book covers with messages I hoped she would notice, excited at the thought of my jotter going home with her for the night. Staying in her house. On the front of my biology book, I wrote out the words to the speaking part from Elvis in the middle of 'Are You Lonesome Tonight?' At the bottom I added, 'And I am.'

JUST IN CASE SHE DIDN'T GET THE MESSAGE.

I wrote her millions of letters and poems. I would go to the staffroom every single day to deliver them. I don't think the poor woman got a proper tea break in her entire career. She'd sit down and there'd be a knock at the door.

'Joan!' One of the other teachers would shout over their shoulder. 'It's your shadow again!'

She would stand in the staffroom door with a cup of coffee in her hand and a bewildered expression on her face as I presented my offering and told her, 'I adore you, I absolutely love you.'

When it became clear that this tactic was not having the desired result, I thought I'd impress her by finding out everything I could about her. Then I would stand in the staffroom doorway and recite everything I'd learned by rote, in an even monotone, like some sort of demented robot presenting *This Is Your Life*.

'You were born on August 17 1955. Your father is called Daniel. He is a doctor. Your mother is called Phoebe. She is a medical secretary. You were born in Edinburgh. You lived there until you were six.'

She would stare at me. Appalled, freaked out, stunned. Waiting for me to update her on what I had recently unearthed about her life. I thought that this relaying of information would draw her in and make her love me. I suppose I wanted her to sink to her knees and profess undying gratitude for my being so diligent in my obsession. That's not the reaction I got. But how the fuck is anyone supposed to react to an individual who not only knows your bra size, but where you buy them, how much they cost and how many blue ones you have?

When this proved to be an utterly pointless line of seduction, I decided that she would only pay attention to me if I became a celebrity. So I knocked on the staffroom door and while she stood, coffee in hand, bewildered expression in place, I told her, 'I've decided I'll become famous and then you'll love me. Do you believe me?'

'Believe what, Rhona? That you'll be famous or that you love me?'

'That I'll be famous,' I replied. Completely convinced that by attaining the former I would secure the latter.

'Yes, Rhona,' she replied, 'I do believe that you will one day be famous.'

As the world's most dedicated stalker, perhaps.

In between lessons this poor hounded woman would dive into the storeroom and light up a soothing cigarette. Standing there, drawing on it so hard that it crackled, she looked like a woman smoking her final fag before the firing squad opened up. The year before this, my dad had had a series of chest infections, and had been ordered by his doctor to give up smoking before it was too late. I was terrified that smoking was going to kill everybody I loved, so I would lecture Miss Carlisle about sneaking a crafty fag between lessons, until she relented and washed it under the tap.

If we had to go to the lecture theatre to watch an educational film, there was a specific seat I would use. It was the one she had to squeeze past in order to operate the projector or change the reel. There can be no doubt that out of all the things I did to make her life miserable, this was the one that pissed her off most. It meant her having to press her arse up against my stomach and groin every time she went by. But she had no choice in the matter if she was to go about her work.

I was oblivious to any distress I may have caused her. She tried all manner of tactics to dissuade me, but nothing worked. I was delighted with the extra attention. She would throw things at me in the classroom when I misbehaved. I would retrieve them – chalk, key rings, pencils, board rubbers, whatever – and take them home to put them in a box with a label on it:

Things Miss Carlisle Has Thrown At Me.

I would take them out lovingly one by one, to touch them, smell them and relive the memories of how each precious article, once held in her hand, had whizzed past my head and sometimes bounced off it.

To try and prevent vandalism and glue sniffing, the head teacher passed a law that year which meant we had to have a note from a teacher before we left the classroom for any reason. Every lesson with Miss Carlisle I would tell her that I was ill or needed to use the toilet. She would write me a note, which I would keep to touch and smell. I got another box and labelled it:

Excuse Notes Miss Carlisle Has Given Me.

Miss Carlisle played hockey for a club in Edinburgh somewhere. One day I discovered through Jean Anne Hunter, a sporty girl, that she was playing in a match in Musselburgh that afternoon after school. Joy, oh joy! I couldn't believe it. Neither could Miss Carlisle. I turned up in the middle of winter, alone, in my thin school blazer, with a gormless grin on my face because I was getting to see her thighs.

I stood alone, the sole spectator. At first, there was a slight spit of rain. As the match went on, the rain became heavier. An umbrella would have helped. I knew I should leave, but I couldn't.

Some time passed. I stood. I stared.

I rooted for her. She played. She ignored. The rain went from heavy to torrential. I remained, soaked to the skin, my moccasins full of water, my cold wet feet encased in tights. I could barely see through the rain. But to leave then would have been too defeatist. Anyway, the rule was she had to leave first, at all times. And she did. But not before I begged her, face pressed up against her car window, eyes squinting through the downpour, for a lift.

Without the use of words, but with a simple head shake, she declined – and I was left to suffer the further indignity of standing in the car park alone. I watched the last piece of red on her back lights fade in the distance.

Only then did I turn around and walk towards the gates that would lead me out on to the streets of Musselburgh, and to my path home, where I would once again face the music for not having the dog walked, the table laid and the potatoes on.

If I was ever off school for some reason, I would rush up to my bedroom at twelve minutes past four and stand poised with my binoculars, because I knew that she would be driving home down the road at the back of my house at around that time. I would be rewarded with a four-second glimpse of the blue Datsun Cherry Estate, registration number PUS 338W. Or the car before that, the turquoise Datsun, registration number YGE 330S.

If only I could have used all these great feats of memory, initiative and research to get my fucking exams, I'd have been out of that town five years earlier. Instead I just used to hand in exam papers covered in poems and song extracts on the off-chance that she would look at them before they went to the examination board.

BIOLOGY. PAPER ONE.
FOR JOAN CARLISLE

You're once, twice, three times a lady
And I love you ...
Yes, you're once, twice, three times a lady
And I love you ...
I love you ...

BY RHONA CAMPBELL

There was some sort of biology going on there, I suppose. And to this day I can recall all the details of the seven stages of cell division, the equations of photosynthesis, how to germinate peas and every-thing there is to know about osmosis. In an exam situation, however, I was empty. Either because she was there and I was looking at her, or because she wasn't and I wished she was.

I failed biology because she was invigilating and left the room halfway through to go and teach a class. I put my pen down and rushed out so that I could accompany her up the corridor for another half-minute or so.

'Miss! Miss, hiya!' I was out of breath and panting as usual.

'Rhona! What are you doing? You can't have finished!' She looked really alarmed.

'Doesn't matter, Miss, I'm not bothered. I just wanted to see you.'

'Rhona, you're jeopardising your entire future, just to spend a few more seconds with me?'

'I don't care,' I told her, in a desperate attempt to impress her. 'It's worth it, Miss. It's the holidays soon and I won't see you for ages.'

Which, of course, only served to disturb her even more, make her think about giving up teaching and drive her further away from me.

t he worst times of all for me – the best of times for Miss Carlisle, I imagine – were the summer holidays when I had to live without her for six weeks. Every other kid in the school was desperate to get out of the place, and in recognition of the fact that we would be impossible to teach on the last day, we were let go at lunchtime. I stayed on my own, skulking around the empty building trying to find her, crying over my impending, loveless summer.

The holidays were like a prison sentence. I'd cycle down to the school two or three times a week to stand in the empty teachers' car park and gaze at the space reserved for her. Occasionally, I would bend down to dip my fingers into the pool of oil her car had left behind. Then, rubbing it between my thumb and forefinger, like an expert tracker, I'd stare out into the distance longingly.

But this holiday, there was skiing. Even before we got there her ordeal started. We had to attend preliminary tuition sessions at Hill End Dry Slopes near Edinburgh, and Miss Carlisle drove us all up there in the school minibus and supervised our training. There was a hut where we had to hand in our shoes and get ski boots in return. Miss Carlisle always wore highly fashionable and desirable clogs. While we were skiing, someone stole them. For once it wasn't me.

I knew that we had the same size feet (imagine that!) so I offered her my trainers. She accepted, and I was overjoyed at the thought of my shoes encasing her feet. We were joined at last. She somehow neglected to return them when we got back to school, and I walked the mile and a half home in my socks. In March. If I couldn't get her on the obsessive relaying of information, perhaps she would fall for the selfless sacrifice of my footwear.

On the week leading up to the trip, I suffered from my usual bout of pre-trip hypochondria. I'd first experienced this two years previously, when I was due to go to Germany for a week with the school. I had suddenly been struck with the worst case of constipation I had ever known. Eventually I was bedridden with stomach pain. My mother was beside herself as I lay crying, convinced I was dying. My friend Charlene made many bedside visits, often in tears, worried she would lose her best friend for the trip and have to sit on the bus all the way to Germany with someone else. I began talking about leaving all my favourite things in the event of my death. Finally, my mum ran out of patience and lost her temper with me. Fortunately the short, sharp, shock treatment worked. I rallied round, had a shit, and left the next day for Germany.

The trip to Italy was no exception. The preceding week I developed a cold, which I automatically assumed was pneumonia. I lay in bed watching *Crown Court* and eating tomato soup. When my mother left for work, I would bandage my chest and lie with my pyjama top open, pretending to be a hero with Alison, my lady, at my bedside.

ME: It's no good, you'll have to go without me, I'm not going to make it.

ALISON *(weeping)*: I couldn't possibly go without you. It wouldn't
be the same. Nothing will be the same without you.

ME: I'll be fine, don't worry. It's nothing – just a few bullets.

ALISON: My darling, you are so brave. You must eat your soup
to keep your strength up.

Alison feeds me some spoonfuls of Heinz.

ME: Pass me my cane and help me to the window, will
you? I want to see the trees.

ALISON: No, you mustn't. It's too soon to try to walk. You are
so brave, but you know what the doctor said.

ME *(angrily)*: Those doctors …They know nothing! I will walk
again, I will!

We ended up, Alison Calder, me and fourteen other pupils, in a
village at the foot of the Italian Alps called Aprica. It was full of
British schoolchildren. The first thing we had to do when we arrived
was wash the swastikas that some of the boys had drawn off the side
of the bus. After this, and a lecture about representing our school and
country abroad, we explored our accommodation. The lodge had
been specifically designed to cater for school trips, so it had all the
ambience of a school canteen with snow.

Outside there was a porch and some sort of decking with

armchairs on it. Inside was a vast hall where we all ate. Corridors joined the three wings that made up the sleeping accommodation. We slept two or three to a room. The walls were all scratched and scraped. It was fairly grey and cold.

From the outset of the journey I began my intensive photographing of Alison: Alison at the door of the hotel, Alison in the distance, the top of Alison's head next to the bus.

The whole school was by this time aware of my sexuality, and I was used to daily abuse, but luckily for me everyone in the skiing party was more tolerant. I shared a room with a girl called Elizabeth Riley, and somehow I avoided becoming obsessed with her, so she had no cause to freak out and start hating me. She was a laugh – and the first among us to learn the Italian for 'fuck off'.

I also had a sort of boyfriend(ish) thing going on with a nice guy by the name of Derek Hamilton. Snogging was our shared interest. It was all we ever did. I don't even remember having any sort of conversation with him. We locked lips on the bus on the way to the airport. I think we disengaged for meals, and an occasional trip to the lavatory, but other than that we kissed for the whole seven days. I didn't mind snogging boys at this age; their faces hadn't become rough with stubble yet so if I kept my eyes closed, I could imagine I was kissing a girl, and Derek Hamilton was the most girly kisser so far. Smallish in appearance, with soft, full lips.

The skiing holiday had the potential to be a really happy time for me. I was accepted by the group. Some of them even seemed to find my sexual dilemmas impressive. I had a boy to snog, and one of my female fixations on hand to stalk at closer quarters than I had ever had before. Plus, I had another ace up my sleeve.

Swimming had given me exceptional upper body strength. Cycling at speed around town, trying to keep up with Mrs Calder's silver Mercedes, had given me powerful leg muscles. As a result, even though I was deceptively small, I was able to lift people much bigger than me on to my shoulders. I used to stand in the corridor of the ski chalet wagering passers-by that I couldn't lift boys twice my size. It had the dual benefit of making me the centre of attention and subsidising my holiday spending money.

The downside was the skiing. I turned out to be the crappest skier in the school. Plus I had the crappest outfit. Alison Calder's parents, because they were rich due to the two lorries, had bought her a top-of-the-range ski suit and branded accessories. In the tuition sessions we had before we left, I had proved to be so awful that my mother saw no point in investing any money in my skiing career. Consequently, I wore a free Municipal Borough of Musselburgh orange cagoule. In blue felt-tip lettering on the back it said 'Please Return To Outdoor Education Department'. I also got some big black plastic sunglasses from Woolworths and a new pair of white tracksuit bottoms. From a distance I looked like a Solero ice lolly. Close up I looked like a little lesbian in a shit anorak.

Throughout the week, I remained rubbish at skiing, never managing to progress beyond the basic 'Snow Plough' position. Subsequently, I was put in the poor skiing ability group, a group which consisted of only three people: me, Elizabeth Riley, and a very overweight boy named Bob. Alison Calder, on the other hand, was a great skier. She was in the advanced group. The poor group were never supposed to venture beyond the nursery slopes and had special supervision at all times while attempting to ski.

Unfortunately, it was unusually hot that spring, and the snow on the nursery slopes – where I should have spent the entire trip – had melted. Consequently, the beginners and hopeless people had to move up the mountain. Every day, the snow cap got higher and we moved up until we were practically on the main piste. Which is where advanced skiers like Alison Calder were to be found. So I obviously wasn't complaining.

Towards the end of the week, while I was pottering around trying not to fall flat on my arse, I happened to look over my shoulder and saw Alison Calder whizzing past at high speed. My reaction was as swift as her skis. Knees bent, I swivelled around, adopted my version of a traditional skiing position, and launched myself down the mountain after her. The warning shouts of my instructor faded behind me as the wind filled my ears.

I was catching up very quickly. Still locked into my original crouching position, I was actually the fastest-moving person on the slope. I was also, however, the most out of control. There was absolutely no way anything other than a tree could stop me now.

Alison became aware of me at the very moment I passed her. As I did so, I turned around to look at her. I just managed to catch a glimpse of surprise on my sweetheart's face, and then, whack! I crashed head first into that tree. Which, incidentally, was on the other side of a nine-foot gorge I had sailed over first. I bounced off the tree and into a heap of snow, skis sticking straight up in the air, my ears ringing and spots of light dancing in front of my eyes. I could see faces leaning in, Alison Calder's among them. I could see their lips moving, but I could only barely hear them asking me if I was alright. Of course I wasn't alright. I was almost dying right there in the snow from the shame of having humiliated myself in front of my true love. There was only one thing to do in order to cope. Pretend to be unconscious.

The first-aid people who rushed to the scene held up fingers and stared into my eyes. It was difficult to keep them closed as they forced open the lids. They said stuff in Italian. Mr Arthur, one of our teachers, arrived, and in broken English they explained I was concussed and would have to go to hospital. Because we were quite high up the mountain – and because people who fetch you down mountains and into hospital take all that kind of stuff very seriously – there followed a full-scale emergency operation.

A squad of Italian mountain rescuers with walkie-talkies and tool belts strapped me into a stretcher and hauled me up the slope a few hundred feet. We then had to wait there for about half an hour until an emergency services snowplough came up the mountain to retrieve me. The stretcher was attached to the back of the plough, and I was dragged pathetically up the hill. Everything happened so slowly, and I was dying to open my eyes to see who cared the most. I squinted slightly as they transferred me to the ambulance, but all I was aware of were hundreds of people dotted around the slopes watching the idiot in the bright orange Musselburgh Council cagoule making a fool of herself. I had no option but to remain 'unconscious'. In the ambulance were a couple of other casualties: a Welsh boy with the skin peeled off the palm of his hands and a very small Geordie lad with an enormous egg on his head. As the van drove off he pressed his two fingers against the window at his classmates.

In truth, I wasn't that badly concussed. I only had to spend the rest of the afternoon in the hospital, although much of that was taken up with lying, strapped on to the stretcher, in a corridor. I remember trying to make a nurse understand that I was desperate to use the toilet. She brought me a bottle, the sort a person with a penis would piss in. She thought I was a boy, which under normal circumstances would have probably made my day.

W hen I got back to the hotel, I was totally mortified, and disappointed at the general lack of interest in my absence. My pride had taken some heavy bruising, and I resolved to keep a lower profile for the remainder of the trip.

Later that day we all had a free session, and spent it in the café area. There was a jukebox, and a bar selling juices, and little tables with people dotted around talking about who fancied who and what was number one. I walked in and there was Alison Calder, glowing in her expensive ski kit. I ordered a lemon soda and a tube of Smarties. Convinced I had the appeal of a handsome boy and the charisma of a young Sean Connery as James Bond, I strolled over to the jukebox and put on The Commodores tune 'Three Times A Lady'.

Thanks for the times that you've given me
The memories are all in my mind
And now that we've come to the end of our rainbow
There's something I must say out loud

This was mine and Alison's tune. She had no way of knowing that, of course. It was something I had told her during the course of one of our many imaginary conversations. In reality, I had very few non-imaginary conversations with Alison. Come to think of it, I can hardly remember a single word she ever said in real life. 'No, I won't kiss you' is about the sum total of her side of the dialogue.

Lionel Richie was warbling away, Alison paid no attention to me whatsoever, and I played out this fantasy in my head. She had been my lover of many years. I stood at the bar, leaning with one foot crossed over the other, as if it was a real bar, and took hefty, dramatic swigs of lemon soda as if it was a real drink, and I was really drinking to forget her. All the while gulping down the Smarties as if they were real pills, pills I needed for my Alison pain, and washing them down as if I was really taking an overdose of real painkillers.

Somehow Alison remained completely unaware of all this drama, and carried on chit-chatting to whoever about whatever. But I figured that if I ran my finger seductively around the rim of the lemon soda bottle, she would notice and melt into my arms.

It's possible that this tactic would have eventually worked if I hadn't got my index finger stuck. Two embarrassing incidents in 24 hours was more than I could take, so I skulked off to try and remove the bottle in private. Disguising my panic as a casual walk, I moved across the café floor cleverly carrying the bottle with one finger.

I decided to take the backstairs route to the bedrooms. The steps were narrow and steep. I was wearing my great clunking ski boots. Holding on to the banister was impractical due to the finger in the bottle situation, yet my heel kept missing the stair. I tried crossing my arm over to hold on to the rail, but ended up descending almost sideways, which was even more dangerous. Slowly turning around and attempting to go down backwards, so I could hold on, proved too dodgy to be practical. I was carefully working through my options when my foot slipped and gravity took the decision out of my hands.

I did the whole stairs from top to bottom in a couple of seconds, bouncing on about every fourth one. The noise attracted the attention of the others, and I was soon looking up at another collection of puzzled and concerned faces, Alison Calder's among them. Me flat on my ass, ski boots wedged into the corners of the landing. Lemon soda bottle still intact, firmly fixed to my finger, the contents dribbling down my face. Must try harder.

there was a big party of Welsh kids also on a half-term skiing trip at the resort, and I woke up one morning and decided that I had fallen in love with one of them. She wasn't even my type. No blue eyes. No blonde hair. Actually, she was a brunette girl from the Valleys called Jacqueline Ashworth. She was very beautiful and very mature.

We hung out for a while, although I have no idea why because I quite clearly wasn't like her other friends. I should have realised that she wasn't available to the likes of me, because she appeared to have pulled the Italian ski instructor, who was quite old (nineteen), muscled, looked like Leif Garrett (result!) and constantly wore white lip cream to stop sunburn.

Nevertheless, I suddenly decided I fancied her rotten. I couldn't think of anything else. This was the new crush. It replaced all previous crushes in an instant. She was the biggest thing in my life. 'Forget Alison. I'm over Miss Carlisle,' I told myself. 'I'm going to make a new start with Jacqueline.'

As with all the others, I somehow convinced myself that she knew how I felt, and that she probably felt the same way. I longed for the day when I would declare my love for a girl I was obsessed with and she would say, 'I am so glad you said that. I have been meaning to declare my love for you also.'

However, the memory of the disastrous episode with Susan Tyler loomed large enough to make me approach Jacqueline with a degree of caution.

For a couple of days I would go up to her and say, 'I have something very important to say to you, but I can't tell you what it is. It's a very important thing, but I'll tell you another time.' Maybe I was hoping that she'd catch my drift and say, 'Oh, I do hope that you love me, because I love you too.'

The day before we were due to leave I stepped up my campaign by telling her more often – about every twenty minutes or so – that I had something important to tell her.

She may never have learned what it was if I hadn't realised that night, while lying awake thinking of her, that this was my last chance. A ridiculous impulse kicked in and I leapt out of my bed. With everyone asleep and the whole skiing complex dark and quiet, I sneaked out of my room and made my way to hers on the other side of the lodge. The Welsh wing.

I nervously knock on the door. She opens it, and greets me with a smile. This is all going well. In the other two beds, her roommates are asleep. Perfect!

'What was this thing you have to tell me?' she asks as soon as I walk through the door.

'I'm not sure I can tell you now,' I say, the memories of Susan Tyler, Alison Calder and Miss Carlisle in various states of distress in my head.

'It's OK, I don't mind. You can tell me.'

'It's very hard to explain. I'm very nervous.'

She seems very warm and friendly and understanding. I am convinced she knows what is really on my mind.

'I'd rather write it down on a piece of paper.'

'Fine.'

I get a scrap of paper and a pencil, think for a moment and write:

Dear Jacqueline, I think you are so beautiful. I have fancied you ever since I first saw you. When we are together, the moments I cherish with every beat of my heart, to touch you, to hold you, to feel you, to need you. There's nothing to keep us apart.

    p.s. Can I kiss you now?

I smile as I hand her the note.

She takes it from me and sits down on the edge of her bed, back to me, one long leg folded over the other. Very grown up and womanly.

She takes a long time to read the contents of my note. Maybe two or three minutes. I watch her and prepare myself for the beautiful moment when another warm smile will appear, far warmer than the others. She'll look up at me, reach out her hand to mine and give it a long reassuring squeeze.

Instead she looks up at me, reaches out her hand to fend me off, opens her mouth, fills her mighty Welsh lungs and gives a long, most unreassuring scream. And she carries on screaming. At the top of her voice. The only other circumstances under which screaming at that volume could possibly be valid would be a rape or a fire. It is definitely an over-the-top reaction to a corny love letter from a small, confused, Scottish lesbian.

I back myself into the corner of the room, fearing that being any nearer to her will make her more hysterical. Her roommates sit bolt upright in bed and immediately leap to her rescue.

'What have you done? What have you said?'

'Nothing. I mean, something silly. SSHHH!'

I'm straining above the racket.

I try to talk to her. 'I thought you knew.'

'I thought you were trying to tell me you fancied my boyfriend. But this –' holding up my note, my poor pathetic harmless note '– this is DISGUSTING!'

She passes it to one of the other girls. She reads it, shows disgust, and comforts her further.

I move forward slightly out of the corner, nearer the bed, with my hands outstretched. This makes her shriek her head off again, and for some strange reason, one of the other girls starts crying. I wait for the inevitable and shameful consequences. Within seconds, all the Welsh teachers are at the door along with most of her classmates. A minute or so later, my teachers are there too, closely followed by my classmates, and eventually the entire staff and management of the lodge. I peek through my fingers, and for the third time in a week see a crowd of puzzled and concerned faces (including Alison's) clustered around me. Must try harder.

The aftermath was actually quite an anticlimax. The screaming that this girl had produced was followed up with a bout of wordless sobs. The note was produced, I was removed and trudged off down the corridor. Hundreds of people in their pyjamas stood gawping at me as I passed.

'So what was that all about?' I heard one of my classmates say.

'Oh, it was nothing,' came the reply. 'Rhona Campbell just told some Welsh girl she fancies her.'

There was a definite feeling from my schoolmates that this was an event so commonplace as to be almost mundane by now. But I didn't go down to breakfast on the last day – I hid in my room – and I somehow managed to sit quietly all the way home without disgracing myself further. But I did ensure that from my seat I had a good view of Alison Calder. Just in case she said or did anything that might be useful for my Fact Files.

back at home, surrounded by silver anniversary gifts, I kept silent about my embarrassing exploits, answering my mother's questions with the briefest of responses.

'Did you have a lovely time, Rhona?'

'Was good fun, yeah.'

'Did you do lots of skiing?'

'Yeah, loads.'

'Did you like Italy?'

'Yeah, it was nice, thanks.'

'Meet nice people?'

'Alright, yeah.'

'For heaven's sake, Rhona!' she shouted, exasperated. 'How do you expect to get along with people if you have nothing to say to them?'

Clipping from the *Musselburgh News*, March 1979

The Italian Alps was the destination of a party of pupils and teachers from Musselburgh Grammar School during the Easter holidays.

A party of 16 pupils from second and third year and four adults spent eight days in the town of Aprica in the Italian Alps.

They travelled to Glasgow by coach where they caught a plane to Milan and then a coach on to their destination.

They shared the holiday with 200 Welsh visitors so they had plenty occasion to speak English, although some did pick up some Italian words and phrases.

The grammar school party spent the days skiing, with entertainment laid on in the evenings. This included fancy dress parties, swimming, discos, and pizza evenings.

Mr W. Devine, who led the party, said, 'The trip was an overwhelming success and everyone seemed to thoroughly enjoy themselves. There were some bumps and bruises gained on the ski-slopes but no serious mishaps.'

four
april

DATE: 6 April **DAY: Friday**

Today was the best day of all. After school Valerie and I went to Guides and next to the Guide Hall round the back is an old house with a garden, with pear and apple trees leaning over. Captain told us to collect leaves but instead me and a few others went and climbed trees but Captain gave us a row. On the way home from Guides we saw Stewart Smith rushing out of his house and he shouted to us and pointed up to the sky. We looked up and we saw a U.F.U. It was smaller than a plane and it had white lights all around with a red light at the top. It was flying low and it swirled round and back and forward making a hoovering sound. But know one believed us but it's true.

Every single photograph I had taken on the school trip to Aprica was a surreptitious shot of Alison Calder. In some she was whizzing blurrily past on skis, in others I hadn't had time to look through the viewfinder properly, so there would be a corner of her shoulder and mass of background. My mum put them in an album.

'What a lot of pictures,' she said. 'There's literally nothing in most of them.'

It might have seemed a harsh thing to say to a fourteen-year-old, except that I had already shown some aptitude with the camera and had got my Photography Badge at the Girl Guides two years previously. I was a prolific badge-getter, mind you. Part of my competitive nature, I suppose. By the end of my Guiding career I had amassed eighteen in total. Plus three 'Service To The Community' flashes. My particular service to my community was to clean out the church hall.

I loved going to that little Guide Hall on a Friday evening, especially after the events of the ski trip. I felt secure and comfortable there. I would go as far as to say that I almost fitted in.

The very fact there was a uniform was one of the big things for me. We had badges and insignia, and on big occasions – Remembrance Sunday, for example – we got to march in them. I would pull every stunt I could think of to ensure I led every march.

The banner fitted into a harness on my waist and I imagined I was a handsome Royal Marine marching in a victory parade. I took Remembrance Sunday very seriously, and my position as Standard Bearer for the 'Platoon' was paramount. The whole military thing was crucial to my fantasy. The drums. The bugles. Folk at the side of the road waving. I always tried not to look down at my feet in case I caught a glimpse of the white patterned knee-socks my mother bought in bulk from a catalogue and the navy-blue skirt reminding me that I was really a teenage girl from a third-rate Guide group.

The Guides were pretty much the nearest thing I had ever got to complete fulfilment as a child. It harnessed the company of girls with military order. It was heaven. I was convinced that I was able to live entirely in a world without men, except for:

My father
Elvis Presley
The minister at our church (who looked like Richard Burton)
Steve Austin
Bruce Lee
Morecambe and Wise

There were no nightmare personalities at the Guides. We were all kind and caring, with a sense of fun. There were no bullies, and no one spoke of boyfriends. We just wanted to care for the elderly, 'serve the Queen, help other people and keep the Girl Guide Law'.

And to take the piss, in a nice way, out of the Captain behind her back.

I was the leader of the Daffodil Patrol. Every meeting we'd begin by standing in a circle and saying a prayer. Then we'd all get out our Guiding boxes. The box was usually an old Rover Assortment biscuit tin that your mum had put tape over with your name on it. It contained all those items essential to the craft of Girl Guiding: a manual, a book of rules, some printed thing about the Queen and God, a little first-aid box and some string to practise knots on. No one ever added anything to the box. And in all the time I was there no one ever removed anything from it. Nevertheless, the first item on the agenda was always the taking of an inventory of the contents and ticking them off on a little checklist. The last item on the agenda was always a prayer followed by me playing 'Taps' on my harmonica. Order, ritual, uniform, prayer, ceremony. All key elements in making me feel secure.

It was, however, a slipshod outfit. Although everyone in our group was lovely, there's no doubt we were a dishevelled gang of misfits, freaks and fat girls. Whenever there was a larger gathering of Guides, the other packs all seemed so much smarter and more regimented than us. One Remembrance Sunday, as we came marching up a street, I overheard one of the parents remark, 'Here comes the *Dad's Army* mob.' It totally screwed with my Victorious Marines Entering The Conquered City fantasy. It was also on those massed Guides occasions that I'd get to see Alison Calder with her Company. All of them gleaming and perfectly laundered, and all of us tatty and slightly grubby around the edges.

I suppose it was partly the fault of our Captain, Susan Thomson. She tried to keep us in hand, but always failed. She was a short, dumpy woman with big glasses and a great sense of humour. Occasionally she'd come back from some sort of Central Guide Leader Meeting where she'd been bollocked for having allowed us to become an undisciplined rabble. So she'd embark on a programme of shouting and establishing of order for a while, but we'd always wear her down after an hour or so.

We were at our most disorderly whenever we went on a Guiding expedition. We would all go out to the countryside and stay in one big tent together. To try and keep us in order, Susan Thomson would recruit a couple of Queen's Guides, Norma and Glenda, to lend a hand. Norma was tall and gentle and always got the giggles. Glenda was short and dumpy and a bit less posh than Norma, although equally as giggly.

There were a couple of things that made these trips so thrilling. I was an only child and used to being on my own, even on holiday. I yearned for brothers or sisters – so much so that when I went away in the caravan with my parents, I used to beg them to let me sleep on the top bunk, so that I could pretend there was someone below me. Guide trips was the nearest I was ever going to get to the experience of having siblings.

Best of all, of course, was sleeping in a big tent with a bunch of other girls, as well as the Blessed Norma and Glenda. This was about as close as I ever got to heaven. The presence of so many women in a confined space was so exciting I would become manic. It wasn't really a sexual thing; it was more of a feeling that I was in an environment free of bullies and sexual games, an environment where I felt free and powerful, where being myself seemed to make me popular.

Here, I could study women at close quarters. I could learn what made them tick, how they viewed the world and, crucially, how they interacted with me. But specifically what they thought of me. To this end, at night-time I would stay awake longer than the others but pretend to be asleep, so I could try and hear Norma and Glenda talking about me. Which they did.

Norma: 'Aw, look at her, she looks so peaceful.'

Glenda: 'Aye, she's an angel when she's asleep. You'd never think she was a handful, lying like that, would you?'

Norma: 'Aw. Bless.'

They were right, I was a handful, but I knew they loved me and understood me. Hoorah, hoorah, for the Queen's Guides.

I was the one who invariably initiated the midnight feasting on sweets and Cremola Foam. I was the one who became so hysterical with excitement and laughter I'd end up wheezing my way into an asthma attack.

I was the one who tumbled headfirst into nettles after being chased by a bull while leading an illicit excursion into a field. And I was the one who instigated the running feud with the Farmer 'Mad Tommy Broon'.

Tommy Broon was indeed mad. He had a constant temper that would escalate very quickly. He had a bright red face, beady eyes and National Health specs. His teeth were big and yellow. There was talk of him brandishing a shotgun. We all imagined that we'd seen it at one point. He wore wellies the entire year round. He was excellent value for taking the piss out of and gave great chase.

If we were bored, especially in the summer, we would say, 'Fancy getting a chase off Tommy Broon?'

There was never a time when you couldn't be bothered. It was too exciting. So we'd go up the fields by the farm and hang around until he spotted us. He'd arrive in the distance on a tractor. We'd wait till he got much nearer before the chase officially began, even though from a mile or so away you could make out his arms waving angrily. He'd get down off his tractor and run towards us, and then we could make out what he was saying, which was only ever:

'Fucking little bastards.'

When the white spit started to gather at the corners of his mouth it was time to run.

'Shotey!' (Meaning 'beware'.)

'Tommy Broon!' one of us would shout, then we were off.

A highly addictive mixture of sheer terror, nervous hysteria, laughter at the sight of mad Tommy chasing us in his wellies and your friends completely shitting it, there was nothing quite like a chase with Tommy Broon. He never caught us – once we got off the fields, through the hole in the barbed-wire fence and over the wall, we were home and dry. We did this time and time again, totally convinced that if he caught one of us, we would be shot, killed, arrested or kidnapped. Or worse – made to live with him and the mad witch woman at the end of the farm road. Of course, there was no witch – just an old woman, living alone in one of the farm cottages, who happened to wear a black shawl and rarely went out.

The other thing I loved about Guides was the Assistant Guide Leader Mrs Davison. I think Mrs Davison is the first woman, in flesh and blood terms, I found sexually intriguing. She had jet-black hair, attractive made-up eyes, a larger-than-life personality, and the brightest orangey-red lips I had seen to date.

Mrs Davison was a grown up, but fooled around constantly like one of us. She was always late, and would burst through the swing doors of the church community hall, pinning her Guide Leader hat to her hair. She was very heavily perfumed. I was struck by the effort she went to just for us. All girls. I appreciated it.

We would often play a game that involved us sitting on the floor, opposite one another, legs flat on the floor, the soles of our feet touching in order to create a ladder effect. While in this position Mrs

Davison would always interrupt, walking up the ladder, hand on hip, exaggerating her walk, over-feminising it. Then she'd air-kiss to us all and go:

'Oooh, Marilyn Monroe, ooh, Marilyn Monroe.' It totally mesmerised me. The others laughed.

Mrs Davison was also the inspiration behind my desire to earn an Entertainer's Badge. The Entertainer's Badge was such a big deal to me, and I decided to utilise my impersonator skills to put on an entire show where I played all the characters. My mum was to direct and choreograph. My repertoire began with Clement Freud, where I just stood centre stage, doing the 'Mince Morsel' ad. Then a quick change into Frank Spencer, for which my mum gave me a nylon coat from my dad's work with a belt tied around the waist. A beret came from one of the Brownies. Then Max Bygraves. No outfit was required for this, as I wore a neutral, makeshift dinner suit, although mum insisted I hold a bunch of tulips whilst singing Max's most famous number, 'Tulips From Amsterdam'.

Al Jolson, again in dinner jacket. Down on one knee, hands clasped, singing 'Sonny Boy'. This was inspired by a seven-inch single my parents had for many years called 'Sammy Davis Impersonates'. We discussed blacking up at this point but it would have been too complicated to get the shoe polish off my face in time for the Jimmy Cagney finale. For Jimmy, I sang 'Yankee Doodle Dandy' while waving two miniature American flags that my mum kept in the drinks cabinet.

My props were in an old suitcase on the stage with me. I was word perfect. My mum had cleverly devised all the links with me. She was so excited, and I was extremely nervous. This was a big showcase for my talents.

The audience (some other Guides and five tables of old people from the church) loved it. But I knew the girls my age only got Frank Spencer. I was completely aware I was doing impressions that only the over-50s would appreciate.

Mrs Davison applauded madly at the end, and wolf-whistled from the tea and coffee counter at the back of the hall. My mum went teary eyed, and I passed with flying colours.

Getting the Entertainer's Badge was my second best day ever at Girl Guides. The best one had been in September 1976 when I had turned up with Joe Bugner to open our annual fete.

My mum was behind that coup as well. Most of my teenage life she worked as a secretary for Ladbrokes, the betting organisation. But her hard work and enthusiasm allowed her to take on an unofficial role in the PR department. It was there she became friendly with Joe, who was to become heavyweight boxing champion of the world, and was the only man ever to go fifteen rounds with Muhammad Ali. Twice.

Mum had somehow convinced him to come up to Scotland to do some promotional work at a Highland Games event sponsored by Ladbrokes. He got paid £31 (I always wonder why he got the extra quid). He came to our house, this big beast of a man stuffed into our tiny living room and chatting happily to us wee people. Within seconds of his arrival, Auntie Kay and Uncle Jim were visiting us, and it seemed like the entire estate had gathered in the street outside to gawp at this giant through our window. He was obviously smitten with my mum, and took very little convincing to stay an extra day or so in order to accompany me to the fete.

I remember little about that day, other than the glow of basking in Joe's celebrity, and the sense of power I felt. The respect I got from that event carried me through my entire Guiding career.

Before he left, he handed the cheque for £31 back to my mum, countersigned it and told her to use it to buy me a new bicycle.

DATE: 7 April   *DAY: Saturday*

I got up at 7 o'clock and went swimming. When I came back I washed Uncle Alan's car and then read books with Valerie. Afterwards about 2.30 Alison, Valerie and I decided to go to Portobello open air and the shows. Mr Duffy drove us there and we only went in the pool twice it was so cold. We had a hot shower, got changed and went to the shows. When we arrived at the shows Valerie was showing off that she wasn't scared of the Big Wheel and that she only liked it when it went really fast and when we got on it she started to cry. After that only Valerie and I went on the walsers and Valerie was also scared then. Then we came off them and went into the house of horrors which was scary. After that we got the bus and went home. When I came in I watched Butch Cassidy and the Sundance Kid. Then I took Hector out, gave him his meat and then I went to my bed.

DATE: 8 April   *DAY: Sunday*

Today I chummed Valerie to see her granny (Nana) off on the train. Then we spent the whole day down the street. Later I stayed in and went down the grassy bit with the gang about 9 o'clock. Valerie arrived and she looked attractive I think, maybe, I'm not sure. Valerie and I spent the rest of the night tidying the caravan. Then we decided to stay the night in it, and went to sleep at 12.00.

DATE: 9 April   *DAY: Monday*

After school I went along for Valerie, we listened to records and I drew her. Later on we went down the street and we saw lots of nice boys today but I like that boy Miss Carlisle teaches. Later on we went to see my Uncle Hebbie but he was asleep. We met quite a nice boy called Andrew Scotland, and we'll keep in touch, I think he likes me. We went home and played records. I think I like boys more now!!!!!

Soon after I got back from my fated skiing trip to Aprica, Mum and Dad took off to Benidorm for their first holiday abroad in years. It was a belated silver wedding gift to each other. They left me in the care of Auntie Kay and Uncle Jim, and that meant I would also see a great deal of my gran, granddad and Uncle Hebbie too. My Uncle Jim was my gran's youngest brother. He was married to my Auntie Kay, who was on her second marriage. In theory she was my mum's auntie, and, therefore, my great aunt.

I remember very little about Uncle Jim, other than he was kind and gentle, a small, balding, elderly man who drove Auntie Kay to and fro. Auntie Kay, on the other hand, was something of a force of nature: a strong, tall, slim woman who wore trousers. This was unheard of in a woman of her generation. She had a very dry sense of humour, a sharp tongue, and took no nonsense from anyone. She wrote poetry that marked every occasion and kept it written up in a big book.

I always found it strange that my gran, who was from a generation of women who believed a hat should always be worn in church and that washing on a Sunday was immoral, lived with her husband and other brother (Herbert) her entire married life, yet neither of them would speak to the other.

'Why doesn't Granddad sit at the table with you, me and Uncle Hebbie?' I'd ask her constantly.

'Because your granddad likes to take his tea on his lap,' she'd reply.

'Why doesn't Granddad ever talk to Uncle Hebbie, Gran?'

'He likes his chair, that's all.'

I never asked my granddad. I don't remember ever asking my granddad anything. He was a man of few words, and a lot of coughing. He watched cricket and liked Nana Mouskouri, and I only ever remember seeing him smile when he was about to start eating a Fry's Chocolate Cream. He wore beige trousers and a cardigan, drove a white Cortina, and peed in a bottle at the side of the bed in the middle of the night. This, and tea every night in his chair on a tray, seemed to be his life. He was a postman all his days. He got awarded the highest order a postman can be awarded, the Imperial Service Medal for Faithful Service, and when he retired, the Post Office presented him with a gold watch. He was a heavy smoker, and as a result coughed up phlegm loudly every morning.

I knew he hated my uncle, but no one would tell me why. My mum tried to fob me off with half-arsed answers as well.

'They've always been like that. Your granddad doesn't like to speak to him, that's all.'

I don't know why I never asked my Uncle Hebbie. Maybe even then I picked up that it might have embarrassed him to tell me. I also sensed it was more Granddad hating him than the other way around.

How could you hate Uncle Hebbie? All he ever did was keep to himself in his little bedsit room, and teach me 'I Do Like To Be Beside The Seaside' while drumming with his sticks from the war on his card table. He went to his partially disabled club twice a week to make things out of deer horn. But he did slurp his food very badly and spill lots of it down himself and over the tablecloth. I suspected this was something to do with why Granddad never sat and ate with him.

He would also yawn a lot and mid-yawn say 'Aye … Aye …' in a really drawn-out way. His room stunk of cigarettes and Vick. He owned very little. At his window was a boxful of tools for his deer-horn making. He sat most days, collar and tie on, waistcoat with pocket watch on a chain, hands clasped over his enormous stomach, with the TV on, blaring. Sundays were his favourite, because he loved *Songs of Praise*. And would sing along to all the hymns.

'Why doesn't Uncle Hebbie have a wife?' I tried a different angle with my mum.

'Never married.'

I thought this was very odd. I'd never known anyone older not to be married, unless their partner had died. The only other unmarried grown-up person I'd met was Edith the missionary, niece of my gran's lifelong neighbour, Mrs Auchenleck. And our Guide Captain.

'Has Uncle Hebbie ever had a girlfriend?' I wasn't going to give up.

'He used to go around with a couple in the band, years ago. Mr and Mrs Mackenzie, I think.'

Oh my God, what was my mum telling me? Uncle Hebbie was in some strange situation with a man and a woman in the Salvation Army band? Was this why my granddad didn't speak to him in nearly 30 years? Because he felt so morally outraged? I never found out.

I sensed that Auntie Kay was at the bottom of much of the intrigue. She was an old-fashioned East Coast Scottish disciplinarian. Like many childless people, she believed that the raising of children was an exact science, which all the parents in the world – specifically mine – had got entirely wrong. By the application of a few basic principles, it was entirely feasible that one could raise well-mannered, tidy and regimented offspring who spoke only when they were spoken to.

Consequently, over the years, Auntie Kay and I had an awful lot of rows. Many of them after we'd returned from shopping expeditions for my clothes. Because my mum worked full-time, and Auntie Kay didn't, she was occasionally entrusted with the job of taking me shopping. I quickly realised that her eyesight was so poor that I could con her into buying me boys' clothes.

She wouldn't even be able to make out the name of the shop, so I used to get her to buy me things from army surplus stores, and she would be none the wiser. One time we were in Goldberg's, browsing through some boring girls' stuff, when I spotted a pair of brown hipster boys' pinstripe trousers. I tried them on and insisted that they were the ones my mum felt I needed. She squinted her eyes, holding the trousers up to the light.

'Are you sure they're girls' slacks?'

'Yes, Auntie Kay, of course.'

Only when we returned home, and my new trousers were inspected by my mum, would Auntie Kay learn that they buttoned up the wrong side. She would be furious. Obviously, she never understood why I wanted boys' trousers in the first place, but it was my lies that really wound her up.

Deep within my Auntie Kay there was a misery that struck a chord with me, even as a kid. Beneath her dominating demeanour, I believe there lay a truly crippled soul. Perhaps it was that she had been consistently thwarted in her attempts to live a creatively rewarding life – her obvious intelligence and artistic bent crushed by the dutiful care of my Uncle Jim. Or, as rumour had it and I preferred to believe, perhaps it was because her first husband had left her for a man.

Evidently, he had been in the army and returned to the marital home somehow transformed into a rampant queen. I only ever got half-truths and diversionary clearing of the throat whenever I asked my mum about him.

'Mum, why did Auntie Kay and her first husband get a divorce?'

'Oh, he went off to the army, and that was that.'

'Mum, what do you mean, that was that?'

(sighing) 'He was a peculiar fellow.'

'How come?'

'Well, she got a letter from him.'

'Where from? Where was he?'

'India.'

'Then what?'

'He said he needed some money for stuff, and she sent it.'

I interrupted, sensing I was getting to the bottom of it.

'What stuff?'

'You know, erm …' She stuttered a bit at this point, obviously editing. 'Vests and things, he needed new vests, said he was running out, you know, so she sent it anyway, and here he was going through it like nothing else on earth.'

Mum carried on making one of her soups for the thousandth time, hoping my line of questioning was complete.

'Going through what? Vests?'

'NO. MONEY! The vests were just a front.'

'What do you mean, a front? Front vest? Why didn't the army give him vests?'

'It wasn't just vests. He said he needed things, and here she was sending the money over and he was running up a bill, with other things, and that's when she clicked. So that was that.'

That was certainly that for me, because I knew it was the most I was going to get out of her on the subject.

It is fair to say that Auntie Kay hated homosexuals. When I was going through stuff with my mum later in life about being gay, she wrote me one of the most vitriolic and malevolent letters imaginable. Yet I always picked up a slightly dykey vibe from her. She had a brusque masculine approach to life and she always wore trousers, which was a pretty rare thing in our family, or in that part of Scotland in 1979. Although apparently nothing could be further from the truth: I was later to learn that during the war she had conducted a rampantly heterosexual campaign to do her bit for morale.

We did have a lot of happy times together, though. She was the one who taught me how to swim. I'm not sure how. She never entered the pool, just encouraged me from the side. I loved her creativity, wit and imagination. She wrote poems about everything that happened to us, no matter how trivial. If I stayed with her in Edinburgh, we would work together on fantastic blueprints of massive spaceships. They were intricate in detail and ambitious in scope, and she encouraged me in the way of someone who genuinely understands a child's imaginative processes. She had an over-the-top neighbour that I loved, called Jean Munroe, who smoked like a chimney and swore constantly. She lived across the stairs from her. Whenever I stayed with her I would beg to see Jean, just to hear her mad stories, where 'bloody' and 'fuck' was every second word. Then she'd take a drag of her cigarette, look down at me and say:

'Excuse my French, by the way.'

And I would laugh my head off, and so would my Auntie Kay because she knew why I found it funny.

But Auntie Kay scared me slightly. There was a part of her that wanted to control me, that felt I should be disciplined. She thought I was too much to cope with and therefore should be taken more in hand. When she looked after me while my parents were in Benidorm, she walked in with an attitude that said, 'Right, young lady! I'm in charge now. Let's do things my way!'

Timetables of housework were drawn up. Curfews imposed. Rules and regulations explained and executed with immediate effect. Punishments and penalties enforced swiftly and without mercy. It felt like a gaol sentence for me. And I was looking to escape.

the spring fair was held every year at the Musselburgh Racecourse, and the lure of the big lights, the big wheel and the big tunes was always going to override any fear of what Auntie Kay would do to me if I gave her the slip. This year I went AWOL with my best friend Valerie for the afternoon and most of the evening.

Valerie Duffy lived next door but one to my mum and dad's house and was a year or so younger than me. We hooked up together because she was also an outsider, albeit for different reasons. She was no dyke, but her look was headed in that direction. She was a little dumpy, she had braces on her teeth and, like me, she favoured the tomboy look in clothing. We were very close for a few years and tried everything we could to dress the same. Both of us were besotted with Elvis, and wore matching memorabilia on the anniversary of his death. Our mothers would attend the same Pippa Dee parties (a common occurrence on housing estates), where a Pippa Dee rep comes with catalogues and all the mums meet in someone's house, have snacks and drinks, then bond with the rep who seduces them into buying lots of clothes that are cheaper than in the shops and get delivered in a truck a few weeks later. Valerie and I used to pop our heads in for a while and beg our mums to order the same clothes.

We spent loads of time together. A lot of it just giggling. We played tricks on people. When we visited other areas, we had our own language. We'd pretend we were foreign, and speak to each other in our own made-up tongue.

As a special treat I'd beg my mum to let us spend the night in the caravan at the bottom of the garden. At night, with the lights off, we'd play a fantastic game. We'd start by drawing the names of pop groups on each other's backs. Which was nice. It was like having a massage. There was a subtle agreement going on; whoever was having the name drawn would say, 'I didn't get that, do it again slower.' Even if it was something really simple like 'Mud'. Then it would be, 'No. Still not got it. Again.' It would feel oh so dreamy, Valerie's fingers up and down my back. I willed her to try The Brotherhood of Man.

We hung out on the Grassy Bit together a lot. The Grassy Bit was an area of grass, just behind Jamie Ritchie's house. It was a useful place for us teenagers to hang out because, due to an uncharacteristic quirk of Wimpey Homes' landscaping, it was not overlooked by the front of any houses, and was hidden by fencing.

A few of us would gather pretty much every night and just talk and flirt a little. Maybe there'd be the odd bit of fighting or snogging, but nothing like the action that took place down the side of the youth club, or under the Roman Bridge.

There'd be me, Valerie, a couple of girls called Hazel, and Carol Cowan – the most beautiful girl in the school – and whoever else happened to be around. And then there was King Jamie Ritchie, entering each evening via a swashbuckling route from his bedroom window, along the garage roof and down the side of the fence. He would return the same way when he'd grown bored of hassling me and Valerie. She didn't get it quite as bad as me, but I remember Jamie waving her pants triumphantly in the air on several occasions. One of the reasons he hung back when it came to humiliating Valerie was because she had an older brother, Jonathan.

Jonathan didn't join us too often down the Grassy Bit. He was a bit of a geeky kid, unable to tear himself away from his CB radio set long enough to develop social skills. But he did look out for Valerie, and she carried that 'I Got Brothers' aura that I so envied. Their family dynamic did confuse me a little. While Jonathan was highly protective of his sister outside the house, inside they fought physically, constantly and dangerously. His standard greeting on entering a room and finding her in it was to creep up behind her and kick her backside as hard as he could.

Over the years, Valerie developed the most extraordinarily strong muscles in her arse, because she would tense her buttocks whenever she sensed her brother behind her. He quit kicking her when she was fifteen. One day he sneaked up and planted his foot on her behind with the usual force, but Valerie tensed her arse so tightly that Jonathan broke his foot. He told everyone he did it playing football, but we revelled in broadcasting to the whole world how Valerie had done it to him with her bum.

Most of the time we wore the same clothes. For daywear, it was navy-blue sweatshirts and drainpipe dresses, for the disco we wore our hideous matching grey jumper-dresses and stilettos. For special occasions we had our identical hacking jackets, or the denim dungarees we'd ordered from the catalogue at the same time.

My friendship with Valerie was the closest I ever got to a normal relationship with a girl, and it wasn't obsessive and wasn't driven by sexual desire. We squabbled, we rode our bikes, we had asthma attacks, we recorded *Top of the Pops* off the radio, we got off with boys, we dared each other to hold peppermint essence in our mouths for as long as possible. We went to see our first proper shows together. The first was *Elvis The Musical*. Afterwards we queued up in a line of about 40 girls outside the stage door and the guy playing Elvis came out and snogged every last one of us. The second concert was Shakin' Stevens in 1980. OK, I know now that Shaky is really the Anti-Elvis, but we were young, The King was dead and Prince Stevens was the closest we were ever going to get. And then, of course, we went to the fair, or 'shows' as we referred to them locally.

In truth I wasn't a great fan of the fair. For most people I guess it was a place of great sexual intensity. For me it was, essentially, another miserable school disco, but outside.

I did feel excited, though, as we approached the racecourse.

From a distance, the music and screaming of folk high on the rides would make my heart pound. But once I got there the reality was very different.

Cocky boys wandered around in packs, and all the girls found that somehow appealing. Of course, everyone falls for a Fair Lad at some point; those strange gypsy guys who strolled through the spinning machinery with studied nonchalance, as if operating a rickety old roller coaster was the ultimate in career achievement.

The Waltzers were the focal point for many of the girls. We'd huddle into the little spinning cars and someone would shout at the nutter years ahead of his time:

'Mister! Spin us! Spin us!'

And if he fancied one of the girls in your carriage, he'd amble over and with a casual flick – one thumb in his belt loop – send you round so fast the force would close your eyes for you.

It was difficult for me to buy into the whole dating game aspect of the fair; the girls passively standing and giggling behind their hands, the boys examining the prospects before strolling over and asking, 'Do you wanna go on the big wheel wi' me?' Rarely did I get the opportunity to go on a ride with a boy, I guess because I never quite worked out that boring passivity, as practised by Alison Calder, was a sure-fire way of luring them. I don't how I hadn't figured that out. After all, passive dumb blondness was a sure-fire way of attracting me.

The main fairground attraction for me was allied to the constant movie in my head. I wanted to be one of those moody and delinquent figures who always ends up at the fun fair in movies. Wandering around with a really good haircut, looking tortured. Having a go at the shooting range, proving to be a crack shot and winning a giant pink teddy bear, which I'd give to a little kid. I wanted to be that guy. I wanted to be James Dean, or Warren Beatty in *Splendour in the Grass*. Most of all I wanted to be Elvis, who seemed to spend a lot of time at the fair in his movies.

I adored Elvis. The best-looking man that ever, ever lived. It is impossible for any other man to get close to how attractive he was. I knew what it felt like to see the world through Elvis's eyes. Elvis was my god. I wanted to fuck Elvis. I wanted to be Elvis. Guess what? A lot of the time, in my head, I was Elvis.

I had a pair of Elvis-style wrap-around shades and I would wear them in the back of my parents' car, pretending I was The King in the back of a long, black limousine. Left alone in the house, I would dress up and wander around, pretending it was Graceland and that I was the occupant, moody and missing Priscilla.

I once went to the Guides fancy dress party as my idol wearing a leather jacket that I borrowed from a friend's brother. In 1957 Elvis was mean and magnificent, like a better-looking young Marlon Brando. I copied the look, and put so much of my dad's Brylcreem on my hair that my head was stuck to the pillow the next morning. I had to take a half-day off school because that's how long it took my mum to wash the slimy muck out of my hair.

Even from the age of eleven, it was a regular occurrence for me to round up all the little kids in the street and put on an Elvis show for them. I'd reconstruct scenes from the movies, which I'd studied at great length so I could get the moves down exactly right. I taught the little kids to scream at me and reach out their hands as if trying to touch me while I was on stage. In my head it was exactly like the scenes from the concert footage in *Elvis – That's the Way It Is*.

I don't know where this thing came from, this overwhelming absorption with the guy. A lot of Elvis fans can tell you exactly where they were and what happened to them the first time they saw him. I couldn't. He just seemed to have always been in my life, like God or my parents. It was certainly nothing to do with them. They weren't too keen on him. He'd swung his hips in 1955 and bumped Perry Como and Frank Sinatra on to the sidelines. My folks had ignored him and carried right on playing their Sinatra and Como records.

I, on the other hand, had transformed my bedroom into a shrine for The King. Flying in the face of all that was fashionable with my peers, I lived my whole life as I imagined my idol would want me to.

Indeed, the previous year I had successfully carried out a plan to bring that fantasy closer to reality.

throughout my childhood I had gone on a series of very depressing holidays to my gran's friend's house in Carnoustie, so my dad could play golf. I'd be stuck in this fucking big, claustrophobic, old lady's house that smelt of mothballs for a whole summer. How much fun is that for a twelve-year-old? I'd be totally bored out of my mind, playing card games in the garden with my gran, and all the while driven to distraction by my overpowering sexual desire for girls.

In 1978, the first day I got there I saw a poster that said 'Children Wanted For Summer Job Picking Raspberries'. So for the whole two weeks I bent my back and got blackened fingernails and a reddened neck from picking damned raspberries. All because I had seen this sleeveless puffer jacket in an army surplus shop. I knew I had to have it, and I knew my mum wouldn't buy it for me. My mum hated to even hear the words 'army' and 'surplus'.

On a practical level, I was pretty sure this jacket would hide my breasts. Those breasts were becoming a real problem. Prior to their arrival, I was frequently mistaken for a boy. People in shops would say, 'What can I do for you, son?' That was a good thing. The tits just gave the game away. I was a girl who looked a bit boyish. That was a bad thing.

So, with the raspberry money, I get the jacket, and parade up and down looking like Mork from *Mork and Mindy*. And when the fair comes to Carnoustie, I hit the dodgems. Now I am that boy. The loner, shoulders hunched, angst seeping from every pore, ready to win the big pink teddy bear. I am Elvis in *Roustabout*.

I exaggerate my walk to make it even more boyish. I hang around on the edge of the dodgems, looking as moody as I possibly can. I catch the eye of a pretty girl and her two friends all squashed up in a dodgem car. I can tell she's interested, and there are no boys around, so no competition. I smile my sideways smile I've been practising in the mirror. She smiles back, and her friends laugh a bit. This feels good. The dodgems all stop, and I use it as an opportunity to get nearer to them. The gypsy man shouts out for another round of dodging, and I gesture to him. He steers a car over towards me by the big long pole that fixes it to the roof, and I get in. I move my eyebrows up and down a bit, like Steve Austin, in order to attract the girl further.

And it fucking works.

This is almost too much to bear. My heart is pounding with adrenalin at the thought of being discovered. I perform the universal symbol for 'Get in' with the side of my head over my shoulder, and she does.

Bingo. I've caught a girl, for the first time ever. I can't believe it. I pay for the ride by pushing the money into the gypsy man's hand, and we're off. She doesn't say much at first, thank fuck, because I don't know what to do if she does. So we ride around, speechless, but she is officially mine because she thinks I'm a boy. I've put my arm along the back of the seat behind her back and she doesn't mind! Then the conversation begins, and how beautiful it is, and how long I've waited to be in it.

Her: 'What's your name?'

Me: 'Ian.' And I feel a bit guilty, cos that's the name my mum told me I would have had, if I'd been a boy. But then I think that's weird, because if I'd been a boy they wouldn't have adopted me, because they were waiting on a girl. So this cancels out my guilt.

'What's your name?' I ask, really upping the stakes, driving carefully so as not to spoil the moment.

'Janet.'

'Right.'

'Do you live here?'

'Holiday, with my parents.'

'Whereabouts?'

I point in the other direction for fear of her ever finding me again after this, in a fucking dress, playing Donkey with my gran.

'Are you coming here again, Ian, maybe tomorrow?'

'Maybe.' I'm shitting myself.

'Gotta go get ma tea.'

Her friends start calling her, the dodgems slow down, it's all over so quickly. I tense my jaw like Elvis, hoping she'll see the muscle moving in the side of my cheek.

She leans over and kisses me on the cheek, then skips off. I keep the jaw thing going, and walk casually away from the park, thinking it best that I quit while I'm ahead.

I don't remember anything on the way back to the house. I am in a complete trance. My mum asks me if I had a nice time, and I say yes and then go to bed. I want to be alone for a while with my thoughts.

Oh my God, I did it. I now have special powers, just like Mork. And for once I feel as though I have found my planet. Elvis would be proud of me.

by 1979, though, even my puffer jacket couldn't hide my sexual identity at the fair. I was back to role of bystander, watching the real boys get the real girls. Valerie and I spent a couple of hours hanging around, not being spun too hard by the Waltzer guy. Just hard enough to make her cry, and then we trudged home singing 'That's The Wonder Of You' and looking out for the U.F.O. which we definitely saw on the Friday. It never came back, and I didn't half catch a row from Auntie Kay when I crept in some two hours after her curfew.

When Mum and Dad returned the next day, Mum looked very pleased with herself.

'Wait till you see what I've got,' she said, opening her case.

'Oh, I don't know if we should give it to her,' teased my newly bronzed father.

'What is it, what is it?' I shouted, excited at the prospect of a gift.

Then Mum pulled out a tan leather bomber jacket with the most enormous collar I had ever seen.

I had been on at my mum for ages to buy me a leather jacket. But this? The Fonz would never wear this, and it was tan and strange, with huge buttons, and cuffs. I hid my disappointment with a fixed grin as I tried it on.

'Do you know, I had to wear it underneath my own jacket when I went through customs!' boasted Mum.

I didn't understand what all that meant, but did think Spain would be glad to get rid of it. But I looked at Mum's face and realised how much she tried to please me with things, and meant well, and I loved her for it, even though she was way off the mark.

'I love it,' I said, giving her a hug. 'I'm going to show Valerie.'

And I left, bracing myself, wearing the jacket, praying that Jamie Ritchie wouldn't see me.

'She doesn't deserve it,' said Auntie Kay as I sloped off.

five
may

my dad's increasing smoking habit was starting to really concern us all. He took ages to recover from bouts of colds and flu, which often turned into chest infections and left him weak and even thinner for weeks on end. My dad had a fag in his hand more often than he didn't. When I was really little I got burnt in the palm of my right hand when I reached up to put my hand to his, not knowing it was clutching a lit cigarette

That was bad smoking, but there was also good smoking. When we were on long drives in the big old blue Ford Zephyr, with one long seat in the front, every 30 miles or so my dad would say, 'Light me a fag, Spar.'

Spar was my dad's name for my mum. When they first married she didn't eat very much and had very skinny legs, so Spar was short for sparrow. I loved it when my dad called my mum Spar – it was very casual, very cool. So, my mum would reluctantly press in the cigarette lighter. I'd be in the back, chewing Juicy Fruit, watching them perform their old light-up routine. It was like the routines I'd seen in old movies in the afternoon on the portable black and white Sony TV, which I was only ever allowed in my bedroom if I was ill.

Mum would put the cigarette in her mouth, just for a second, just long enough to light it, then put it in Dad's mouth. It was a beautiful moment to me, the viewing of such great familiarity between them.

My dad smoked Benson and Hedges, just like Joan Carlisle. Either that, or Regal King Size – a truly Scottish smoke in both its strength and its affordability in comparison with other brands. He saved up his coupons with the Regal packs and subscribed to some cigarette magazine which provided us with gardening stuff in exchange for the tokens. This gave him something to smoke towards.

My mum hated the smoke – she suffered it all her life with him – but he refused to stop. The house stunk of smoke, and the car, and all my dad's clothes. He would sit in his chair reading the paper, laying it on the ground and leaning down with his elbows on his knees, glasses resting over his nose, not noticing the ash falling on the floor. Then my mum would shout.

'BILL!'

There was no way my dad would ever stop smoking, no way he would ever listen to my mum. He was from that totally inflexible generation of Scottish men.

Like many Scottish men, he loved all things bad for him. The only time he would eat fruit would be very occasionally on a Saturday night when we were all sitting together on front of the television. He would ask me to throw him an orange, which he would then dip in sugar before eating. That was about as healthy as it got. He demanded chips with every meal. No matter how tired my mother was, or what shift my dad came home after, out would come the chip pan. Every night, the house would smell of deep fried fat.

Often, after the late shift, he'd arrive home around 10.30. I'd be in my bed, but as soon as I heard the motorbike engine and the wrought-iron gates swing open, I'd race downstairs in my pyjamas to share some of his chips. Dad and I, much to my mother's disgust, took our chips the same way. An unnatural amount of ketchup, with tons of salt and pepper. I, of course, would copy my dad in as many ways as possible. His world was always fascinating to me. He seemed to do the same things over and over again in his life, rarely deviating from his routine. He'd work, a lot. He'd play golf every few weeks with his brothers, my Uncle Sandy and my Uncle Joe, except in the summer holidays when we were caravanning, when he'd play the entire time. Every second Monday of his life he would go into town to meet his best friend Jimmy Sinclair, also a mechanic. God knows what they would do, because neither of them drank. I constantly asked my dad what happened on the Jimmy Sinclair evenings. He told me they went for coffee, and I remember feeling slightly disappointed that my dad never drank a pint of lager with his friends like Jamie Ritchie's dad did.

But nobody knew the pitfalls of drink more than my father. His father, my grandfather, was a real bastard by all accounts. A publican, he was a drinker and a bully, given to disappearing for days at a time on massive benders, leaving my dad to look after the bar from quite a young age. During the Second World War, the eldest Campbell had joined the navy and been captured by the Germans at Tobruk. My grandfather used this as a reason to take to his bed, rising only occasionally in order to drink himself back into a stupor.

Apart from his afternoons with Jimmy Sinclair, my dad didn't socialise. He chose to spend most of his time alone in the garage with the door down, tinkering on the car, making things. Sometimes he would make pretend spying devices for me: magnets stuck on wood, mini fake radios. My dad totally bought into my spy obsession. On the first Tuesday of every month, he would take me to the local cinema to watch re-runs of James Bond films. Nothing was ever as exciting as those Tuesdays.

Like most men of his generation and class, my dad had deliberately failed to acquire any domestic skills whatsoever. Cooking, childcare and the folding of laundry were considered to be both beneath and beyond him. That was women's work. My dad was a man.

His attitude wasn't unusual for men of his age in that part of Scotland, even in the late seventies. And the women didn't seem to mind. Even if a wife and mother worked full-time, as mine did, it was her role to take on all of the household duties. My father did nothing in the house. If he came in from work, he would drop his clothes on the floor and my mother would pick them up. That's the way it was and that's the way it had always been.

Dad only cooked two things. One, a strange and unhealthy ancient Scottish cake called Clootie Dumpling, which he would make once a year. Two, spaghetti bolognese (also an annual event, and the only foreign influence I was to experience until I left Musselburgh – unless you include chicken pineapple at the Chinese restaurant when I was fifteen). My father did the dishes on Christmas Day so my mum could put her feet up, and that was his entire contribution to the domestic set-up.

My dad was funny. He cracked jokes all the time and he did tricks. He could make his finger look like it was falling off, and could shake his hand until his fingers made a strange cracking sound. He was good with a football, had a special whistle for the dog, and sang 'Would You Like To Swing On A Star?' almost every day. Despite all this I knew there was a sadness in him. I detected his regret and bitterness from very early on. He told me stories about his school-teacher belittling him. I knew he was disappointed at the outcome of his life, that he could have been more. He was incredibly bright, and would teach me bits of Latin, and quote me Shakespeare. His favourite quote was kept for those occasions when I would come home with lines for misbehaving at school.

On presenting them to him, he would shake his head and say, 'Let me play the fool,' then begin his speech from *The Merchant of Venice*.

I would tell him stories about what had happened to me at school. He would suggest that I talk less, then tell me a fable about an Indian in a circle of other Indians. This Indian said very little, yet when he did, his words would interest and therefore influence the group more than the constant talkers. I loved my little sessions with my dad. I viewed his wisdom as the kung fu student viewed the bald blind man – essential to my growth and journey into the future world.

It's fair to say I idolised my father.

my parents would often humour my little fantasies. Sometimes, at dinnertime, they would take parts and play along. I would stand in the corner of the living room, perfectly still, staring ahead in a military fashion. With one arm outstretched, folded at the elbow. Draped over my arm, a tea towel. My mother and father watching television in their usual seats. My father sitting by the window, the dog at his feet. My mother resting on the chair in the corner nearest me. Some time passes; no one speaks.

'Would sir or madam require anything?' I ask in a robotic, servant-like fashion.

'No, thank you,' says my mum in a friendly, polite way.

'Actually, I fancy an ice-cream drink,' pipes up my dad.

This pleases me – one of my favourite orders, because it requires the pulling down of the door on the drinks cabinet, so I can pretend I am a cocktail waiter.

'An excellent choice, sir, if you don't mind me saying.'

'I don't. Now make my bloody drink!' jokes my father, causing my mother to laugh. I can't laugh, however. It is not appropriate to share a joke with your employers.

In the garage, I reach into the back of the cabinet for the special lager glass only used at New Year for a visiting lager drinker. Opening the freezer, taking a little longer than necessary, dragging it out, I hear a noise. *They* have come for me.

HOOD 1:   You could end up in that freezer if you're not careful.

ME: Ssh! You'll get me fired. They'll hear me.

HOOD 2:   Thought about our proposition at all?

ME: I don't need to think about it, I know the answer.

HOOD 1: Think you're pretty smart, don't you?

HOOD 2: He's been learning Latin, haven't you?

ME: How do you know that?

HOOD 1: We know everything about you. Which is why we'll always have one over on you. You wouldn't want them to find out about your past, would you?

At this point I want to kill them.

ME: I don't talk about my past with anyone. What's done is done. Leave me alone, or I'll kill you both. I'll never work for you. I'm just going to do my time here, keep my head low, then I'm out of here …

HOOD 1: Well, here's a little something to help you decide.

(From my back pocket I bring out my trio picture pack, of Jodie Foster, Barbra Streisand and Tatum O'Neal. And show it to myself.)

One of the hoods brings out a photograph. I can't believe it! I know they've got me on this one. I'm left with no choice, for the photo I see before me is of the three great loves of my life, the reason I'm still on the run, the place I'm running to, everything, my world.

My love! My loves! If anything were to happen to you …

ME: You bastards!

(I put my pictures back in my pocket.)

HOOD 1:   Think about driving for us, one last job.

They leave the garage. And, battling in my head with the life I had then and the life I have now, I take some of Luca's ice cream out of the freezer and go back into the home of the good people I work for to make one of them a Red Cola ice-cream drink.

I make up the drink, carefully layering bits of ice cream with sections of cola. I stir it, add some more ice cream on the top, place the tea towel over my arm, open the sliding doors that separate the kitchen from the lounge, compose myself, and take the drink in to my father.

He thanks me. My mum looks over and smiles again. I go back to my place and await further instructions.

'Rhona, come and sit down, will you. We want to talk to you.'

Uh, oh. You never want to hear that from anyone. It can only be bad, or embarrassing or a mixture of both. Coming out of character, I sit down on the sofa. A parent in either corner.

My mum draws in a breath.

Fuck, I think. What's happened? Has my guidance teacher

phoned my parents and told them I fancy girls? Has Alison Calder broken down in tears and told her parents? Did she see me with my binoculars on the bowling-green roof? Has there been a phone call from Wales? Has word got home that I'm a cow, a slag?

My dad still slurps his ice-cream drink and half watches television. As usual, he leaves important moments in life up to my mother.

'What?' I ask hurriedly.

'Your dad and I have been thinking ...'

Lie. Only my mum has been thinking.

'You do know that if anything happened to your dad and I ...'

'What? No, I don't care, I mean, I don't want to ... I mean, yes. Yes?'

'It's alright, we just want you to know what to do, that's all. Where things are kept. All the documents are upstairs in the loft, and if anything happens to us Uncle Sandy is the executor of our will.'

Would I have to go and live with Uncle Sandy, and Gillian and Fraser? I go along with it for a bit, curious as to where I would sleep, because Gillian is bad tempered and three years older than me, and Fraser's room is very small, and I'm not interested in his only interest, *Star Wars*.

'Yes. Don't worry, nothing's going to happen. We just want to make sure you understand things. You're getting older now, and your dad and I won't be here for ever.'

'I do understand, and I'm not worried. But I don't really want to hear any of this.'

'OK, OK, it's alright. We just have to make sure, that's all.'

Dad says nothing. Mum smiles, but her eyes are slightly teary. I feel very upset, and become aware I've been holding my breath while she's been talking. I want to get away from them; get to my room where I can breathe and cry. And, obviously, worry. I wait for a moment, then I get up, trailing the tea towel, now so utterly redundant. And I go upstairs.

When I got home from Italy, my dad had the flu again, but this time it stayed around much longer than usual. It didn't, however, stop him smoking – although my mum banned him from smoking in the bedroom. So he would have most of his cigarettes in the garden, or while walking the dog, or in the garage. His time in the garage increased and his interest in going places stopped. When we were in the car together he'd rely on me more and more to turn the steering wheel while he parked and he would wince with pain every time he turned around, clutching his ribs. Towards the end of May, he got a cough that just wouldn't go away. He came home from work early one day, which was unheard of, and took to his bed. We set up the portable TV, and he lay there for over a week.

Mum was working as a rep in Ladbrokes, so her hours were flexible, but she needed some extra help with Dad and me. I was a very independent child, however. From the age of nine I had a door key. I was never any trouble getting up in the mornings and enjoyed going to school. I did, however, require a lot of driving back and forth to swimming, so Mum asked Gran to stay the odd night, to keep an eye on my dad until he got better.

I loved my gran staying. She would share my room, her in my bed and me in the camp bed that we kept stored in the attic for emergencies such as these. Lying in bed at night I would ask my gran about the war. She would tell me odd stories, never finishing the end of her sentences, missing out vital information.

'Here, the young fellow would stand in the square every day, with a huge bear, great big thing it was. A dancing bear, very tame it was, nice fellow, very polite. "Morning, Mrs McLeary, how are you?" "Fine, thanks," and he'd be there, and, well, you thought nothing of it. It had a collar, I remember that. Well, the war went on, and I heard that he'd been taken away ...'

'Why, Gran?'

'He'd been spying for the Germans. The bear had been in on it. He'd kept the codes and stuff, the secret information. Anyway, it was in the collar the whole time.'

I couldn't believe, or understand, half her stories, but I loved lying in the camp bed, all tucked up in a sleeping bag, listening to her voice. By my bed I kept a huge ledger that I got from the old lady who lived opposite my gran. I never knew the old lady's name – my gran simply referred to her as the 'old lady', and that's what I called her. She lived in the top flat, like my gran, but on the other side of the road. Every morning at ten past ten, which I thought was a strange choice of time, my gran would go to the window and wait for the old lady to appear and wave. This was to check that she was still alive. Sometimes my gran would still be in the bathroom and would shout through to me.

'Rhona! Check the old lady's waving, will you?'

The day the old lady received a letter from the Queen when she was 100 years old, Gran and I went over to wish her well. She sat on a chair, profoundly deaf, and waited for a huge red light to flash on her mantelpiece to indicate whether the doorbell was ringing or not.

It was then she gave me the ledger, in which I began writing a story, about two brothers called The Conways, trying to escape their criminal past. At the back of the ledger I wrote down lyrics to countless war songs that I asked my grandmother to sing for me at night while lying in the bed next to me.

'Sing slower! Sing slower, Gran!' I pleaded, as I scribbled away the likes of 'Keep The Home Fires Burning'.

With my dad in bed, Gran stayed for five days, a record stay, although she would have to make trips home to make sure my Uncle Hebbie had enough food. I could tell Mum was getting stressed because she scratched a lot more with her psoriasis, and didn't eat much. I wanted to ask her about my dad, but I was scared and thought it best instead to gauge things by the escalation of her skin complaint.

The mystery flu and chest cough didn't stop my dad sneaking out to the garden in his dressing gown and having a fag. No one spoke about it, but daily more cigarette butts appeared on the grass. When I got home from school I would go up to my dad's room, which was always dark, and smelt of man and menthol. He looked older without his Brylcreem, his grey hair showing through. He had lost weight, if that was possible, for he was always painfully thin. I was fascinated to see my dad in his pyjamas – indeed, in any outfit other than a security man's uniform.

I rarely saw my dad's body and I wondered what it was like. He was never one to wear little. Even in the midst of summer he would sit on a deckchair, trousers rolled up, white shirt on. Once, and only once, my father purchased a pair of swimming trunks, much to my excitement. The idea of going swimming with my dad felt so modern. We were in Blackpool the month Elvis died, and Dad and I went to the outdoor pool. My dad was by far the thinnest and whitest dad in the pool, which caused me and everyone else to stare at him with fascination.

'I'll show you how it's done, kiddo,' he shouted from the diving board.

My mouth open, I watched my father salute me as he ran along the board and threw himself into the water. His legs bent over his back, smashing down on the water. It was a bad dive, and left him under water for a worrying length of time. I dived in to rescue him, but he came splashing and gulping to the surface, wincing with pain.

'I'm alright, kiddo, I'm alright.'

We laughed about this incident, as did my mum when we told her, and embellished it for entertainment purposes for years to come.

d uring my father's absence from normal daily life, his new bike stood, untouched and abandoned, in the garage. I would sit on it from time to time, imagining I'd just arrived home. I washed his Cortina at the weekends. I would be allowed to sit in the driver's seat, unlock the handbrake and steer the car back on to the driveway. This was high up on the list of things to look forward to.

My dad had been ill for a good two weeks now, staying most of the time in bed. He'd completed a course of antibiotics, but still coughed his guts up day and night. It was getting worse, and now he was running a temperature.

One night it was particularly bad. I lay in bed listening to all the sounds in my parents' room, trying to work out what was happening. My gran lay in the bed next to me, trying to distract me by reading aloud 'Wag the Dog' in the back of the *People's Friend*, in her most animated voice.

There was much more shuffling around than usual. I could hear my mum talking on the phone. Gran and I stayed in my room until the ambulance arrived. I could hear Mum answering the door and lots of feet clambering up the stairs. But no word from my father, except coughing.

After everybody had vacated the house, my mum and gran had a conversation downstairs. I watched from my parents' bedroom window. I saw three ambulance men lift my dad into the van. He was strapped to a chair/bed thing, covered in a red blanket. He was sitting upright, which I took comfort from. He didn't see me watching, didn't look up. A few neighbours were also watching from their bedroom windows. My mum left the house in some unusual clothes – trousers, which were rarely worn, and a raincoat, kept in the study for unexpected downpours.

Gran joined me upstairs.

'That's the ambulance,' she said, stating the bloody obvious.

And I went back to my camp bed, to scribble in my ledger.

six
june

DATE: 28 June   **DAY: Thursday**

Today was the 2nd last day of term. It was quite sad really but I tried to see as less of Patricia McDonald as possible because, she's been acting too nice to me. Afterwards was the prize giving. It was sad to see the school at its best, with all the staff. Susanne Flynn got a prize and Louise and Richard. Later Susanne, L, Janet and I went to the chip shop and Susanne bought us chips.

DATE: 29 June   **DAY: Friday**

Today was the last day of term. I broke my nose when I was playing in the park. Patricia McDonald got me home and she gave me a poem about love or something. It was crap so I just ripped it up.

Later I was very sad to leave Susanne. I went to the hospital and I saw Susanne when I came back.

I'm not a Homosexual but I admit I do have homosexual feelings and tendencies towards Susanne but I'm not queer.

DATE: *30 June*   **DAY: *Saturday***

This morning when I woke up I felt that I had to go and see Susanne and I also found out that if I dream I'm in love with someone, when I wake up I am in love with them. I still have a crush on Susanne. It's just my age. And yesterday I swore on the bible that I don't fancy Leslie. I don't. I like her a lot.

I was dreading the holidays. I just wanted to stay at school all the time. I was some kind of weirdo who just loved school. Most of my schoolmates didn't even bother to turn up towards the end of term. The last day was a half-day, when most normal kids took to the beach and the park. I, however, was there until the bitter end. Because the majority had given themselves the extra two days of holiday, it meant that whoever did come to school tended to be sensitive and well behaved. I felt that the morons had been separated out, leaving only the lovely pupils – the ones who would actually get something at the prize-giving ceremony.

On the last day, cast out, I wandered off in the general direction of Luca's Ice-Cream Parlour, but was intercepted at the school gate by Patricia McDonald, who had been waiting for me.

'Come and play football in the park with us,' she ordered.

I agreed. Patricia slightly frightened me – she was the hardest girl in the school.

She was from the rough part of town. A hefty girl who stank of cigarettes. She was uncomfortable with her body and ill at ease with her gender, flushing red with embarrassment at any display of girl-ishness in her or around her. She followed punk music, though didn't dress accordingly. She, like me, was part of a rare group who chose to wear her uniform. At my school you could wear whatever you liked: most people were mods, goths, heavy rockers or punks. The rest were too poor to be anything, and just wore a cagoule as a winter coat. But Patricia was no swot, so I presumed her choice of uniform wearing was also based on a soft spot for the military. Patricia wore her tie in an unusually fattened knot. On her neck she wore an out-of-character necklace, as a choker, with Patricia written across it.

Patricia was keen on me to the point that she asked me out for a fight pretty much every other day. Naturally I declined. If I wanted to get beaten up I could stay at home or just hang around the Grassy Bit and wait for Jamie Ritchie to appear.

I had no desire whatsoever to enter into a punch-up. I didn't want to get hurt. But that didn't stop the challenges. One day it reached an extreme. The class was history on C floor. The teacher had left us for a while, something I dreaded, as it encouraged the lunatics to go mental. Most of the time we had no choice but to go along with their pea-brained ideas. A popular trick was to all leave by the classroom window, level permitting, and laugh at the reaction of the teacher when she came back to find the classroom entirely empty a few minutes later. Ha fucking ha.

Patricia was subversive in a different way. She was clearly quite disturbed, and would frighten teachers verbally. She had a command-ing, threatening presence – not manic and hyper, more slow and controlled. She didn't like to move quickly at all and always refused PE – self-conscious about her big thighs and enormous tits, no doubt. Whatever, I'd always assumed that Patricia was just like me, and I really didn't need to see that played out in front of me. It was very ugly. I was aware that I was the only one who noticed it.

This particular day, the room felt hyped up; there was something spreading through the class. Nervously, I tried smiling across at Patricia. She just scowled back. This pretty much confirmed my fear that I was about to be asked for a fight with her. A few minutes later, Roger Watson, a small curly-haired, half-Italian boy who was completely under her control, appeared at the side of my desk.

'This is from Patricia.' He passes me a note. Great, I think, knowing it's not an invite to her fucking birthday party. The note reads:

After school – fight. You and me. 3.45. You die.

I don't react. The teacher returns, missing the whole thing, and for the remainder of the lesson I stare ahead, trying to zone her out.

At 3.45 the bell goes. I remain seated, not leaving with the others. Patricia brushes past me, pushing into me. I smell her cigarettes, I feel the tension from her. The class has gone, her leaving last, turning around at the door making that dragged finger across the cheek sign that means 'you die by knife'.

The teacher has finished packing her bag. I am the only one left in the class, left with no option but to confess.

'Miss, can I walk out with you? Patricia McDonald wants to fight me.'

'Oh, for goodness' sake! Come on.'

And we leave together. I walk out of the school and up to the teachers' car park about an inch away from Miss Hall, Patricia and some class members shouting obscenities in the distance. Miss Hall drops me down the High Street, and I walk home, avoiding my one hundredth invitation to fight.

throughout that term Patricia McDonald had been a constant presence in my school life. She just seemed to be there. Always appearing at my side to ask for a fight or just invading my space. She made me feel claustrophobic and somewhat repulsed, as she followed me following Miss Carlisle, and made me miserable with her obsessive attention. The irony of the situation completely passed me by.

Up until then, she was the only other girl apart from me that I thought might be a lesbian, and her whole persona depressed me. If I were to ever take that route would I be facing a world full of Patricia McDonalds? Even more worrying, she was very much like me. There was a depth to her, something tortured in her soul. She so obviously viewed being a girl as a curse.

Patricia was butcher and harder than me. I didn't like her trying to fight me. I didn't like her following me. I didn't like her liking me. But I was also scared of her and consequently tried to keep on the right side of her. She was one of the nutters in the school – and there were so many of them – who could suddenly turn into a violent psychopath.

I loved football. I loved physical sport of any kind. It made me feel free from judgement. Football was particularly special because being allowed to play it with the boys was, for me, a way of staving off growing up into a nice, young, boring woman. Which I knew I had no chance of ever being.

Which is presumably why I took up Patricia's offer to join her and some others in a kickabout in the park across the road from the school. Unfortunately, on this occasion, I simply managed to deflect my head off Kevin Telford's boot. I was trying too hard to impress them, to keep up with the boys. Kevin was the only mixed-race kid in the whole school. He was considerably bigger and stronger than even the sturdiest of boys in my class. He played football enthusiastically and competitively with no regard at all for anyone else's size or sex. So, as he came charging through me towards the goal, I bounced off his legs and, landing on my backside just in front of him, half sat up at the exact moment he tried to jump over me. There was a crack and a searing pain that travelled right through to the back of my head. My nose started throbbing. With each throb, a gob of blood spattered my shirt, and then my eyes started watering too.

'Don't worry,' said Patricia before anyone really had time to take in what had happened. 'I'll see she gets home OK.'

With that, she dragged me to my feet, grabbed my arm firmly, and started frog-marching me in the direction of my house, a good mile and a half away. We made our way through the town in silence, with her propelling me by my arm as if she were a soldier helping a wounded comrade through no-man's-land. I trotted beside her, snot and blood and tears streaming down my face, keeping silent in case she decided that what all this intimacy needed to make it perfect was a good fight.

Halfway over the Roman Bridge she wheeled me around and stood glowering at me as I cowered and waited for her next move.

'Here,' she barked, fishing into her jacket pocket. 'This is for you.'

She handed me a folded-up piece of paper, which I was too terrified not to take, and then she pissed off without another word. I opened the note and read it. It was a love letter. With a poem. Some girl, who frightened and repulsed me with her weird hanging around and stalking my every move, had suddenly and unexpectedly declared her obsession via a couple of badly written verses, rhyming 'You' with 'True'. What pathetic behaviour!

I certainly wasn't interested in taking things further, so I threw the letter away and dodged Patricia for the rest of the summer. By the time we got back to school, she'd got the message and shunned me, probably out of embarrassment. Of all people, of course, I should have realised how much she'd taken out of herself to write and present that poem.

It all made me even more determined not to be queer. If I was alone with other straight girls, I definitely felt different from – and attracted to – them. On the other hand, when I encountered Patricia McDonald, I felt like the most normal girl on earth, and upset by the idea that we might be the same.

I somehow managed to find my way over the Roman Bridge with my bloody nose. My poor mum had just returned from visiting my dad in the one hospital, and she had to drag herself all the way to another to get my nose seen to. It was broken all right, but there wasn't a whole lot they could do about it. They offered to put me under anaesthetic and knock it the other way, but I reckoned it had been bashed around enough for one day.

the encounters with Kevin Telford and Patricia McDonald were the beginning of a long, baking, miserable, Carlisle-less summer by the sea. It also began to dawn on me that my dad was very ill.

I didn't go to see him very much in hospital. I was discouraged from visiting when he was too ill, because Mum thought it would be too much for me. Shortly after he was admitted, he fell into a coma. Nobody expected him to pull through.

Days after, he came to, and I went to visit. Not for long, just in and out. I stayed long enough for him to tell me a bit about his coma experience. He had been walking along a dark corridor towards a light. He described a long line of people he'd not seen for many years: people from all parts of his life, from Sunday school to the present day, all of them dead. He spoke of a tall, old, white man beckoning him from the front of the queue. As his finger gestured for my father to come towards him, he grew increasingly weary, unable to resist the old man's hypnotic pull. But my dad being a hero, as always, somehow turned around.

'I was walking through the valley of death, Rhona,' he said, 'and then I heard your mum calling from behind me. Just as I was about to step through the gates, I turned around and your mum was there, and behind her were all these huge snakes. That's why I came back. To protect your mother from the snakes.'

He had woken up to the sound of my Auntie Ella, my dad's brother's wife, repeating, 'Bill, Bill, come back to us.'

I was fascinated, relieved and comforted by all this, but I could see that telling me the story had worn him out. He was barely awake. Mum told me visitors exhausted him. From the corridor, I looked at my long, thin, pale father lying flat out, full of tubes and wires, as my mother tidied around him, replenishing Lucozade and arranging flowers and opening cards. I obsessed over the 'Intensive Care' sign on the door to his room.

he was ready when we got there, sitting in a chair in his room, reading the sports page at the back of the paper. Today we would be taking him home.

'Dad, Dad, I polished your car, and I checked the tyre pressure,' I said, pre-empting anything my mother needed to say.

'Well done, kiddo. Let's have a look at that nose.'

He moved my head towards the light and squinted as he studied the bruising.

'What are we going to do with you, eh?'

Mum thanked the nurses and doctors, as they do in happy endings, and my dad joked with some men in the ward. The three of us left the hospital, me looking in as much as I could to scenes of far sicker people in little rooms along the way. I wondered if they were about to join a queue of dead people.

My dad wore a sports jacket and an open-necked shirt (his version of very casual, almost relaxed). All his clothes were too big for him by now.

'Have to put another hole in the belt, kiddo,' he said, pulling out the waistline of his trousers to show us the gap.

We had taken Dad's car to the hospital – his idea – because he was worried it hadn't had a run. Mum never got to drive Dad's car, but this was one of those rare exceptions. I watched with fascination as my mum steered, more carefully than usual, the big, red, man-size car that I hoped one day would be mine. I would beg my dad constantly to keep the car for my driving lessons in four years' time. He didn't reply much to my persistent pleadings; instead, he chose to ramble on about how proud he would be when I was eighteen, a young lady, his daughter, whom he'd walk up the aisle one day. The proudest dad in the world. He also promised to buy me a large, white, double-doored wardrobe. For some reason. Like most dads, Dad was very strange with gifts.

The oddest gift of all was a hand-size lump of marble with a mini claymore stuck through the middle. It was intended to be a letter opener. My dad bought it for my mum in 1977. He presented it to her in the lounge on the evening of her birthday, with great pride, and a build-up that lasted all day. As usual, there was a long, compli-cated story that went with it.

'This began its journey ...' started my father. I lost track. It was like a history lesson.

'...and the man was left on the ship clutching it, the last one in Britain. And it's yours, Spar.'

Mum looked perplexed.

'There's not another one like it. A Scottish hand and the half sword.'

They'd kissed. My mum had thanked him, trying to hide her disappointment, and I'd looked on in admiration of my father's quirkiness.

I was so happy to have him back, to have us all back. A family of three in my dad's red Cortina. Mum had been told by the doctors to 'build him up'. So, on the way home, we stopped at the chemist and bought a load of Carnation Build-Up, The Powder Drink To Help Underweight People Gain Pounds. Mum also stocked up on steaks in the freezer.

When we got home, he sat on his chair, which had become my chair in his absence, and stroked the dog. I watched him out of the corner of my eye, wanting to ask him about his coma, but too frightened I'd upset someone. Mum fiddled about in the kitchen and appeared carrying a glass of Strawberry Build-Up. He finished it and went to bed.

I was left with Mum. It was a Saturday evening on the last day of June. It was getting hot already, and summer was around the corner. My allergies had started: sneezing and wheezing as a reaction to various pollens.

The summer meant the hayfields were in full bloom, and all the secret snogging and fingering would commence.

Our estate was surrounded by hayfields. They were so beautiful. I was aware of that back then. Each summer the hay grew taller than any of us. It was thick and gold. It didn't move in the wind, the strips as thick as bamboo. This is where you went for kissing. Nobody could see you lying down once you were in there. From high up a tree that overlooked the sloped cornfields, you could see flattened areas where people had been getting off together. From the highest point you could see our estate. You could see our parents standing at the top of their drives, shouting on us. Then you would head home, lifting your knees high as you walked to get through the thick of it. Grabbing pieces of hay in your hands as you moved. Sometimes chewing a piece hanging outside your mouth. Though this was traditionally a boy thing. Girls, I noticed, toyed with the hay more, gently brushing it around their chins as they lay in another newly created flattened circle, giggling at everything their date was saying.

When summer arrived, we'd all head down to the harbour on our bikes in our cut-downs. No top if you were a boy, bikini top if you were a girl. It was a bit of a race – we'd cycle along the edge, and some of the boys would keep on cycling off the pier into the water, still on their bikes. Then we'd all dive in. The water was murky from the boat fuel, oil and sewage works along the coast. One time, Andrew McIrish came up with a dog shite on his head.

This summer, I knew, would be the worst. I felt awkward with my mum. She was very stressed, caring for my dad and taking unpaid leave from work. Yet I felt unable to comfort her, or talk to her about Dad. I would become anxious while left alone with her, scared of her crying. I decided it was best to keep myself busy. Nothing to take my mind off things like a bit of car washing or shoe polishing.

It was always my job to clean my father's shoes. He had at least ten pairs. All in excellent condition. Mostly black, but a couple of brown pairs. Some of his shoes were from Spain, and were still preserved in their original boxes from the sixties when he bought them.

'Always keep your shoes clean,' he would say to me when he put them on.

'It means you respect yourself. People notice dirty shoes, you know, and it just means you don't give a damn.'

I loved polishing them. I would place them all downstairs at the kitchen door, lay them out on newspaper and begin giving them a first coat. Then I would brush them up with the special brush marked 'no polish'. Finally, I would buff them with a soft brown velvet cloth. Then I'd lay them all out again and ask my father to inspect them. Once they'd been given his seal of approval, I'd put them back in his wardrobe with a tremendous sense of achievement. After polishing my dad's shoes, I always felt that I had to ask my mum if she needed me to clean some of hers. I secretly hoped that she didn't, because her shoes were ladies' shoes, strange and small and patent, often with bows, which was all, of course, entirely unsatisfactory from a shoe-cleaning perspective. Luckily she'd rarely take me up on my offer.

I knew I'd have to occupy my time this summer with as many activities as possible, to get through this intense indoor period with my mum and dad. I decided to up my car maintenance as a way of escaping the house.

One evening, I decided to wash my mum's car, a gold Fiesta, to make up for my not polishing her shoes. I rigged up the equipment. I liked to drag out the car wash, and while others would merely give their cars a quick going over with a sponge and some soapy water, followed by a quick rinse, I would offer a superior service at my garage at the side of the house. I'd prime the garden hose and blast the undercarriage around the wheels to loosen the dirt. I would pretend to be a welder, and a mechanic. Anything to keep me in work, anything to keep me clean and away from the criminal life I had led before.

The Italian/American welder is busy at work. It's evening, early summer. This guy's trying to do some overtime when, from his crouching position, he notices a pair of feet. He turns around and sees two guys standing over him in a threatening manner.

HOOD 1:   Bit late to be working, is it not?

ME: I take the work when I can get it.

HOOD 2:   *(sarcastic)* How touching.

nineteen seventy-nine

ME: This is becoming a habit.

HOOD 1:   Yeah, one we'll have to break.

ME: OK, wise guys, cut the crap. What do you want?

HOOD 2:   Lost your memory, have you?

HOOD 1:   You said you needed some time to think while the old man was away. Well, he's back now, so time's ran out.

HOOD 2:   You'll always belong to us, Tony. *(I loved the name Tony at this time. It was always on American cop shows.)*

HOOD 1:   Yeah, the sooner you accept that the better. You're our driver and we want you back. Either we have to drag you, or you walk out with us now.

I was getting tired of this. How much can a man take? They were right, I'd never be free from them. They had too much on me. I could never escape my past. I could run but I couldn't hide.

I had to think on my feet.

ME: OK, just give me a minute to put this stuff away.

HOOD 1:   We knew you'd see sense.

Mugs. I bend down, pretending to gather up the hose. Instead, I quickly wrap it around each hand, get a tight grip on it, jump up and fix it around the neck of the one standing nearer to me. I pull him towards me, choking him. Whilst I have him, I jump up and karate-kick the other guy in the face with my right foot. He goes down. But the guy I'm holding knees me in the stomach and breaks free. I bend forward, wincing in pain, when I'm delivered an under-the-chin blow that knocks me back on to the bonnet of the car. Both the men set about me. My head is banged repeatedly off the car. There is a lot of blood running down my face from above my left eye. (At least, I hope so, because it's a very attractive look, that, a small boxer's cut just above the eyebrow. Like Rocky.)

I manage to push both the guys back with one kick. I bounce back, using some expert karate. This is always a last resort, because black belts like me are lethal, and my skills should only be used when absolutely necessary.

I catch one of them under the chin with my elbow, and with the other hand punch the guy so hard he passes out. It's all over now.

They are beaten.

HOOD 1: *(in pain)* You shouldn't have done that. The Boss is
gonna come after you.

They were right, I shouldn't have, but they pushed me too far.

From now on, though, I won't be able to rest, to sleep, to turn my back or let my guard down for one moment ...

'Rhona!' Mum shouts. 'What on earth is all the racket? Your father's in his bed.'

'Sorry, I dropped the hose when I was wrapping it up.'

I have always hated the month of June. Since way back then. A prelude to summer. A taster of the frustration and loneliness to follow. I don't think I've enjoyed summer since I developed breasts. Before then, it was all fine, everybody running about in shorts and vests, little difference between boys and girls, no puberty shit fucking with your head. Now it was all about boys pretending to be men, girls pretending to be women. The summer accentuated all that was problematic for me. The break from school allowed us all to roam free of structure. This led to boredom and, inevitably, pathetic mating rituals, underage drinking parties, vomiting, fighting, and tears. And, for me, many days alone indoors, full of antihistamines and Ventolin, lying down with a cold flannel over my forehead, battling another bout of hayfever.

The June before, I had started my period. Another one of life's blows. I was playing up the end of the railway with a girl called Sandra Halliday. Sandra and I drifted in and out of a casual friendship that year. Nothing very memorable, just some tennis which we played all summer in her street, and some Kerbie (where the football is thrown from one side of the road to another, with the aim of it bouncing off the kerb opposite and back to you). There was also lots of going to the chip shop on a Saturday night for a sausage supper, a huge amount of laughing at everything, and a fair bit of her chumming me up the back road to stare at Alison Calder's house.

Sandra was small and tomboyish and very relaxed with my oddness. One June evening, we were up the railway, hanging around under the bridge near Alison's, when I felt something sticky in my pants. I told Sandra to walk on while I went for a piss under the bridge. I feared the worst and I was right. My fucking period. I got all worked up. I didn't feel any of that elated 'I'm growing into a young woman' shit. I just felt dread, anxiety and concern that I wouldn't be able to spend the next few days and the rest of my life on a bicycle.

I came out from under the bridge shouting.

'Sandra, guess what?'

'What?'

'I've started my fucking period.'

Sandra started absolutely pissing herself laughing and didn't stop all the way back down the back road and home. When we parted at the railway fence she was still doubled over. I went home, really tense, and waited for my mum to come home from work. When she did, I sheepishly told her.

'Oh, that's OK, dear, there's some things in my wardrobe.'

She took me upstairs and handed me a packet of Kotex Simplicity, absolutely massive sanitary towels. I took them and miserably walked into the bathroom to stick my first one in my pants. What a future, I thought, as I prepared my nappy, perplexed as to how the word Simplicity got on the packet.

all the car washing and shoe polishing in the world wouldn't take away from the fact that, inevitably, my most important summer project would arrive in the form of another obsession about another girl.

FACT FILE 4

SUBJECT:	SUSANNE FLYNN	
AGE:	15	
HAIR:	BLONDE	
EYES:	BLUE	
FAMILY:	FATHER –	STEELWORKS MAN
	MOTHER –	HOUSEWIFE
CAR:	NONE	
REGISTRATION:	N/A	
ACTIVITIES:	PUSHING BABY SISTER IN PRAM	
	BRUSHING HAIR	
	WALKING OVER BRIDGE	
ADDRESS:	FLAT 6, 30 WELLS STREET	
PHONE NO:	665 3404	
MOVES:	4.00 PM	WATCHES TV
	10.30 PM	BRUSHES HAIR
	10.45 PM	GOES TO BED

Susanne Flynn was one of those girls with what I would call class. Style and sophistication. She was gentle, quiet and studious. She had kind eyes, and beautiful hair. She hung around with another nice girl, though not so pretty as her. And the two of them, just genuinely I think, knew what I was and felt sorry for me. Whatever, I didn't care: they were just another oasis of temporary sanity for me. Susanne had great posture and, like many lovely girls, attended ballet in her younger days. I would watch her in the mornings as our school walking paths crossed.

I would walk across the Roman Bridge, Musselburgh's historic pride and joy. Not many people used the bridge any more. Many chose to take advantage of the new shortcuts brought about by various road developments, but I continued to use it even if it meant a longer route. I thought it was very dramatic on that bridge, going over the cobbles to school, a bridge where Bonnie Prince Charlie was injured in 1736, and where Susanne Flynn could be seen four times every school day, most upright, her long blonde freshly brushed hair blowing in the wind.

Susanne lived in a flat across the bridge above one of Musselburgh's betting shops. Musselburgh was your classic small Scottish town. A mass of bookies and pubs. Practically all the pubs' names were based on themes to do with the river or the sea. The River's Edge, or The Sea Shore. Either that or they were named after famous footballers. And all the hairdressers were named after popular women's Christian names, broken in the middle with a hyphen to add character.

JILL-IANNES

SUZ-ANNES

The River Esk flowed under the Roman Bridge and, where it widened to join the Forth, the much-loved swans nested. Nobody, but nobody, touched the swans. In fact, everybody in that town went out of their way to see that those swans were alright. Even the hardest of nutters wouldn't dream of touching the swans. In the summer, folk would go down to look at them in the evening. We would feed them, photograph them. Local artists would paint them. Musselburgh loved them. They were given a special position in our lives. And Susanne Flynn lived near them, which I always think suited her. Both being things of natural beauty.

Clipping from the *Musselburgh News*, July 1979

SWANS ARE 'QUITE SAFE'

The Musselburgh swan and her two cygnets are safe and well – and living further up the River Esk.

Fears had been running rife in the town that something had happened to the swan and her young after they disappeared from their usual stretch of the water beside the Roman Bridge.

The swans were adopted by the people of the town when the cob – the male bird – was killed earlier this year shortly after the eggs were lain.

Since then, residents have kept an eye on the swans and protected them from attacks on land and water.

However, last week, the swan and her young suddenly vanished, worrying many of their protectors. But Mr Rob Morgan, one of the people who started the 'Save Our Swans' campaign, announced this week the swans were quite safe and had only moved up the river a little. He said, 'It looks as if they have been frightened by the workmen who came down to tidy the river for the Honest Toun's Association Festival. I've been up to see them and they're quite all right. There is no cause for concern.'

seven
july

DATE: 16 July   *DAY: Monday*

Today I had to come home and I left Elie at eleven o'clock, I was in Edinburgh at 12.10, I was very sad on the journey home I kept thinking about Wilson and how much I'd miss them all. I know now that I love Wilson and I really miss him, because we had so much fun together. I know that it would have to end sooner or later.

DATE: 19 July   *DAY: Thursday*

Today was very boring with Jacqueline, we done nothing really, it was raining in the morning so we had to stay indoors. At night I got a phone call from Gillian to say that Leslie wasn't going with Stephen and that Wilson was coming back to the site,

I do miss him and I'm worried in case he fancies Loretta.
Gillian says that Leslie wrote something on the back of a piece of
paper. I do miss them all but I'm getting Leslie's address.

July was dead hot. The pollen count was high. I was bored with
summer as early as a few days in. It was the Trade's Fortnight and
nearly everyone was away, including Alison Calder, Susanne Flynn
and Miss Carlisle. I know because I checked. I made a few trips up
the back road, climbed on to the bowling club roof, stared through
my binoculars, but no sighting of Alison was made. The blinds at the
Calders' were firmly shut, the lorry parked on the piece of land at the
back of their mansion, and the large white Graceland-type gates
padlocked. Even so, I stared at her bedroom window, looking for
something Alisonesque, but to no avail. I would have to make do
with the ski-trip photos for my daily fix.

Even Susanne Flynn was away, and her nice but not-so-nice-look-
ing friend and neighbour, who was becoming increasingly nice-look-
ing. I cycled down to the Roman Bridge a few times and stood there,
pretending to look at the swans but really straining my neck for any
sighting of a Flynn. Nope, nothing going on there. And Miss Carlisle
was always away the minute school broke for the holidays. I knew
this, but still I made the odd call, in a time before answerphones,
when I just listened to the endless ring, imagining it to be a bit more
Miss Carlisley than other rings.

I was truly alone for the summer, and began moping around
accordingly.

I got up in time to watch *Belle and Sebastian*, a fantastic
Scandinavian series that was shot in black and white in the sixties,

with a cute little boy with big eyes who I took to be an orphan (Sebastian). He had a St Bernard named Belle. There was also a pretty girl in it called Angelina. Basically, the boy worried constantly about the threat of 'The Avalanche', and Angelina worried (a sister or mother figure) for the boy worrying about it. Eventually it happened, and Belle saved the day. But not without the boy crying 'Belle! Belle! The avalanche! Look out!' about a hundred times, his words slightly out of sync with the movement of his lips. I loved it, and wanted, of course, to be the cute, young, vulnerable boy with this fabulous dog that everybody fussed over all the time. I thought very long and hard about entering a Scandinavian phase. This consisted of me making enquires to my mother about knitting me a fawn jumper, with a complex jig-jag pattern down the front.

'Maybe in the winter, dear. I'm not knitting in this heat.'

During the day, I hung around, dragging my feet, picking the melted bubblegum off the boiling hot tarmac with an ice-lolly stick. Or played swingball. Alone. Occasionally, I would give myself a cheeky little unexpected serve. Then react to it as though it had caught me off-guard.

When Dad was out of bed, he would doze in the garden on the deckchair with his sleeves rolled up and Foster Grants on. Or read his Alistair MacLean book, which was usually his holiday read.

Mum would make salad to go with Dad's 'build-up' steaks. We only ever had salad for one month in the year. It was a sign of extreme heat in Scotland if the iceberg lettuce and egg slicer appeared.

Despite, however, me eating salads, and Dad eating steaks, he seemed to be getting thinner, and I seemed to be getting fatter. Swimming was finished for the summer, and I was bang in the middle of puberty. That sink or swim time. Jamie Ritchie, I noticed, was completely unaffected by puberty. I became obsessed with the fact that some people would always look good, always come out on top, while others would always remain losers. That year's winners in puberty were:

Jamie Ritchie: Looks never changed. In fact, got better. Good skin, good hair, great body, always smelt nice.

Carol Cowan: Started life looking like a young Natalie Wood, during puberty became a slightly older young Natalie Wood. Always had a perfect figure. Never a spot or a blemish.

I, on the other hand, suffered from a series of embarrassing and extremely painful boils that would appear on my bum and my inner thigh. Each boil would start as a normal spot, then after a day would get a massive yellow head on it, then suddenly grow to the size of a tennis ball, leaving me limping to the doctors to have it lanced while my mother looked on.

After 'The Avalanche' had covered all the central characters of *Belle and Sebastian*, and Belle had dug them all out again, there really was nothing left to live for. Even Mad Tommy Broon had taken a break and was off chasing for the time being.

Then the big red phone at the foot of the stairs rang.

It was my Auntie Muriel, my mum's sister-in-law, asking me if I wanted to go on holiday for a week with my cousins Gillian and Fraser, in their caravan in Elie. I absolutely loved seeing my cousins, and didn't get to see them nearly enough. I also loved the fact that they were both adopted, each from different families, making them the only other children in my world the same as me. It was very frustrating for me that our parents only seemed to make about six trips a year back and forth to socialise.

I had missed out that year on our usual caravan outings, due to Dad being ill. Every year since I was born, the three of us had taken off around the country as avid followers of the Caravan Club. We Caravan Clubbers would often drive to a club 'rally' (our name for the gatherings) in single file along the motorway.

'Flash your lights at him, Dad!' I'd shout excitedly as we spotted another set of caravanners pulling out of a side road. The caravan trips were heaven to me, a great time of closeness and comfort. I loved lying in bed at night, the curtain pulled across for my parents' privacy; my dad stirring gently a late-night cup of tea, using one of the many teaspoons with the crest on it of another town we'd camped in. His deep voice, murmuring to my mum, whispering so as not to wake me. But I would be awake, my eyes heavy, but loving the moment too much to sleep.

We had lots of caravan procedures as well. We would eat tinned potatoes, to save my mum the extra work in a confined space, corned beef, and tinned Goblin hamburgers. It was the only time the dog would eat tinned dog meat. There would be orange squash, and Kellogg's Variety Packs, which my mum felt were overpriced and would never buy when we were at home. In the caravan, I'd excitedly plan in advance my cereal choice for every day of the trip. There was a lot of maintaining the van to be done on these trips, and the responsibilities would be divided among us. Dad, obviously, would drive, Mum would navigate, and I would be in charge of distribution of all travel sweets and barley sugars. On the way we'd play 'I Spy' and sing 'There Was An Old Man Called Michael Finnegan'.

When we got there, we would go to the warden and be allocated our lot on the site. First of all, Dad would need to reverse, which was really tricky, so Mum and I had to stand at the back of the van and direct him. Then, once parked, I would spring into action with the jack, and wind down the four stabilisers so that we could get Mum into the caravan as soon as possible to get the kettle on. Even the kettle was completely different from our electric one at home: it had a loud whistle that added to the perfection of everything.

Dad would separate the towbars and park the car next to the van, and I would pull the big water carrier on wheels (which was as tall as me) to the water station to fill it up. When I got back, Dad would have set up the toilet, and placed a pail under the waste tap underneath the van. The table that would become my parents' bed was put on its hinges, and three cups of tea would be waiting on it. Then our holiday would begin.

They were, without a doubt, the happiest times of my childhood. I would love lying on the top bunk, with the rain pattering on the roof. I would love it when my mum set the caravan door to its half-door position and leant over it, shouting outside to Dad and I, who'd been kicking a ball around, that it was time for our tea.

If it rained, we'd go to the cinema in the nearest town, or to a local crafts shop, or tearoom. If it was really bad weather, we would sit in and listen to Radio 2 and play mini dominoes or snap. Sometimes Dad and I would practise sign language for the deaf. For a while, Dad was the foreman at his garage and when a deaf man was employed, Dad attended a course on signing. To make it easier for him we'd learnt it together. I picked it up very quickly, and we'd sit for ages making each other laugh by annoying Mum because she didn't understand what we were saying.

We made friends with other families on our various trips. Some that would become great friends for the rest of our lives. Like the McAlphines, who had a daughter called Rhona. She had got lost one day, at the same time as I had, and when my mum was looking for me, both mums ran into each other shouting, 'Rhona!' They became friends and have been ever since. We attended events, like fancy dress parties, and races put on for the kids.

In 1969 at the age of four I was crowned 'Rose Bud Princess' by the other caravanners, in a competition I never quite understood. Basically, all the children lined up and the judges picked the cutest. A crown was put on my head, a rosette pinned on my swimsuit, and I held hands with another girl, a runner-up, for a snapshot in the *Montrose Gazette*. One of the rules was my parents had to grant me anything I desired, within reason, for the day. While other children may have chosen vast amounts of ice cream, or a trip to a fun park, I requested that I be allowed to put my shoes on and off for the duration of the day without undoing the laces and my mum nagging me about it.

At the end of each 'rally', I would take the addresses of various friends I'd made, and vowed to write. Then, on the way out of the site, we'd purchase a flag, or badge, to mark our visit, and when we got home Dad would unscrew the plastic panel above the foldaway table/bed and place it in there.

When we were not on trips, the caravan was parked at the bottom of our garden, and I would beg all summer long to be allowed to play in it. Our caravan was an Astral Ranger, four-berth. I was disappointed at the Ranger part of its model name, due to my dislike of anything associated with Rangers Football Club. But I thought Astral sounded pretty and sparkly.

When Mum sat me down at the age of eight to tell me I was adopted she asked me whether I had any questions.

'What did my other mother say?' was all I could come up with at short notice.

'Well,' my mum said slowly, choosing her words thoughtfully, 'she said that she was glad that you were going to a good home, and that we had a caravan, because she couldn't afford anything like that.'

I didn't really believe, even then, that a caravan was the talking point of a woman who was just about to say goodbye to her baby for life, but I understood what my mum meant by it. I often looked at the caravan as a safe and happy home, where everything was perfect, much safer and much happier for me than the one at the other end of the garden.

My cousins toured with us regularly before they bought the stationary caravan in Elie. We would drive in convoy and toot the horn at each other, taking it in turns to overtake, so Fraser and I could wave at one another. On one particular trip, a car sped around the corner in the other direction, almost smashing into us. When we lurched around the corner there were a handful of people bent over a figure in a crash helmet who lay twisted on the ground. Over by the wall lay the wreckage of his mangled motorbike. My dad went to get out of the car, but a man from the crowd shook his head. Dad got back in the car and Mum told me we would have to pass it and not look. I turned around to see my Auntie Muriel peeling Gillian and Fraser away from the back-seat windows as they strained to see. Dad drove slowly past the incident. Mum looked away. I put my hands over my eyes but kept my fingers wide apart in one hand. His arm was in an unusual position, one a conscious person couldn't manage, and under his helmet trickled a long stream of blood, which flowed away from the scene down into a nearby ditch.

I knew he was dead, and couldn't wait to talk to my cousin Fraser about it.

Sharing time with people I could call 'family' was, as an only child, an experience I loved. I got on best of all with my cousin Fraser, who was the same age as me, also adopted and also, like me, a peculiar mixture of male and female with little interest in the opposite sex. Perhaps we were so close because we somehow recognised each other's sexuality from an early age. When we were very little we used to walk around holding hands, and often asked our parents if we could marry each other when we were grown up. In Elie that summer, with Fraser, I finally got to fulfil my fantasy of sleeping in a bunkbed with a real live person, who was close to me, on the top bunk.

Around this time I used to go with Fraser and see all the X-rated films. Although he was my age, he was an enormous bloke. I would borrow make-up off my granny and plaster it on at her house, take my saddle bag (a ridiculous fashionable bag at the time, that came in many sizes), and we'd pool our money and put it in Fraser's wallet so he looked more of a man.

Both of us adored films and took every opportunity to slip off together to see *Friday the Thirteenth*, *The Bitch*, or *American Gigolo*. Afterwards we'd go down to the Hollywood Hamburger Joint, a restaurant done up with film posters, to get a burger and Coke, and read the latest issue of *Film Review* magazine.

It was *Star Wars* though that really blew Fraser away. He never moved on to girls, but stuck to Han Solo figurines and his *Star Wars* pyjamas, wallpaper and duvet covers. We both shared a passion for

James Bond, and on occasions visited exhibitions containing props from the films.

Fraser's teenage sexual confusion caused problems with his father. Uncle Sandy was strict, like my father, and uncomfortable with Fraser's campness. He used to bully his son, which I suppose he considered might act as some sort of 'cure'. When Fraser hit his late teens and his homosexuality became more obvious, he and his father rowed increasingly. On one occasion, my uncle even punched Fraser, but then one day, just after he was seventeen, Fraser just punched him right back. His dad never touched him again.

The night I arrived in Elie, there was a teenage disco on the caravan site. The three of us decided to go. Even at thirteen I had already developed a real neurosis about clothes. I got into a terrible state about what I should wear, and my holiday wardrobe didn't cater for a disco. I had brought nothing fashionable. I say brought, but really I didn't own anything fashionable whatsoever, nothing that was considered cool. I was distraught. Gillian was a lot girlier than me, so borrowing anything of hers was out of the question. In the end I had to pick an item from Fraser's wardrobe.

Maybe I'd have been better off wearing one of Gillian's dresses, but the opportunity to dress as a boy was always too much to resist. I borrowed brown cotton matching jacket and trousers. The jacket was boxy and zipped up the middle. It was two sizes too big for me. I sat outside the disco not really wanting to go in.

Everyone laughed at me. Even I had to admit that it was funny. Had I not been on holiday and surrounded by my family, I'd have been mortified. But I wasn't out to impress anyone, so I didn't worry too much over it.

The next day, it was raining heavily so we stayed indoors playing cards. Every so often we stopped to laugh about my night-before outfit.

Uncle Sandy and Auntie Muriel went into town for groceries. It went fairly quiet for a bit while we concentrated on our game, but I couldn't resist the opportunity to ask the others about IT.

'You know we're adopted, don't you?' (Imagine if they didn't, I think, just after saying it.)

Fraser looks at Gillian, to see what to say next, because she's very much in charge, the older sister.

'Yes, they have told us,' Gillian replies, uptight already.

'Do you ever think about it? I mean, who your other parents are?'

'I never think about it. It doesn't bother me,' Fraser chips in, as he deals another hand.

'It's my turn to be banker, Fraser.' Gillian tries to bring the focus back to the game. But I'm not having it – this is the only chance I have to talk to anyone about this, let alone my own cousins who are alien babies like me.

'As far we're concerned, our real mum and dad are the ones that brought us up. We have no interest in the other stuff.' And from that I take it that Gillian wants to end the conversation. So I stop probing, jealous that she can apply the word 'we' to her family set-up.

Soon after that, the car pulls in at the side of the van, and their parents arrive back. I watch them intensely, unpacking the items, wondering what their story is, and what Gillian and Fraser's original sets of parents look like.

The next day, when the rain had stopped, the three of us went down to play on the beach. Standing on the edge of a rock, skimming stones, were two boys, one short and dark, the other tall and blond.

We got talking, except Gillian started acting all weird and shy, which she really wasn't. The blond boy turned out to be called Wilson De La Mare. His friend was called Stephen, and we agreed to meet them both the next day, down on the beach again, in the same spot.

Wilson was something of a poet, and we spent the next two weeks hanging around together. We even held hands.

Wilson was a couple of years older than me, and a nice, gentle boy. He was cool because his leather jacket stayed on his back wherever we were and no matter how hot it was. We had a sort of mini-romance for the rest of my holiday. It consisted mainly of holding hands and having our pictures taken together in a photo booth. I may have kissed him a couple of times, but that was about it. Cousin Gillian hooked up with his friend, Stephen, and the four of us hung out together. Nothing sexual ever occurred and I suspect that I only really liked him because he was another of the boys I wanted to be. Especially if it meant I could wear a leather jacket.

At the end of the two weeks I went back to Musselburgh on the train. When I got home I somehow convinced myself that we had had a passionate and tempestuous love affair; how fate had torn us cruelly apart; how I'd struggle to live without him.

All bollocks, of course. In three days I'd forgotten all about him. Or I would have, if his friend Stephen, Gillian's boyfriend, hadn't called me out of the blue about a week later and asked if he could meet me. I agreed because he was considered quite handsome with his little bum-fluff moustache and yellow crash helmet. He looked a bit like the swimmer David Wilkie.

Stephen drove all the way from Elie – about two hours away – on his little yellow Yamaha 125, parked up in the lay-by behind the railway track and waited for me. I went down and we sort of scuffed our feet a bit and looked into the distance and after about ten minutes of us not even bothering to make eye contact, he headed off for the two-hour drive back up the coast. I never saw him again.

On my return from holiday, I found my dad to be a bit stronger. He'd even started going for little walks with the dog, which made me feel secure about his recovery. My mum, however, though tanned from sunbathing in the garden, looked tired. I also noticed she was scratching much more, which was a sign of stress. That didn't stop my perpetual questioning about things I'm sure she'd rather have not talked about.

'Mum? You know how Gillian and Fraser are adopted and there's two of them?'

'Yes, dear.'

'Well, did you never think about getting a brother to go with me?'

'No, we wanted a little girl.'

My real interest in a brother was to have someone to fend off Jamie Ritchie, and someone to give me their clothes to wear when I wanted to look like a boy.

Almost as soon as I got back, I checked to see if my three love interests were back too. I went out on my bike and checked Alison first, but the gates were still firmly shut. Then I cycled down to Susanne's, by the swans, where there was also a phone box. Here I called Miss Carlisle, killing two birds with the one stone. But all my loves were missing. On the way home I wished I could have stayed with my cousins longer, in order to tide me over until things went back to normal.

The next day Valerie came along to tell me that there was a new person in our lives. It appeared that the large house in the avenue, usually rented out to people of no interest to us, had a new resident for the next few weeks. An American.

And so the beautiful Wesley McAllister breezed into our lives, with his Fonzie jacket, all ready to destroy Jamie Ritchie's leadership.

I really fancied Wesley. Everyone did. He was so much more attractive than the Scottish boys. He was cooler, whether spinning a basketball or just the way he wore his socks. But he never dated a single girl for the six months he was in Musselburgh. He just played sport non-stop.

Quite clearly, the basis of my slight crush on Wesley was that he had curly hair and an American accent, just like Paul Michael Glaser. At that age, had I been able to have a sex change operation and look the spit of Starsky, I would have accepted with open arms.

My obsession with boys, or men, on television was based on wanting to be them, in order to attract a string of girls and women, ranging from Angela Mitchell in my primary school class to Farrah Fawcett-Majors. In my tiny child brain, I thought that given the right clothes (always of American influence) this was entirely possible. Like James Bond, I believed I could get any girl in the world. All I had to do was study the clothing and manner of Wesley McAllister.

Wesley had olive to brown skin, beautiful lips, a perfect chest, and a great bum. He was good at all sports. I don't remember one word he said. I don't even know if he spoke at all. He must have, if only to explain the rules of basketball. Wesley could spin a ball on his index finger, like the Harlem Globetrotters – a skill that was passed on to King Jamie before Wesley's departure. Jamie and Wesley got on very well, which was predictable and disappointing. They had an unspoken respect and instant mutual admiration the second they met. Perhaps, back in the USA, Wesley was king of his suburb, as Jamie was here. Two kings from different lands meeting. I never quite worked the Jamie/Wesley thing out, but it must have been pretty massive because Jamie never asked Wesley for a fight, which was unheard of. After Wesley left, Jamie wore tube socks and cut-downs every summer for a long time. He carried the torch; his skin even got browner. In return, Jamie gave Wesley his most treasured possession – the fucking miniature wooden Viking axe his Orange Lodge-attending father had made him. I was glad to see it go. I'm sure Wesley was touched by this gesture, but probably dumped it at the back of his garage along with all the other gifts he'd collected from his trips to various lands. What need would he have for an axe in his world, a world filled only with sport?

Wesley was a powerful and charismatic individual who influenced all our lives, mine in particular. The things he brought us included:

Basketball
Tube socks of a sporting nature worn with cut-down denims
Levi's
No interest in violence
The use of the word 'cool'
A laidback approach to everything
Cans of Coke bought in bulk at the cash and carry by his parents.
    These were readily available and always chilled

The last one was the best. Scottish parents only bought large economy bottles of fake cola from the supermarket. Wesley's mum got the

Real Thing in cans, and put it in a fridge, a special fridge, just for keeping cans of Coke in. And the fridge was in the garage!

This was great because garage life featured regularly on all American films with children, and most American sitcoms.

Imagine this. It's a hot day. You ride around to Wesley's house on your bike. His garage door is open. At the side of the garage Wesley is shooting hoops in his NYC T-shirt and cut-off jeans.

'Hey, Rhona!' He breaks off and stands there whizzing the ball around on his finger. 'Fancy a Coke?'

And he tosses you an ice-cold can, and you lean against the garage wall and drink it. Suddenly you're in every American sitcom and teen-based movie you've ever seen. Especially towards the end of the summer, when Wesley took to wearing his leather jacket. The one that was exactly the same as the one sported by Arthur Fonzarelli.

America, and all things American, were great. First, and always, there's Elvis. Then *Happy Days*. Then *Starsky and Hutch*. Now Wesley, real flesh-and-blood proof that there is a nicer place somewhere far away from here that makes people like him. A place where foodstuffs are replaced by groceries, and the groceries are placed in cardboard bags, just like the ones Hutch used to pick up on the way home to his apartment. A place where, if you are delivering newspapers, you can throw them on to lawns from the seat of your bike. A place where dads are like Ryan O'Neal in *Paper Moon* and daughters are like Jodie Foster in *Freaky Friday*.

At this point we were reading *Shane* in English, and I loved it. Shane was everything I wanted to be, and everything I wanted in a father. Of course, I convinced myself that Shane was quite like Wesley.

I naturally cast myself as the little boy hankering after Shane/Wesley, hanging on his every word, learning from his every move. In all my writing at this time I overused the phrase 'like a tightly coiled spring' to describe not only Shane's emotional frame of mind but almost everything. It crept into my diary:

> *I don't know what's wrong with me at the moment. It's as though I'm like a tightly coiled spring.*
>
> *Miss Livingstone got very angry with me and shouted at me in class today. She was just like a tightly coiled spring*
>
> *Took Hector for his walk. He saw a cat and barked at it like a tightly coiled spring.*
>
> *Mum is like a tightly coiled spring. I have to be quiet and walk around the house like a tightly coiled spring.*

After school, when I walked the dog, we took a new route – down to the big tree with the stuck-out branch. I would sit on it, put the dog's leash under it and pull it up like a rein. I was able to touch the ground with my feet while sitting on it, and push myself up to create a horseriding effect. I'd ride in silence for a bit then stop as the imaginary cavalry captain approached me. The conversation never changed. It went like this every day:

CAPTAIN: Will you help us?

ME/SHANE/WESLEY: Captain, let me tell you something. The wolf will protect the lamb from the fox, but one day the wolf shall eat the lamb itself.

God knows where I got that from, but the general idea was that I was this wise mystical outsider, neither cowboy, nor Indian, but friend to both. A peacemaker with a dodgy past. Full of hurt and now completely self-reliant. It was me the captain would turn to for help in leading the cavalry through the treacherous pass; I was enigmatic and would give nothing away. Just like Wesley. Where was he from? What was he hiding? If only I could bring him here and explain my game. Or, better still, he could take me back to America with him, where I would escape this monotony and fit in with nice families who have a laugh, like the Cunninghams.

Suddenly everything about life in Scotland was shite. I wanted to protect Wesley from any Scottish influence. It was embarrassing. But I already knew I was too late and somehow Jamie's Rangers propaganda had seeped through into Wesley. He started wearing more and more blue, and even went down to the bloody Sea Cadets (the mock paramilitary wing of child Rangers supporters) with Jamie one night.

Disillusioned with the Scottish Dream, pining for Miss Carlisle and, of course, keeping a tight lid on the awful fear I felt for my dad, I knew that this summer was going to be the hardest yet.

eight
august

i sat on the large branch, half torn off the tree, looking at the hayfields in full bloom. I stared over at the estate, my dog sniffing around beneath me, the sun making the road on my street look like it was made of rubber. It was very hot and I was in my cutdowns and a vest – the official least-I-could-wear outfit.

I always hated August, a month that was a wasteland of heat and despair. This one was no different. No one was around – people were still in Blackpool, Great Yarmouth or Benidorm. But even if they had been back it would have only meant I could pointlessly pursue their affections. Only two and a bit weeks of the prison sentence left until the start of a new school term, was my general thinking, as I bounced around on my imaginary horse, who was thirsty and tired.

My father was getting slightly stronger, and becoming bored of the same flavour of Carnation Build-Up every day. Mum decided to move him on to banana flavour, so they went to the shops to get some. Mum and Dad had begun venturing out on little trips: down to the seafront, out with the dog or to the shops.

I used the time alone in the house to play blaring sad and emotional music, while dressed in my father's shirts. I also wore my sunglasses the moment they were gone, pretending I was Elvis in his later years. Whatever I was trying to be – I think it was a broken-hearted fallen star, famous but deeply unhappy – I had to be it quickly, because they never went away for very long. I'd stand at the window and wave them off, then leap upstairs and rifle through my father's wardrobe. He had two Hawaiian shirts from the sixties, which were perfect for my Elvis impressions. I'd put them on, wet my hair and slick it back a bit, then put on my sunglasses, place a rolled-up hand towel around my neck and mime to 'American Trilogy'. I'd splash water on my face, every so often, from the kitchen sink, to make my face look sweaty from my performance. Sometimes I'd encore with 'Suspicious Minds', depending on whether my parents went down the road to Fine Fare, or ventured further afield to Asda.

We had one stereo in the house, a small High Fidelity player that sat in the corner of the lounge. My parents never used it, unless the family visited, when they'd put on Frank Sinatra or Tony Bennett. In my bedroom I had a small Hitachi tape recorder, which seemed fine because it was what I was used to, but for full dramatic effect during my mock concerts the record player was essential. The rest of the time I wanted to play records I had to make do with sitting in the lounge with the headphones on, struggling to remain subdued in front of my parents.

Mum and Dad returned home. Good news. Well, they didn't know they had news of any kind, but I could see they were each carrying a cardboard bag. I couldn't believe it.

My local supermarket had gone American. It was too perfect.

'Where did you get this?' I shouted, grabbing the bag off my father, practising carrying it.

'Fine Fare, of course,' replied Mum, unimpressed and totally missing the point.

'Bloody useless, they are, though. No good if they get wet.' This pleased me, because my dad getting opinionated again was a sign he was back to his old self.

From then on, I volunteered to do all the shopping, but not if it was a ridiculously heavy load. Struggling with too many bags would have spoilt the look. But the *Starsky and Hutch* two-bag clutch was a beautiful thing. I took the whole bag revolution down at Fine Fare to be a tribute to the now departed Wesley McAllister.

Mum was really starting to show the strain of the last few months. Her skin condition was much worse, and she had to increase the hoovering to twice a day to clean up the scales on the patch where she sat in the evenings. She was well past the time of her usual hospital visit, and even my gifts of Milk Tray and Dairy Milk didn't seem to lift her. Finally, my gran offered to come down and stay for the next week to help her out. This meant us sharing a room again, which I wasn't in the mood for, partly because of the heat, but mainly due to my need to be alone to pine for Miss Carlisle and Susanne Flynn. Plus I needed to be alone to enable me to practise snogging on my arm, at night, rolling around the bed, telling a pillow that I loved her. I begged to stay in my gang hut in the garden shed, to which my mum replied 'No'.

'How about ... Oh, please, please ... How about I sleep with the camp bed in the study, then? Oh, pleeease, Mum?'

'Oh, alright. But only while Gran is here.'

'Yeeees.'

'You'd better get it down from the loft, then.'

I was beside myself with joy. The study was a tiny room, big enough for a coat stand, which was always toppling over with the weight of my dad's motorbike jacket. There was a small, fold-up bureau where I did homework and where my mum kept all our paperwork and bills. The idea of being able to camp down there, on the ground floor, with a small window that overlooked the driveway, was like another holiday for me. Perhaps I could get a friend to sneak out at night and throw small stones at the window to wake me, and, like Tom Sawyer, I could sneak out and we could go exploring.

Gran arrived, in her usual way, grabbing my face with both hands, pulling me towards her and rubbing our noses together. Then she would sit down, reach into her handbag and give me a pear drop. The dog always went mad to see her. I loved Gran being there. I hoped she would make us her bizarre Russian salad: lettuce and onion and cucumber and tomato all chopped up really small in a bowl, mixed with sugar and salad cream. My gran cooked her own weird, but highly enjoyable, versions of my mum's meals. Gran never drank anything except tea or sherry. In the morning, she had a cup of boiling water and porridge, with lots of salt, then a stand-up wash before covering herself in talc before dressing. I loved Gran staying in my room, and very soon it smelt of her – talc, mints, and Tweed perfume. Whenever anyone arrived in our house it was customary for me to invite them upstairs to view any recent additions to my poster collection since they last visited. I grabbed my gran by the hand and rushed her excitedly up the stairs. Gran treated it all like an exhibition she was visiting.

'Oh my word,' she'd say, fixing her glasses on her nose from the gold chain that hung permanently around her neck. She would go up really close, trying, for my benefit, to show a real interest. I had always been poster mad, more so than anyone else I had ever met (apart from Stevie Gilmore, who had no walls left at all, all obscured by Black Sabbath posters). But I was a close second. My walls were mainly full of Elvis. But the longest part of my wall was covered by Lee Majors as Steve Austin, and Roger Moore sitting in a hanging basket-chair with a gun near his cheek. I moved my gran over to my most recent finds.

'What on earth?' She stopped at Bruce Lee and contorted her face in disgust.

'You can take that thing down – I'm not sleeping with that in the room.'

I giggled, and Gran made more over-the-top yuck noises as I peeled off my Bruce Lee covered-in-cuts-and-blood poster, rolled it up and placed it on top of my wardrobe out of harm's way.

'Sorry, Gran.'

'What have you got tripe like that on your walls for?'

'Everyone has, Gran.' (Lie.)

We all sat down to have dinner. Mum got out Arctic Roll as a treat. Dad had his with the cream-of-the-milk, which he shared with me. We ate in silence, never being great conversationalists during dinner, and rarely even pausing between main meal, pudding and washing up. Afterwards, Gran told us the latest news from her stair:

about how Mrs Stewart, the Irish lady with the lisp and drawn-on eyebrows, made a fuss over the stair-cleaning rota; how Mr and Mrs Cow, her neighbours of 30 years, had bought a new car; who had got a parking ticket that week (when Gran wasn't busy she would stand for hours looking out of her window on to the street obsessing over traffic wardens and double yellow lines).

I felt happy that night, with Gran staying. It made everything better, sort of lighter, and I worried less about everyone. The dog was different too – he was calmer, and let my gran lift him up, the only person who was ever allowed by him to do so.

I was happy making up my camp bed in my new room. I already felt like an American boy at college or something. It was hot in the evening, so I changed into my Adidas shorts and a vest. It was quite late, but we all sat up chatting.

'What are you wearing that at this time of night for?'

'I'm hot,' I said, embarrassed that my mum had noticed my outfit change, and that she might detect the real reason behind it, i.e. that I felt like an American boy in boxer shorts.

Usually, I wore pyjamas from the good old Kays catalogue to bed. I had to make do with stupid girls' pyjamas, which were short at the sleeves with lace around the neck. Which, let's face it, was designed to make it a kind of nightdress. I hated nightdresses. I hated the idea that the dress theme was meant to continue through to your sleeping time.

Dad went to bed, and Mum and Gran followed, both clutching their handbags that they'd sat with all evening. They took them upstairs with them at night-time in case of burglars.

And I was, at last, in my new sleeping environment, with the Kays catalogue for company. It always stayed in the study in the bureau. At night, I would escape to the boys section, and pick out all the clothes and underwear I would wear if I was a boy. I was only allowed one item from each page. (I felt the game needed some structure.) The boys in the catalogue were all handsome with good bodies and contented expressions. No wonder. I would be contended if I could go to bed at night wearing karate pyjamas. And guess who had a pair of them? Yes, Jamie Ritchie.

Imagine all the girls I could get if I was one of them. Then, once I'd picked my clothes from every page of the boys section, I'd pick a bike, and shoes, and finally the inflatable swimming pool at the games section at the back. Then I'd dream about what I'd do next, now that I was perfect. Thinking about tracksuits, and Y-fronts, white cotton vests, red karate pyjamas with black piping down the front, and me on a brand-new Chopper riding around with Susanne Flynn on the back, I drifted off to sleep on the camp bed.

he next morning I woke with the worst hayfever of all time. My eyes were extremely itchy, and the back of my throat felt red hot from me making this funny sound in order to scratch it. I could barely speak for sneezing. Mum, uncharacteristically, had a long lie-in, while Dad sipped his strong, sweet tea in his dressing gown. Gran was up before the rest of us, stirring her porridge, even though it was August. I had Sugar Puffs, with the cream-of-the-milk. Between bouts of sneezing, I wondered what to do with the day.

'Well, did you sleep well in your wee cubby hole?'

'Yes, thanks, Gran.'

'You're a daft wee thing.'

Everything my gran said was extra cute and lovely. On this occasion it made me feel slightly weird and guilty about my catalogue fantasies.

It was a predictably blistering hot day. The beach would be packed full of people from visiting towns, the harbour benches all taken up with the elderly snoozing, in their versions of summer clothing. The hayfields were particularly golden. The air was still, unusual for Musselburgh, which always had a slight breeze from the coast. This must have been the hottest day of the year, and it only served to magnify all the lust, longing and loneliness I was feeling. On days like this, the anxiety surrounding my various infatuations totally overtook me. I seriously believed that my love was a prison, and I had no way of escaping. I would never properly lay down next to a girl that I loved, who would love me back. Nothing else mattered to me as much as that; all the rest was padding.

After breakfast, I kissed Dad and Gran – who were sunbathing in the garden – goodbye, and set off on my trusty three-speed Raleigh Vindec. Now I was getting on for fourteen, I'd noticed I was one of very few girls who still cycled everywhere, let alone attached football cards to the spokes to create an engine sound. I cycled down past my old primary school, through the back streets and straight to Susanne Flynn's flat. I knew she was still on holiday, but I had to be near her as best I could. In this instance, her stairwell would have to do.

I drag my bike through the main door into her staircase, so as not to draw attention to it. Imagine if she and her family arrived home at that moment. What would I do? What would I say? I'd be innocently knocking on her door to see if she was coming out. I would ask her if she'd like to come to Luca's for an ice cream. In the morning? To arrive at someone's house you hardly know in the morning has a terrible sense of urgency about it. Like you've been awake all night thinking about seeing them, and as soon as it's morning you race there. That's exactly why I was there. Who was I kidding?

Standing for a moment in the stairwell, these concerns and anxieties send my heart racing so hard I think that someone upstairs might hear it.

Occasionally I open her letterbox and take in a noseful of air, to see if Susanne is mixed in there with the other smells. Mainly I smell dust, slight traces of food, but mostly nothing. The stair banisters smell of polish. Shafts of light shoot through the fire escape window at the top, creating moving dust particles. Watching this makes me dreamy. The stair is nice and cool compared to the street. I am content standing there, leaning against the wall, pretending in my head I am a boy walking her home after a perfectly normal date. There'd be no need to sneak around and follow her the way I had. I turn around and put my arm up against the wall, folding it so that my forearm is the same height as my face. I start to kiss my arm, imagining I am kissing her. This is my latest thing, the arm kissing. It comforts me. I make up our dialogue in my head, and speak my bits out loud, though in a whisper, so as not to alert the neighbours. There really would be no talking my way out of this one, might I be caught.

SUSANNE: Thanks for a lovely evening.

ME: Pleasure. You're a beautiful girl, Susanne, and you
                deserve the very best.

SUSANNE: I loved my knickerbocker glory. Can we do it again sometime?

ME: Of course.

A bit of kissing begins again.

SUSANNE: You are the best kisser.

ME: I could say the same for you.

Susanne's dad, being a normal protective father, shouts to us.

MR FLYNN: It's about time you were inside.

ME: He's right, it's getting late. We've got school in the morning. We must concentrate on our homework, get good marks, then leave this town together.

SUSANNE: I just hate to be without you for another night.

ME: Me too, but we have our whole lives ahead of us.

(I must at all times be patient with her. I wouldn't want her father to think I was disrespectful.)

SUSANNE: Wait, one more kiss before I see you off on your motorbike.

ME: OK, then.

I move into the arm. My nose starts to itch with the hayfever, made worse by the dust in the stair. I give out a massive sneeze that I try to stifle for fear of anyone hearing me, which makes loads of snot explode from my nose. That's my cue to leave. I kick my bicycle off its stand, push the stair door open, and pedal off.

dad was spending less time in bed during the day, so the black and white Sony portable television, used only for caravan trips or illness, was placed back in the wardrobe. I loved the portable. And I decided to use my hayfever as an excuse to view it. Hayfever did, after all, constitute being unwell. Therefore, in terms of the family rules, I should be entitled to have it placed in my temporary bedroom. I won my case and quickly moved it down to the study. The obvious joy of having your own TV was watching whatever you fancied whenever. And, with the privacy of sleeping downstairs, I could watch it at any time of night. My parents had a healthy and fairly strict attitude to me watching television. I had to be thinking about getting ready for bed after the ten o'clock news, and I was never allowed to watch *The Sweeney*.

I didn't have long to wait for Valerie to come back from her summer holidays, and was excited at the thought of celebrating the anniversary of Elvis's death in a few days – although I felt bad about being excited, because the mood would be sombre. But that didn't stop us looking forward to wearing our Elvis T-shirts and badges for all the world to see. Two days after celebrating the passing of The

King, school would start again. A new term, a new beginning, and the chance to be in the company of my loves again.

Feeling fairly content at the prospect of all that, I decided to sit out the last week of prison on my tiny camp bed, watching old films as much as I could get away with. I quickly developed a craving for tomato sandwiches with salad cream, and a glass of milk. It was all I wanted to eat for a while.

A film began, an old film from the early sixties, starring Warren Beatty and Natalie Wood, called *Splendour in the Grass.* It was a story about a young woman who falls in love with a rich handsome young man. Although he loves her, and lusts after her, they cannot be together. The boy's father is against their love, and influences him into not ending up with her. They are both distraught, but she comes out worse. He drifts, a broken man. She ends up obsessing so greatly it consumes her, and she is forced to spend time in a mental institution, where she makes artwork until her broken heart is mended. They both waste the prime of their lives with their obsession. In the end, in the most powerful scene, we see he has moved on. He has a wife and children, but seems to feel very little. She can't help herself and must visit him one more time. A friend reluctantly takes her to him. She is deeply affected by their meeting. He, on the other hand, is relatively unmoved by it. They both seem deadened by their loss of one another. Him more than her. She is almost in tears at the sight of him, in his new life, the life she should have had with him. It's a terrible injustice that they are not together. At the very end, she leaves in a car driven away along a dirt track leading from his farm. Half crying, she quotes us the Walt Whitman poem, of the film's title.

Splendour in the grass blew my mind away, and upset me greatly.

An hour later I stopped crying, wondering if I would ever get over the effect the film had had on me. I worried that I was just like Natalie Wood, and that I would spend some time myself in an institution trying to get over some love obsession, probably Miss Carlisle. Just like me, the two characters in this film were victims of life in a small town. At least they could take some comfort from the fact that they were obsessed with each other. My obsessions were a one-way street. On the upside, Natalie Wood did do a lot of pottery and painting during her breakdown, which must have been very relaxing. I weighed all this up in my mind, while making my fourth tomato and salad cream sandwich of the evening.

There was one date in August that kept me going. August 16th. The day Elvis died. The day when Valerie and I would pay tribute to The King.

I adored Elvis. The best-looking man that ever, ever lived. It is impossible for any other man to get close to how attractive he was. I knew what it felt like to see the world through Elvis's eyes. Elvis was my god. I wanted to be Elvis. A lot of the time, in my head, I was Elvis.

I was probably one of the world's most obsessive Elvis fans. No surprise there. The other fans worried me, though. If I ever went to some Elvis thing where they were gathered, they always seemed a bit retarded. There also seems to be a bit of a link between being an Elvis fan and being ugly. There was this ageing, ugly Teddy Boy called Shug who ran the local pool hall. He believed he was Elvis. I told him once, 'You have no idea what went on with Elvis. I can tell by looking at your face. I'm more Elvis than you are.'

This August 16th, Valerie and I had arranged an Elvis schedule. We would wear our matching Elvis T-shirts, the black ones with a

picture of Elvis in the middle, on stage in Hawaii, shrouded in flowers. She would come round for me, and we would perform the ceremony at mine. (Valerie's mum was obsessive about a tidy house, so
we tended not to play there as much.)

In my bedroom we arranged a selection of tapes from our
combined collections. I had previously asked Mum for a power-cut
candle. She allowed me to have it, so long as I promised not to set
my room on fire. We felt tearful as soon as we'd placed our fake satin
Elvis scarves around our necks, the ones that we'd bought the year
before when we attended *Elvis The Musical* in town.

'Are you sad?' I ask Valerie.

'Yeah, I'm dead sad. I can't believe he's gone.'

'Me neither. I can't believe he's gone.'

We begin the prayer, on our knees in front of my dressing table
as though it's an altar, with our Elvis bubblegum cards lined up in
chronological order.

I lead the prayer.

'Dear God. Holy sweet Lord.' (I put that in because it was a bit
Elvisy.) 'We pray for Elvis, that you protect him now, wherever he is.
And thank you, God, for giving us him in the first place. Thank you
for all the joy he brought to our lives ...'

Now we are both in floods of tears.

I light the candle. Solemn-faced we stare at it for a moment, until
I nod.

And then Valerie, with her fingers poised on the play button of
my tape recorder, pushes down, and we hug each other as 'Can't
Help Falling In Love' kicks in.

We join in, singing together through crackly, tearful voices.

At this point we feel genuine grief, there's no doubt about it. I feel devastated at the death of Elvis. Two years ago to this very day, I remember so clearly standing in the caravan shop on a site in Lytham St Anne's surrounded by newspapers, reading 'The King Is Dead'.

We begin clutching our Elvis annuals to our chests.

'I really miss him, do you?'

'I just can't take it in that he's no longer here.'

'Me too.'

We throw ourselves on to my bed face down. Claiming a pillow each, burying our faces in them, to various cries of 'Oh Elvis, why did you have to go?'

Mum bursts through the door, forgetting, on this occasion, to obey the sign on my door. Please knock.

We quickly turn our backs around, pretending to be looking out of the window, because we feel very silly indeed.

'Would you girls like some coconut sponge?'

'Yes. please. Sorry, we just seen someone we knew go up the back road.' I manage to stifle my tears enough to reply.

'I don't know, the pair of you are mad. Elvis this, Elvis that.'

'MUM! This is Elvis's anniversary! Do you mind? And can Valerie stay and watch the Elvis special?'

'As long as you both cheer up, for goodness' sake.'

he next day was the day before school started. I couldn't wait. Everybody was back on the estate. All the cars were parked in their driveways. By early evening I already had my uniform laid out on my chair in my bedroom. My shoes were polished to perfection. My bag was packed, with the obligatory items for a new term in it.

I decided to have one last play out at the Grassy Bit, to mark the end of the summer period. Mum and Dad were still off work, with no sign of returning soon. I couldn't wait to get out of the house. I walked round the corner, full of the joys of the end of the summer holidays, something I knew I was alone in feeling. Jamie Ritchie was there, looking tanned, with the usual gang. He had Andrew McIrish in a headlock as he chatted to Carol Cowan. She giggled every so often, looking as technically good-looking as usual.

It's not that Jamie was always unfriendly towards me, he was more unpredictable. Not with everyone, mostly with me and Andrew McIrish. With Carol, there was a consistency with his behaviour, which never moved beyond doting.

We all do a round of hiyas.

'Where d'ya go on your holidays?' Jamie asks.

'Couldn't go, my dad's been sick. What about you?'

'Benidorm. It was fuckin' magic. Braw birds.'

'Shut up, you.' Carol pretend slaps him, like she's his wife and he's jokingly stepped out of line. This causes him to release McIrish. Jamie begins a mock chase of Carol. Carol makes little effort to escape him. They throw each other around a bit. McIrish and Kev Moffat laugh. I sit down on the grass next to McIrish. While Jamie has hold of Carol's arms behind her, I can see him signalling to McIrish with his eyebrow, his head cocking towards me. McIrish grabs me. I push him off. He, Jamie and Kev chase me round the Grassy Bit. Carol shouts for them to leave off me. Jamie catches me, which is inevitable, rugby tackles me to the ground and sits on top of me. He forces my head down. He holds my hands behind me, as though I'm handcuffed, and lies on top of me. He starts tickling me.

'Don't! I'll get asthma.'

'Oh, shame.'

The others have lost interest; they've seen this a million times before. I get wheezy from laughing too hard at the tickling.

'You're getting big tits.' He half laughs, forcing one hand underneath my body to grab one.

'Fuck off. So what?'

'Let us see them.'

'No, Jamie, please. Another time, I promise.' Knowing there'd be plenty more times like this.

Carol shouts, 'Jamie, let her go.' He does, and I wander off home, feeling that things are well and truly back to normal.

At school the next day many children had new bags and pencil cases. Everybody's hair was soft from washing it the night before. Lots of us bore tans. Some of the female teaching staff had experimented with new hairstyles. The new first years were wandering around the corridor, which smelt of cleaning products, looking lost, wearing stiff new shirts, and blazers too big for them. This made me feel slightly older.

The next term was an important one in our school lives. It was the year we would choose the subjects that we would sit at O-Level. And this, the teachers told us again and again, was what our entire futures were based on. I knew in my first year I would fail most subjects except English and art, and had no interest in anything else other than sport. I also knew, from this time last year, that I was destined to choose biology and A.P.H., for the sole purpose of being in the same room as Miss Carlisle.

I entered my registration class and I saw Susanne Flynn, sitting there with her freshly brushed hair. She looked as radiant as ever. (I decided to use the word 'radiant' to describe her from then on. I'd heard it used in an old black and white film I'd seen on the portable during the holidays.)

I stared at the information sheet that listed subjects available. I considered taking pottery, like Natalie Wood, and wondered if it might help cure me. Art was my big thing. I was practically the best person in my school at drawing and painting, and my art teacher had high hopes for me. The art department was a wonderful place to escape lunatics. It was quiet and mature, yet had an edge to it. All the art teachers were highly unusual in comparison with other staff. They wore cords, and open-neck shirts, and had more of a way with the kids. My art class was full of geeky Led Zepplin fans with bad skin, who spent hours hunched over a board, meticulously copying album covers. The teacher would offer up a Still Life, should anyone care to draw it. The Still Life never changed from a bashed Coke can, a sheep's skull, and an old bottle of Mateus Rosé. I drew whenever I got the chance; even in break times I would often arrange to be allowed to paint there. None of the girls I fancied ever chose art, so it was a haven for me, away from desire, free to do other things for a change.

After school, Dad offered to take me swimming, as he'd had a particularly good few weeks and was feeling fine. Mum stayed home to chat to her long-time friend, my Auntie Rona.

In the changing rooms, two girl swimmers were standing by

Heather Stewart, our club champion, who was drying her eyes with a worn-out piece of toilet paper.

'What's wrong?' I asked, putting things in a locker.

'It's Mr Collins, he's *really* ill.'

Mr Collins was our chief swimming coach. He was English, and slightly older than the other coach. He was dedicated to coaching us all, and planned to see Heather Stewart through to the Scottish team.

'Ill with what?'

'Don't know, but he's been bad all summer, and nobody knew,' sobbed Heather.

I felt sorry for Heather, and knew that Mr Collins was like a father to her. We all stroked her back a bit, until a couple of the boys, Douglas and William, shouted through to her from the antiseptic footbath that she would feel better if she trained.

Training was downbeat; most of us swam in silence. At the edge of the baths, the other coach and a temporary one stood close together speaking intensely, their arms folded. From where I was swimming this all looked very bad.

Dad was leaning against the glass partition with the other parents when, I swear, I saw him put a cigarette in his mouth. I tried to get a proper look as I tumble-turned near him at the deep end. I could see he had it hidden in his hand, which he kept close to his leg. I suppose he thought I couldn't see him from the water, through the steam and splashing. But that cigarette stuck out to me, an enormous glowing white stick. My heart was thumping. I felt sick, and panicked. I used the time in between strokes, when my face was in the water, to cry. I cried out loud and screamed at the top of my underwater voice, and wondered if any of the other swimmers could hear me.

Afterwards, in the car, Dad winced with pain again as he turned the wheel. I noticed he was chewing gum.

'Dad, stop for a minute. I want to ask you something.'

'Sure, kiddo. What is it?'

'If I ask you, will you promise to tell me the truth, like you've always taught me?'

'Of course. Fire away.'

'Dad, were you smoking in there?'

'NO.' He looked surprised.

'Then what was that white thing you had in your mouth?'

He laughed a bit. 'A stick of Wrigleys.'

I said nothing as we drove off home, and hoped if I opened the window, Mum wouldn't smell the smoke from his jacket.

A week after that, Mr Collins, a heavy smoker, died of cancer.

nine
september

mr Collins died of lung cancer very quickly. The whole club was shocked. Heather Stewart was in pieces. The funeral was to be held at Morton Hall Crematorium in Edinburgh. The entire swimming club, bar some very young children, decided to attend.

I had never been to a funeral before. My granddad died when I was nine, but everybody thought I was too young to go to the funeral. I did, however, attend the drinks and sandwiches do at the Co-op function room afterwards. I remember my gran being very sad and drinking sherry. Between bouts of tears she told me a joke to 'cheer me up'. It was very nice of her, I remember thinking then, but I really wasn't upset. His death had little effect on me, having hardly remembered a word he said to me. All the same, I listened intently to my gran's joke, which was about a little girl receiving a watch on her birthday and bragging to everyone about it.

'"Don't be showing off like that at church on Sunday now, about your watch – there might be some children not as well off as you,"' she continued.

'So when the girl goes to church, the minister says to her, "Did you have a nice birthday, then?"

'"Yes thanks," says the girl, "and I won't go on about it too much, but if during the service you hear a little noise and smell a little smell you'll know it's me."'

My gran half laughed, half cried. Other people on the table over-laughed. I was stunned that my gran had told me a fart joke at my granddad's funeral, and thought about how people cope with upset. And whether you're meant to tell jokes to help them.

I rode to the funeral in a car with Douglas Cameron and William McKean, just like a normal swimming night. We had all worn our school uniforms. William never usually wore a tie, but I noticed on this occasion he did. Douglas never spoke much anyway, but he never uttered one word on the journey to the crematorium, during the service or on the way home. He and William looked very handsome, all dressed up inside Morton Hall. I watched them closely during the hymns, to see if they were stifling tears. Douglas had been second closest to Mr Collins after Heather, and he looked very choked up. Heather was comforted by her mother and father and sat in a row behind the immediate family.

The minister spoke of Mr Collins' dedication to his family, to young people in sport, in particular to Tranent Amateur Swimming Club. He mentioned Heather and his hopes for her as the Scottish

Champion. Douglas fiddled with his watchstrap and tensed the muscle in his jaw in and out. I thought about all the times I'd seen Mr Collins smoking, and wondered how much that had contributed to his rapid decline. I remembered his cough, which was fairly persistent, and yet how full of energy he was, walking up and down the edge of the pool, shouting at us all to go faster. I remembered the cigarette I saw my father smoke, how the doctors told him the year before to stop or it would kill him, and how he lied to me when I asked him in the car. By the time 'Abide With Me' started I was in tears, and Douglas looked close to following me.

meanwhile, the 7th Musselburgh Guides Company was dwindling. We had unusually low attendance for the first week back, and no newcomers. Perhaps news had got around that we were a motley bunch, and that our Captain couldn't control us in the tiny back room of a church hall. Mrs Davison wasn't around as much. Her time was taken up by family and church things. Norma and Glenda had left, and gone on to join the police force. Which seemed the next step up.

I had to face the truth. The Girl Guides had lost its sparkle. I guess for some of the girls it was merely a stopgap between childhood and puberty, whereas I would have happily been in it for life. But perhaps even I had to admit my heart wasn't into the pursuit of badges as much as it had been before. I decided this was not good for morale, and I must work towards a couple of awards. I settled on my Artist Badge. If I got it, it would bring my total to fourteen, the age I was going to be that month.

I liked drawing more and more, the older I became. It was so peaceful, and it made me feel utterly content. At primary school, I was the one who designed the school hall for the Christmas party. Admittedly, Robinson Crusoe was a strange theme for that time of year, but it really grabbed me at the time. The teachers were very complimentary as we all danced around the gym hall, covered in huge paintings of bearded men in cut-downs, with their feet pointing out to the sides because I couldn't work out how to draw them facing straight on.

With the start of a new term, and the beginning of the year before our O-Levels, a team of careers officers arrived at school, and we all waited in turn to talk to one.

'Try to have an idea before you meet with an officer what kind of future you would like to have, so you can use the time productively to explore the possibilities open to you,' barked the headmaster at another poorly attended morning assembly.

I feared for my future, and struggled to choose a 'real job or career' that would be acceptable for me to talk about. Basically, I wanted to be a painter, a writer, a cowboy, a spy, an Elvis impersonator or a shoe polisher. I knew none of these would go down well with the careers officer. So I settled on more conventional options that I'd toyed with in my head from time to time in a desperate bid to map out some kind of plan. These options included becoming a vet, because I loved my dog so much, and was an active member of the Junior RSPCA. This, up until now, had involved making use of the emergency phone number issued to me on the back of my membership card every time someone so much as chased a cat out of their garden. They must have been sick of me phoning. The other was a PE teacher, mainly because it wasn't a 'real job' and it was my only shot at turning playing sport into a full-time job. I had always imagined my school PE teachers were lesbians. They were fairly manly, with matching Datsuns and Afghan coats in the winter. They both had flat chests and short hair, and, at the end of every summer break, acquired matching tans. This could be me, I thought, observing them one day high on a rope between the pull-out wall bars, playing Pirates. I could meet my twin, spend a grown-up working day in a tracksuit, and get paid.

The careers officers were positioned in the library, in the study area. And, alphabetically, over a period of a week, we all met with them.

I sat in a booth, looking at a lady with huge glasses.

'Now, then, Rhonda, is it?' She scrabbled through some papers.

'Rhona.'

'Sorry, Rhona. Have you had a think about what you might like to do?'

Real answer.

'Yes, I'd like to be James Bond. Highly skilled in martial arts, able to take on anyone who annoys me and wear a man's dinner suit at any opportunity. I'll have lots of beautiful women, who look like Farrah Fawcett-Majors, in love with me. I'll travel around on a speedboat, involve myself in lots of car chases, get paid millions of pounds so I can buy the house down near the harbour with smoked glass and wooden decking, where, when I wasn't on a mission, I would live, relaxing in a black polo neck, doing lots of meditation.'

The answer I give.

'Well, I love art, and it's my strongest subject. Errr … And I like writing poems. I'm quite good at that.'

'Shall we have a look at your subjects? Let's see now. Not so good at maths. I can see from looking at your progress report that you're in the remedial group for that at the moment. Very good at English. Your history is OK, biology not so strong. Have you thought about college at all?'

Real answer.

'Yes, all the time. An American college where I am a boy, of course, and I carry books under my arm, and wear Levi's and a white T-shirt, and we eat our lunch in a big hall, with cartons of milk on a tray. We each have a locker in a corridor that we cover in various pictures that define who we are. It is these lockers that become the focal point of all teenage conversations. And I drive a sports car like Dustin Hoffman in *The Graduate*.'

The answer I give.

'I've thought about PE college.'

'OK, now we're getting somewhere.' She perks up, and moves her shoulders back, rifling through her books.

'You could go to Dunfermline College to study PE, with the view to becoming a teacher. You would need three O grades and two Higher grades to gain entry for this, which would be a three-year course.'

This didn't make any sense to me. Three Highers to pull out the wall bars when it's raining, take notes from girls at the side of the swimming pool explaining why they couldn't go swimming 'this time', and stand and chat to another member of staff while you send a group of schoolchildren wheezing off on a cross-country run in the middle of winter that you'd never embark on yourself. Admittedly, you did have to learn the rules of hockey and basketball, which would involve having to read a bit, but that could be learnt in an afternoon, surely?

'What about being a vet?' I asked, knowing I would never be able to pass anything other than art, English and possibly history, if the exam paper concentrated more on the Highland Clearances and less on the old infield/outfield farming system.

'Mmm. OK. Let's have a look. Like animals, do you?'

'I've got a dog. I look after him quite a lot, although my gran's the only person whom he'll let lift him ...'

'OK,' she pressed on, abruptly. 'Let's try and concentrate on a couple of options. I do have a limited time with each pupil, but if we don't decide on something for you, don't worry. You will have ample opportunity to discuss it with your guidance teacher, should you find the need.'

Mmm ... Mrs Thomson, with her nice cleavage yet disappointing neck.

'Veterinary college, let's have a look,' she hummed, as she thumbed an index. 'There are a few options here, a number of courses ... Bla bla bla bla, ladi da da da da.'

I lost track of everything she was saying. My eyes drifted over to McIrish, who sat in the cubicle opposite, wearing a Wrangler jacket and looking to be saying nothing at all. His leg was shaking up and down manically. I felt for McIrish, although he hardly said anything to me. I knew his future was ill-fated. He really had nothing going for him, as well as a slight stutter. I wondered what the bored careers officer opposite him was looking up. Perhaps 'punch-bag'. I couldn't imagine him as a grown-up, but if he stayed in Musselburgh, like most young men, he would acquire a moustache. I visualised him at 35, still in his Wrangler jacket. Perhaps married, although he had formed no friendships or relationships with girls, living over the fence from Jamie Ritchie who would no doubt end up with a pretty child-bearing wife, like Warren Beatty in *Splendour in the Grass*. Jamie would give him a good kicking every time he was out cutting the lawn.

'So that would mean a considerable amount of effort.' She was back, and it sounded pretty bleak. The vet thing was definitely out, due to even more qualifications needed than being a PE teacher.

She hurried me off as there was a queue forming of other pupils whose surname began with C. We both agreed that perhaps a foundation course at art college would be my best bet, if I 'played my cards right, and got my head down'.

The careers interview panicked me. Everything was:

Moving far too fast,

I was in a phase I knew would last,

What was ahead but pain and fear?

How would someone like me have a career?

This is what I thought up on the walk back from the library, to the dreaded home economics class. I found the future daunting, and began a phase of writing poetry and lyrics to made-up songs based on that theme. I would sing my latest creation when I was out walking with the dog. The songs invariably contained the word 'insecure', which would rhyme with 'unsure', or 'far away' with 'another day'.

I stared out of the window high up on C floor, in my mini kitchen, stirring the main ingredients of coconut scones, with Mrs Fairclough pacing up and down, occasionally shouting out the next step:

'That's it, and begin folding in.'

Why wasn't I allowed in woodwork, where I could make a tape cassette rack or a nail picture? I just knew that this was the one and only time in my life I would be making coconut fucking scones.

Susanne Flynn was in the mini kitchen next to me. She, unlike me, looked good in her apron. I leant over, still stirring.

'Hey, Susanne, have you had your careers advice talk yet?' I suddenly realised, DUH! Her name is F for Flynn so obviously she hadn't. Still, I continued in an attempt to spend some time with her.

'No, I get mine on Wednesday. Have you had yours, like?'

'Yeah.'

'What was it like, then?'

'Fine. She said I didn't need maths to go to art school, and that even if I didn't want to do that I had plenty of other things.'

'Right.'

'What do you want to be?'

'Dunno, really. A dental hygienist maybe.'

'Right.'

I wondered if we'd all end up in Musselburgh. Alison working for her dad in a secretarial role, going to the dentist on Bridge Street to have her teeth cleaned by Susanne. At least I'd be able to keep track of them, and, let's face it, the rate I was going I'd have the time, because I would be joining the ranks of the long-term unemployed.

dad is sitting on his chair, doing a crossword, when I get home. Mum is in the kitchen, baking one of her sultana cakes. As I walk into the lounge, Dad looks up at me over his glasses.

'Well, then, how was school?'

'Alright.' His question makes me feel bad-tempered. I mask my anxiety about my school future.

Mum comes through from the kitchen, wiping her hands on a towel, taking her place in her chair.

'So, how was your chat at school, then, with the guidance lady?'

'It wasn't guidance. I told you, it's careers. It wasn't important, it was just a talk to see how things are going ...'

I go through to the kitchen for a glass of Red Cola.

'Well, what did she say?'

'I'd better walk the dog first.'

'He's been out,' my father says sternly, obviously detecting my avoidance.

I sit down on the sofa, immediately claustrophobic, terrified that they are catching on to the fact that I am an utter weirdo.

'I told them about art school, and PE college.'

'Uh huh,' says my mum, nodding encouragingly.

'What about veterinary school? Although I think you're growing out of that idea slightly, are you not, dear?'

'Yes, and anyway you need loads of Highers.' (I become slightly hysterical at this point, speeding up my voice and adopting a sense of urgency.) 'I've told you, but you won't listen. I'll fail everything except English and art. I hate everything else. It's so pointless. Now can I take the dog out?'

'No need to get yourself worked up. That attitude is defeatist. You stick in and do the best you can, do you hear me?'

'Yes.'

'What are you going to do?'

'Stick in and do my best.' I drag the words out really slowly and robotically.

'Let me play the fool ...' My father begins his Shakespeare put-down, and I leave the house trailing a dog that has already been walked, imagining that the sad music from the end of *The Incredible Hulk* is playing over me. And I am Dr David Banner forced to leave yet another town, just when I was settling in and making sense of everything.

'Those bloody gamma rays,' I mutter, as I head for the fields.

d ad seemed much better, but still remained off work under the doctor's advice. He drove me more and more to swimming. I watched anxiously whenever I was up his end of the pool, checking to see if he was secretly smoking. But the last time he'd done it seemed to be an isolated incident.

Mum went to the doctor and asked for hospital treatment, as her psoriasis was raging out of control. She was also showing the signs of emotional strain with everything she'd been through. This made her more short-tempered and prone to outbursts of tears.

'Go upstairs and talk to your mum, will you? See she's alright,' said my father, as useless as ever in times of upset. I didn't know what to say to her when I got up there, but she was glad to have me sitting there for a while.

'It's just my nerves,' she'd say. 'They're on end.'

I was very worried about her and, as in all times of trouble, I thought it best to walk the dog.

the following Sunday morning, I decided to give Mum and Dad a special treat by making them a full Scottish breakfast. I got up at 7am, to give me loads of time to prepare, and cycled down to the shops to buy half a dozen soft rolls. Everyone in Scotland ate soft rolls filled with meat or eggs on a Sunday morning. I'd even gone to the trouble of asking my mum for money to buy black pudding the day before.

Excited, I ate some Sugar Puffs while listening to a seven-inch single of Cilla Black singing 'Love's Just A Broken Heart' on the hi-fi with the headphones on.

After a fix of music, I opened my kitchen. I made them bacon, fried eggs, sausages, black pudding, tomatoes, fried bread (for my dad), with warm rolls as the finishing touch. I set the table, put their cutlery in a napkin, made a pot of tea, cut a rose from the garden, put it in a vase on the table, and made my way upstairs to wake them.

the Fisherman's Walk took place every year. A mixture of Musselburgh tradition, which honoured the fisher-folk past and present, and a chance for a piss-up in a different outfit. The Calders (no relation to Alison) were the biggest fishing family in town, owning nearly all the boats. The walk itself originally involved the men and women of Musselburgh who had fishing connections, although by this time anyone who fancied joined in. They were dressed in traditional attire: the men wore hand-knitted blue jumpers that buttoned up the side of the neck, with black wool trousers and boots. The older men wore flat caps. The women, of course, got the bum deal on the outfit front as far as I could see. They had to wear a hideous, almost puff-ball, skirt, a blouse, a floral shawl and an apron. The outfits were hired in Musselburgh, and made by the old women of the town.

For the parade, all the fishermen and their ridiculously clad female family members would march along the town, which was lined with spectators. There were decorated lorries, with bands playing in the back of them, all representing the families who owned the boats. At the very front of the parade was a pipe band. I loved the pipe band, and always felt a lump in my throat when they cranked up.

Mum, Dad and I went to watch. People from all the housing estates made their way down in droves. I took my bike, in case I wanted freedom at any point. I knew I was bound to see the entire Flynn and Calder families, after all, and might, therefore, be able to fit in a bit of quality following and observing.

The event itself was not something I had great interest in. Once again it made me feel like an outsider. I did, of course, want to come from a fishing family (I was totally jealous of anyone that had a right-ful place in tradition). Plus, it was a way, I suppose, of gathering some respect. That and the chance to play on a boat.

The Musselburgh Sea Cadets were involved in the parade, which meant Jamie Ritchie was there.

I spot him, looking deadly handsome, in his military-style uniform, modelled on a naval uniform with sailor-type hat. Having to live in the same small town as the Sea Cadets, who got to go snorkelling, water-skiing and hanging around on boats with girls watching from the shore, and not being able to join them, was another reason to absolutely loathe being a girl. You could guarantee that Jamie would find his way into almost any organisation that involved looking mature, masculine and like he could take anyone on. I watch him march.

'Oh, look Rhona! There's Jamie!' shouts Mum, waving.

'Oh yeah, so it is.' I pretend to have just noticed.

'Who is it?' asks Dad, once again behind on the names front.

'It's the boy Ritchie, Bill. The Ritchies across the road.'

Standing near us, in the crowd, is the Cowan family, with Carol, dressed in shades of white and lemon. I study her reaction as Jamie passes her. She waves and smiles. He gives her a casual wink, and I feel like the jealous queen in *Snow White*.

A couple of neighbours and girls from my class form a line of fisher girls behind a float.

A chorus of 'hiyas' come my way. I 'hiya' them back, wondering how they could bear being dressed in such a way. Although really I know why – because they are happy and normal, and don't think about these matters in the way I do 24 hours a day.

'Don't they look lovely, the girls in their outfits?'

'No, Mum, they look silly.'

'You could go into the parade next year if you wanted. It's not as strict as it used to be – anyone can join in.'

'I don't want to march up and down in tights.'

'You don't have to wear tights, dear. Some of the girls are bare-legged with a sandal.'

'You don't get it, do you?' I am straining my voice above 'Scotland The Brave'.

'I'm only saying. What on earth's got into you?'

'I don't like sandals and I don't like tights. I want to be a Cadet! It's not fair.'

The band is in full volume.

'There's no pleasing you.'

'The Ritchies are at 52, are they not?' We ignore my dad.

'I'm off, Mum, this is stupid.'

And I leave, on my bike, banging my shins against my pedals as I'm jostled by a happy crowd.

I escape to the harbour, which is empty for once, bar a fleet of yachts bobbing around, bells clanking as they edge into one another. I head for the edge of the pier, one leg pushing off the edge of the wall as I sit on my bike. I look at the coastline stretching over to Fife, the noise of festivities in the background. Tonight there will be a party. The men and women of Musselburgh will dance, boys and girls will swig cider and cheap lager behind the Brunton Hall and under the Roman Bridge, then attend the Junior Fisherman's Walk Disco. Jamie will probably go with Carol. I will be no part of it. Because ...

I have no boy to go with

I don't want to go anyway, but it's still unfair

I hate tights

And I have to ship some illicit cargo across the coast for the mafia

Scene: night-time at the harbour. A fog surrounds a small fishing boat. Two suspicious Italian-looking men are standing on the pier. Through the fog, lit up as the nearby lighthouse light sweeps across the cobbled ground, I appear, in a navy-blue hand-knitted fisherman's jumper, with buttons up the side of the neck. I'm smoking. As I approach the two men, I take one last drag on the cigarette then throw it into the water.

HOOD 1: We were worried about you – thought you got scared.

HOOD 2: Yeah, we're real sorry to drag you away from the party.

ME: OK, cut the crap, wise guys. Let's get this thing over with.

HOOD 1: Now you're talking.

ME: Got enough fuel?

HOOD 2: Yeah. But we wait a while. Lie low. We don't have all the cargo. It's due real soon.

ME: No, we must go now. It's too dangerous, we'll get caught. We must leave by midnight. After that these shores are patrolled – it's not safe.

HOOD 1: We call the shots. We'll leave when we have everything on board. You just do the driving. The boss wants it this way.

ME: Now listen here, I won't do it. We made a deal, the deal was I'd do one more job then my debts are paid off. That's when we say adios. Getting caught wasn't part of the deal.

HOOD 2: I'm thinking you're not hearing me properly. We leave when our guy gets here.

ME: Look, no one knows these waters as well as I do. I know this coastline like the back of my hand. I've been a sailor all my life, as was my father, and his father before him. I was even in the Junior Sea Cadets. So don't tell me –

HOOD 3: What's all the noise about? Wanna give yourselves away, schmucks?

A third man I haven't seen before has arrived. With him, handcuffed and with tape across his mouth, is a man with desperate eyes.

ME: That's it, I'm outta here. No one gets hurt, it was in my contract. You said we were just moving some goods.

HOOD 1: We are, but let's say we got a little last-minute addi-tion to our shipment.

HOOD 2: Yeah, a little travel insurance.

ME: I quit.

HOOD 1: Say, hows about we join the party, guys? Pay that pretty Flynn girl a visit.

I turn around and run towards them with my fist clenched.

ME:　　　　Why, you sonsofbitches! Why, I oughta …

I hear a voice cry out. It's Susanne running along the pier.

SUSANNE:　No, wait, my darling! I must say goodbye. I knew I'd
　　　　　　find you here.

HOOD 3:　Looks like she's beaten us to it.

*Susanne looks beautiful in the night; her piercing eyes, her
cheeks flushed from running, her floral shawl clutched around
her.*

ME:　　　　What are you doing here? This is not how it looks …
　　　　　　I just wanna …

She puts her hand over my mouth, and stops me speaking.

SUSANNE:　It's OK, I understand. You have to do this, to be free
　　　　　　of them. I know it's for us. I just wanted to see you
　　　　　　before you …

She bursts into tears.

HOOD 1:　This is all very touching, but we gotta go now. Come
　　　　　　on, sailor boy, get your ass on board.

ME: I promise you, sweetheart, everything's gonna be
             OK. Now you run ahead and I'll join you at the party
             in a few hours.

SUSANNE: I love you. Take care.

ME: Please, I'll be fine. You'll catch your death.

SUSANNE: I'm OK, I'm wearing tights.

*She blows me a kiss. I blow one back and jump on board. The
tugboat pulls off into the fog, until the harbour and Susanne Flynn
disappear behind me.*

I wake up on 27 September very excited to be fourteen. I feel fourteen as soon as my digital clock/radio goes off, playing 'Bright Eyes',
a hit from a few months back. I lie still for a while, my hands folded
behind my head, thinking about the benefits of being a year older,
which so far include being allowed entry into an AA certificate film
at the cinema. But I'd been doing that already.

Mum knocks through the wall.

'Happy birthday, darling, we're just getting up.'

'OK!'

I am anxious to run through to my parents' room to open my
present, but figure I should apply a little bit more reserve, as I am
meant to be growing up. Anyhow, I'd only have to make my dad a
cup of tea, even though it is my birthday. Mum knocks on the door,
as she's been trained to do through the years.

'Can I come in, dear?'

I quickly rearrange my pillows, because I've been sleeping with one long-ways, pretending it's a person, and I'm worried she'll put two and two together.

'Yeah, come in.'

'Happy birthday, dear.' She kisses me and hands me two parcels and some envelopes.

'Thanks.'

'Well, then, how does it feel to be ancient?'

'I'm nearly as old as you.' We both laugh.

Dad shouts through, 'Don't tell her there's no Santa, Spar!'

'I was saving that for later. I don't want to upset her right away.'

We all laugh some more. 'Our Tune' is on in the background, which is a bit sad, so I turn it off, as it's spoiling my celebrations.

I unravel my mum's perfectly wrapped gifts, to find an artist's set, containing pastels, watercolours and a sketchpad.

'Wow! Aw, thanks, Mum.'

Mum gets teary. She grabs the back of my neck.

'Now you stick in there, do you hear?'

'Promise.'

She passes me parcel number two.

'Now, this is from Hector.'

It's an Arena red swimming towel. Underneath are some baby-doll pyjamas. (Mum still trying on the frill front.)

'Mum, these are great.'

'We can exchange them if they don't fit.'

She hands me an envelope.

'This is from your father.'

I open it, knowing it's a cheque, but wondering what the amount is.

'Wow, thanks, Dad.' It's made out for £25, which makes the realms of my spending power endless.

'Hang on, you've got something else.' Mum goes off. The phone rings. I race downstairs to pick it up. It's my gran, singing, sounding like the Queen Mum.

'Heppy Birthday to yoo, heppy birthday to yoo …'

She does the whole song and tells me there's a cheque inside her card, to 'do what I like with'. I thank her, and put down the phone. The second I do, it rings again. It's my Auntie Kay, who proceeds to do the same thing. I thank her for the song and the cheque.

Mum arrives back with a brown parcel, covered in air-mail stickers from the USA. I can see it's from my pen pal, Pamela Maine in Boston, Massachusetts. I can feel it's soft, and therefore must be an article of clothing, which makes me slightly nervous, because I've never met the girl, and she doesn't know what size I am. Unless it's an American flag, which I would be delighted with.

But it's better than that, better than anything I could hope for. The look on my face says it all, as my jaw drops open and eyes light up.

'Oh my God, I don't believe it! It can't be true!'

But it is. A brand new pair of genuine Levi Strauss jeans! I rush to the brown label, checking the waist size, and … it's … correct!

'Yeeahh!' I shout, as I rush upstairs to try them on.

They are miles too long, I can see that the second I unfold them, but Mum can fix that. There is some disappointment in that they are girls' jeans and not boys', so a bit too high-waisted, which makes me sigh out loud. But all this is manageable. I can wear them slightly high, taken up. I feel so happy. My heart is beating fast as I race to school with Valerie, who's made me an Elvis card. I can't wait to get the day over with and rush home to wear my newly taken-up jeans.

The day drags. I'm too excited, and for once leave bang on 3.45pm. My mum has arranged for me and my cousin Fraser to meet in Edinburgh, to go to see *Moonraker*, the new James Bond film. Her and Dad drive me there, and tell me they'll pick me up at Gran's later. As it's a special occasion, and seeing as I'm loaded with cheques, I pay for us to sit in the Pullman seats, which cost an extra five pounds each. There's only a few and they're leather.

The film is fantastic, and Fraser and I love all the same bits, nudging each other during the funny lines and fight scenes.

During the film, when the cinema lights up with explosive scenes, I glance down at my Levi's, and feel content. At the end of the film Roger Moore is wrapped round Lois Chiles, suspended, weightless in a space capsule, draped in a silky sheet. We are transfixed. James Bond turns to a monitor where M has just caught him carrying on.

'I'm attempting re-entry, sir.' And we piss ourselves laughing.

Afterwards, I walk down Bread Street towards my gran's, clutching my *Moonraker* commemorative brochure. I decide to cut through the lane, which brings me out at the house where we used to live, opposite my gran. I look at the doorway, where I used to sit and play when I was little, where an old-fashioned dairy horse and cart would deliver milk, waking me in the mornings as it moved over the cobbled Edinburgh streets.

Yes, I think, putting my hands in my Levi pockets, bracing against an autumnal chill, crossing the street to my grandmother's, I definitely feel different.

ten
october

DATE: 10 October   **DAY: Wednesday**

I haven't written for a while but today was an event I won't forget. I went to the sponsored disco. I confess I have an infatuation about Elaine Duncan. I admit it, I'm in love with her [crossed out and 'fancy' inserted] *but I can't help it. I loved* [crossed out and 'liked' inserted] *her more than I ever have before, she spoke to me a lot and then I met Mark Renton and I went out with him. I felt great. I forgot about her and I went home. I've never felt better for years.*

DATE: 11 October   **DAY: Thursday**

Today after the disco, I've found a cure (boys). If I'm to go out with a boy I really like, I forget about Elaine or Susanne or anyone else I'm attracted to. I was pleased when I got to school and I really felt great and I like David more than ever. But as usual I shot my mouth off about last night. And I don't think I'm going out with him. I feel depressed and I'm still in love [crossed out and replaced with 'liking'] *with Elaine. I'm obsessed with her.*

DATE: 12 October   DAY: Friday
Today (the day before the October holidays) I learnt to keep my mouth shut. I found out that Elaine fancied Mark. She phoned me and she told me to come up. Later we spoke about the past and I told her how I used to feel about her, she took it well at first but later I was in tears, and wished she had never come into my life. Suicide was in my head.

Jackie was the most popular teenage girl magazine around at the time. I reluctantly bought it so Valerie and I could have something to look forward to on a Saturday, which is when we would go down the High Street and buy a copy, then get excited at the pictures of the latest heart-throb, whoever he might be. It was, however, an enormous wrench to move away from a couple of comics called *Spellbound* and *Misty for Girls*, which were aimed at younger girls who weren't interested in boys yet. They were packed with girls' adventure stories, about haunted houses, mysterious places. Plus they gave you the chance to join various clubs by sending them a postal order for £1.50. In return they would send you collectable items, like my plastic Queen Nefertiti necklace, and my mini purse full of calling cards with a masked cat in the top right-hand corner, saying 'Supercat …' And I'd fill in 'Rhona' in the space.

I had often compiled a letter to the *Jackie* problem page, but never sent it off – partly because there was a letter just like mine in the magazine every few weeks, so I knew what the answer would be.

Dear Jackie

I am worried that I might be gay. I like lots of girls and have obsessions about a few of them. I'm also in love with my teacher, even though it annoys her. I think about her all the time. I have always felt like this, and worry that I always will.

Most people at school know. My best friends don't mention it, but I'm starting to get a reputation, and worry that my parents will find out. I would rather not have homosexual tendencies. What will I do?

Depressed Elvis fan (age 14)

'I'm Not In Love' by 10cc played on the radio as I ate my Sugar Puffs.

I loved this song because it had the line 'It's just a silly phase I'm going through', and the word 'phase' was always used in the *Jackie* problem page for girls writing in worried that they were gay. The agony aunt always reassured them, by explaining that their desires, which clearly overwhelmed them as they did me, were simply a phase that they would soon grow out of. Presumably there were millions of girls out there, so obviously gay for life, who felt completely unreassured by the useless advice offered. I was certainly left wondering how long this fucking phase was going to last, given that I was fourteen and so far I'd been in the thick of the 'phase' for four years. I begged for a boy phase, but apart from my pining for the affections of Jamie Ritchie, and the two-week hero-worshipping of a visiting Wesley McAllister, I feared it was never going to really happen.

It's not that I didn't believe the *Jackie* lady. I was sure that she knew what she was talking about. It was just that I seemed to have been bogged down in this infatuation with girls for an awfully long time. I had made – and continued to make – strenuous efforts to move into a 'boy phase', but had found them all entirely unsatisfactory. They were either boys I wanted to be, or they hung out with me because I let them finger me periodically, or they committed the cardinal sin of trying to be funnier than me. Besides, apart from anything else, they just didn't smell as nice as girls.

Elaine Duncan was an attractive, edgy girl who lived in the top estate, half-council, half-private, on the other side of the fields. I'd known her for a few years, and we both attended the same primary school, although I didn't notice her then. We were in the same year, and started hanging around with each other occasionally. I've no idea how we came to be friendly, it was just one of those things you drift in and out of at that age. She was a tough individual, and extremely confident. She wore earrings early on, and lived in the shadow, slightly, of her older sister (who'd left school by then), whom she tried to model herself on. She had short blonde hair, sparkly blue eyes, of course, and nice lips. She had a smallish build and a lovely figure, with very white skin. I was frightened of her, and she took full advantage of it. She had a manipulative streak, almost verging on a stereotypical female baddie in a Bond film.

In a nutshell, she was sexy and she knew it.

Around this time began a game that Elaine started.

One Saturday morning, while my parents were down the High

Street, Elaine rang my doorbell. I was lying on my bed in my dressing gown reading a book of ghost stories that I was too scared to read at night.

I answered the door, surprised to find her standing there.

'Alright?' She was always chewing gum, even early in the morning. Which I thought was strange.

'Alright, yeah?'

'What you doin'?'

'Nothing, just reading.' I felt stupid in my dressing gown.

'Where's yur mum and dad?'

'Down the street.'

'Let us in, then.'

'Alright.'

I didn't know what to do with her now she was in my house. Show her my posters, I suppose.

'Want to see my posters?'

'Go on, then.'

We walk upstairs. I hope she's not looking at me in my dressing gown, because it's an old one of my dad's.

In my room she starts doing that sexually provocative 'I'm mean and I'm bad' act, like Krystle from *Dynasty*. She runs her fingers over the dust on my bedroom furniture. I rarely polished. As a reminder of my two neglectful areas my mum would sneak into my room and write DB on the tallboy, which meant one of two things.

It was dusty enough to write on.

I needed to wash my bra. DB meant dirty bra.

I am very nervous by now, and have no idea what Elaine is doing in my room on a Saturday morning, chewing gum, and not saying much.

She sits down on my bed and looks at me, her head cocked to one side. I'm standing with my hands in a man's dressing-gown pockets.

'Want to see my parents' room?' I have to say something.

'What fir?' Good point.

'Dunno. Just … you know … something.' I shrug my shoulders.

'What's this?' She picks up my book, which I'm relieved about, because it gives me something to talk about, hoping by then my parents will be back. For once I would welcome an intrusion from my mother.

'It's my ghost book from the library. They're all true. I'm halfway through one about a monk who died, in a castle …'

'What you got that fir?'

She starts playing with the dressing-gown cord, wrapping it around her finger as she wraps her gum around her other finger.

'Mine's in the wash. It's just for today.'

She yanks at the cord and my dressing gown opens. I'm not wearing anything and I'm mortified. I grab it back and pull it shut.

'Fuck off, what you doing?'

'Aright, only mucking aboot.'

'What you doin' today?' I change the subject.

'Dunno, goin doon the street. What you doin', like?'

'Probably going down the street later for a bit.'

She gets up again, and walks around the room a bit more, picking up things, still chewing.

'I'm going to get spotlights soon,' I say, pointing up to the light fitting, trying to take her gaze away from my possessions.

Elaine was an attractive girl, and did have a slight Farrah Fawcett-Majors look about her. But I didn't want to fancy her, she unnerved me too much. I couldn't figure her out.

I stand at the edge of my bed and she turns around, pushing me down on the bed. I fall back. She lies on top of me, her face a few inches away from mine, still chewing.

I make no real attempt to get away, but I do wriggle around slightly, not wanting to appear completely defeated.

'You like this, don't you?'

'It's alright.' Of course, it was more than alright, it was the closest I'd got to a girl, apart from the pop stars game with Valerie in the caravan, and holding hands with Angela Wilson at the youth club a year or so back, while playing at spirits in the toilets. However, I was wary of Elaine, and didn't trust her motives.

She moves around more, which makes it more frustrating for me. I feel like Tony Curtis being seduced by Marilyn Monroe in *Some Like It Hot*. The bit where he's pretending to be Cary Grant on the yacht.

'You like it. It's what you want, isn't it?'

'Don't tell anyone.'

'Might.'

'Oh fuck off, Elaine, I haven't done anything.'

I make a concerted effort to push her off. She jumps up, so she's controlling the move. She starts singing a bit and wandering around the room again. Meanwhile I get up and tie my cord tight.

'What are you playing at?' I take the direct approach, which I feel is my only option now.

She doesn't answer. Instead she just does that shrugging the shoulders, raising the eyebrows, fake 'I don't know what you're talking about' look.

I suddenly feel gripped by anxiety. I feel certain she'll tell everyone at school that I started it, and I'll never live it down.

'Elaine, don't blame me, right?'

'Going to the sponsored disco?'

'Yeah.' I'm happy that she's asked me that, because it may mean she's prepared to forget the whole thing.

'Who ye goin' with?'

'Valerie probably.'

'See ye there, then. Gotta go.'

And with that she leaves my bedroom and makes her way down the stairs and out the front door, just as my mum's Fiesta pulls into the drive. I quickly dress, shaking and feeling sick, because I know that something terrible will come from this. I think about sending my problem letter off to *Jackie* magazine, but delay it again.

he sponsored disco, which was in aid of Help The Aged, was at the Brunton Hall. The idea was we had to get as many sponsors as possible, and engage in non-stop dancing for the duration of the disco, which lasted from 7 to 11pm. Usually the discos ended around 10pm, but as this was for charity and would be supervised by adults, we were allowed a late night.

'Have a nice time, then, the pair of you,' my mum says to Valerie and I, as I pop my head round the door to say goodbye.

'Don't overdo it,' says my father.

'Dad, it's a non-stop sponsored disco – you have to overdo it.'

'Let's see what the pair of you look like.'

I sigh, and drag Valerie into the lounge. We are wearing as near to similar outfits as we can manage. We both have on a pair of pegged trousers that are a bit drainpipe at the bottom, with braces and a blouse underneath. We're also wearing our matching hacking jackets, with scarves made from the same material, draped around our upturned collars. I wear no make-up. Valerie is wearing some lip gloss.

'Very smart. Now look after one another.'

We both say 'we will' at the same time and head off.

As soon as we get to the Grassy Bit we can see Jamie Ritchie, leaning against a fence with McIrish and Kev Moffat.

Jamie gestures towards us, his hand masking a cigarette.

'Draw?'

'Aye, aright.'

'Aright.'

'Goin' to the disco?'

Valerie says yes. I nod, because I'm in the middle of inhaling.

'Get yis doon then.'

We all walk down the hill towards town.

'Go the back way,' says Jamie. I know what that means – it means towards the rugby pitch. It means railway, and railway means sex stuff. Jamie makes a trumpet noise through a blade of grass that he's blowing between his cupped hands. Kev does the same, and tries to compete for who can blow the loudest. I feel a bit dizzy from the cigarette. Jamie is wearing a Wrangler jacket and jeans, and a brown Adidas T-shirt with cream piping around the neck. He walks, with Kevin, slightly ahead of me and Valerie. McIrish walks out to the left a bit, picking up shiny bits of paper in case it's money. There is a breeze coming off the sea as we reach the open space of grass that leads to the railway.

When we reach the bottom, Jamie gestures to the railway. McIrish pulls out a bottle of Woodpecker cider from under his jacket and takes a swig. Jamie takes it after him, and it's passed around until we've all had some. We hang about by the big old tree on the outskirts of the rugby pitch. McIrish is peeling bits of bark off while we finish the cider and Jamie has another cigarette.

'McIrish?' says Jamie.

'What?'

'Fuck off the now, eh?'

'Fuckssake.' McIrish reluctantly does what he's told.

Jamie lies down on the straw grass away from the tree. He pats the grass with his hand and looks over at me.

'C'meer. Lie doon.'

I look at Valerie. We both smile a bit, but try to look pissed off.

Valerie lies down next to Kev, and I take my place next to Jamie. There is no more dialogue for a while as we all fall into place.

I wasn't sure whether I was going to be issued with Jamie that night, because often it changed around – sometimes he would prefer Valerie. It all depended on how he felt. However, Valerie was a year younger than me, and out of respect for her older brother, who was older than us, Jamie would do nothing but snog her. I, on the other hand, was always available for anything he felt like.

Tonight is no exception, the cider and cigarettes opening up the realms of possibilities to him even more than usual. We all start snogging. There is little movement anywhere and no sound. Jamie's mouth is pressed tightly to mine. Both Jamie and Kev are small-mouthed kissers.

While deriving no sexual pleasure from this at all, certainly nothing like how I felt with vampy Elaine lying on top of me in a threatening manner, I did feel warm, and content to be engaged and interlocked with my hero in some form. Even if it was a narrow-mouthed kiss. Jamie tasted of tobacco and cider, but it was pleasant. He generally did have nice breath, and smelt nice all over. His hair was clean, his clothes were always fresh on that day and smelt of fabric conditioner, and on nights out such as this he would wear Brut 33, which was very powerful. He wore a thin gold chain around his neck, which his mother bought him for his fourteenth birthday. When he moved around to kiss my neck it rubbed up against my face. I could feel him sucking.

'Dinnae give me a love bite,' I say, panicking slightly.

'Promise, a winn'ae.' And with that, he steered clear of the sucking. Jamie was frequently covered in love bites to mark his various conquests. The marks on a boy's neck stood out as a symbol of sexual popularity. On a girl, however, it was just another way of looking like a slag. During the youth club antics the year before I had many bites all over my neck and tits, but had no desire to live through the abuse that came with it again.

Jamie moved his hand on to my tit. I let him keep it there – it was only, after all, about the hundredth time I'd let him do it. I fear that at eleven or twelve I may have been the first girl at primary school to let so many boys touch my tits, always followed by the pointless request of 'dinnae tell anyone'. Only to find out, in the playground the next day, that the boy, whoever he may be, had told every other male member of his year that 'Rhona Campbell gave us the top half'.

Sadly, it hadn't been long before I'd given them 'the bottom half' as well.

I rarely touched Jamie, however, not unless he asked. It was just something you didn't do, or had no desire or drive to. That came much later on.

This night we wouldn't be doing much, because we had to be down at the Brunton Hall and on the dance floor by 7pm, otherwise we weren't allowed to enter.

'The thing starts soon, we better be goin',' says Valerie, taking a break from Kev's mouth.

'One mair minute,' Jamie says, so we all go back to kissing. He soon stops and jumps up. Jamie and Kev walk ahead. Valerie and I brush the grass off our hacking jackets.

'Have I got any marks on my neck?' I ask her, pulling my blouse open.

'Nuh. Huv I?'

'Nuh.'

We follow the boys.

'MCIRISH!' bellows Jamie along the railway. In the distance McIrish, who's been hanging around, stops, and leans against the wall backing on to the football pitch.

'WAIT THERE!'

the Brunton Hall is packed. In the foyer, there are tables laid out with small bottles of Vimto and Red Cola. The toilets are packed too, with girls smoking and drinking cans of Tennent's. They are all talking about either fights or boys. Valerie and I are waiting in the queue, when Elaine Duncan comes in. We do the 'hiyas'. She's chewing gum. The chewing is bigger than ever. She looks right at me. It makes my heart jump, and I feel all weak and anxious. I long to be back on the bed with her on top of me, playing the ridiculous game. I'm confident now, after the cider, that I'd play things very differently if we did it again.

'Let's see.' She pulls open my jacket to have a look at what I'm wearing.

'Nice pegs.' She nods and chews together.

'Let's see you.' She does the same with Valerie.

'What you wearin'?' Valerie does the same with her. Elaine's wearing tight Omega stretch denim that really shows off her bum shape, which is close to perfect, and a pink Simon shirt with a grey corduroy bomber jacket.

'I like that.' Valerie hooks her finger in Elaine's silver-spangled disco belt.

Michael Jackson's shriek at the start of 'Don't Stop 'Til You Get Enough' begins, and everyone, including us, forgets about the toilets and rushes through to the dance floor, to various shouts of 'A fuckin' love this!'

The DJ spoils the song a bit by droning on halfway through about the Help The Aged campaign, and how we are 'gonna have sore feet tonight!' He also asks, 'Are we havin' fun, folks?', to which a couple of boys shout, 'Fuck off, ya pof,' which makes everyone laugh and the DJ shut up.

Me, Elaine and Valerie dance in a three. Valerie and Elaine look around constantly as we are dancing. I look at Elaine, which makes my heart feel as though it's hurting. I can smell her perfume every so often. I think it's Charlie but I'm not sure. It could be one of the many Avon brands floating around the room tonight. Valerie is wearing a necklace that says 'Valerie', which is all joined up. Elaine's looking over at Mark Renton, a boy in my class with red hair and lots of freckles. I am a terrible dancer and have always had the same dance – my arms come out to the side and over as though I'm doing the front crawl. Elaine is sure of herself when she dances. I catch sight of Jamie, who's dancing with a girl in the year above us. There's no sign of Susanne Flynn or Alison Calder, thank goodness, because I've got enough on my plate with Elaine, who right now is draining me with desire.

We dance for most of the four hours, but the organisers relax the rules and let us wander around the edge of the hall, go out for drinks and use the toilet. Effectively, the sponsored disco has no rules: it's just the same as any other disco, except for the DJ going on about 'Who'll raise the most cash for a good cause?'

'Oops Up Side Your Head' plays, which everybody loves, but I hate. We all scramble around to find people we want to sit behind and in front of on the floor. I end up in front of Mark Renton and behind Elaine Duncan. I want everyone to leave the room, except me and Elaine. I want to be sat there alone with her, my legs around her. The song on this occasion is over far too quickly, and next thing we're up on our feet to The Nolan Sisters. Mark Renton hangs around near us and taps me – East Coast for asking to dance – and the boy with him taps Elaine. I find this annoying, because I want to dance with Elaine, but there is no such thing as tapping another girl. Dancing with a friend, though, is a different matter and entirely normal. I decide I should make the most of it because at least I won't feel odd and different, and by dancing with a boy I won't draw any attention to myself. In fact, if this progresses maybe everyone will forget about all my mistakes of the last year and my queerness will be cancelled out.

By the end of the night I've danced a few times with Mark Renton and Elaine has danced a few times with his mate. Valerie has danced with a nondescript boy from her year I didn't even know existed.

Inevitably, the slow dancing begins, with the ever-painful 'Three Times A Lady'. None of us are taken for this, so we stand around drinking Vimto through a straw. I can't bear to hear the song any more; it's a killer. I wonder, once again, if I will ever have anyone to 'Thank for the times that they've given me' or whether I'll always be locked into this nightmare of fantasy and frustration. Elaine has hardly said a word to me all night. It's as though she's a different person from the one I had in my bedroom the other day.

'This is it, folks, this is the last one. Better make the most of it …'

We all wait with anticipation to find out what the last record is. The DJ stalls playing it for a minute, to keep us guessing. Someone shouts 'GET ON WI IT, FANNY!' and Earth Wind and Fire's 'After The Love Has Gone' begins. I can see Mark Renton approaching with his mate. Valerie's already been snogging for about five minutes without a break, so they just move into the mooning position – East Coast for slow dance. Elaine moons with Mark's mate, very close to Mark and I.

It's nice to dance with a boy. I feel cared for and normal, something I rarely experience. But that's all it is. Nice. The way my body, heart and soul feels when I lightly brush arms with Elaine Duncan, as Mark Renton and I moon around on the crowded dance floor, is very different. That feeling is all-consuming. But I have to try and like Mark more. He is no Jamie Ritchie, but no one is, and I have to face it, I am never going to get Jamie properly. Not when there's a million Carol Cowans in life. I should make an effort. He's a nice boy, though slightly defective with his redness, but if that's all I have to put up with for a quiet life, away from hysterical girls who report me to guidance every ten minutes, then that's the way it has to be. Yes, this will definitely be good for me. I could start wearing dresses again, get more into coffee mornings round Carol's house, study hard, wear a bit of make-up, wear ankle socks and sandals in the summer. I'll stop thinking about kung fu, and like kissing Mark more …

I watch Elaine storm off before the end of the song. I want to run after her, but have to be strong and stay with Mark, who has asked to walk me home. He notices me anxiously trying to find her, my eyes darting around the room.

'Your mate's awright. She's with Davey – he'll see she gets home.'

We leave the Brunton Hall and walk through a lively High Street up to my estate.

Valerie and the other boy are walking ahead of us. Mark and I hold hands, which feels good. I notice that I am making an attempt to feminise my walk slightly, but I am aware that all his mannerisms feel more natural to me than my own. Mark is very tall and walks on the road quite a bit, while I walk on the pavement. I wonder where Jamie Ritchie has walked to as we pass his house, his bedroom light still off.

I stop at the end of the Grassy Bit, not wanting to stand outside in front of my parents' house snogging. We stand still, looking at each other. He bends down and kisses me, in a more probing way than before, because it marks the end of the evening. But it is just as boring as all the other kissing we've been doing. It isn't his fault he's boring, it's mine, and I have to learn to live with it.

a s I went to bed, I marked that evening out as a new period of me making a concerted effort to like boys in general, and Mark Renton in particular.

I felt happy when I woke up the next morning, and managed to put Elaine Duncan, Susanne Flynn, Alison Calder and Miss Carlisle to the back of my mind for once. On the way to school, Valerie and I chatted about the night before. We told each other how much we fancied our potential new boyfriends. I had a spring in my step that day, as I fantasised about all the school discos to come – including the Christmas one with mistletoe – and all the Valentine Days I could look forward to now that I belonged to a boy and was no longer a freak. At school, I told as many people as possible that Mark Renton and I were an item. Then I ran into Mark at break time, looking pissed off.

'What d'ya tell everyone for? I havn'ae said anything yet tae anyone.'

'I didn'ae say anything! Things just get spread around, don't they?'

'I'm no goin' out wi ye, I didn'ae say that. Just take it easy a bit, like?'

'Fine.'

I was hardly heartbroken, but I did feel like a desperado for escalating things in my head so quickly.

Later, at home, the phone rang. It was Elaine Duncan, wanting me to come up to her house. I dropped what I was doing – pretending to have my own radio show in my bedroom – and jumped on my bike, pedalling up to her house on the top estate.

It's a Friday night. Her parents are out. She answers the door but doesn't say anything, except,

'C'mon, upstairs.'

I follow her up closely, looking at her arse as it moves around in stretch denim.

I feel sick and nervous again.

'Sit down.' She points to the bed. This is it as far as I am concerned. No more fucking about. I am not going to be intimidated.

'What's the score with you and Mark, then?'

'Nothin', what d'ya mean?'

'You ken I fancy him, don't you?'

'Elaine, I'm not going out with Mark. He's chucked me anyway. I'm no bothered, you can go out with him.'

I don't understand this girl, and can't make any sense of any of her words or actions regarding our strange and sudden friendship.

'What if I told folk what you're like?' She begins pacing up and down the floor of her bedroom. 'What if I said you came on to me in your room the other day, and that you loved it?'

'Elaine, please stop, I'm begging you.'

'I'm goin' tae phone your mum and dad.' She rushes down to the green phone at the foot of the stairs. I race after her. She picks it up. I snatch it from her.

'Take it if you like, but I'm telling everyone tomorrow. I'll go to your mum and dad's house.'

This is the worst threat so far. I'd managed up till now to keep all my other antics at school and down the railway out of reach from my parents. I had a close shave once, when a fat little boy younger than me stood outside my house for a few minutes shouting 'Lemon!' the year before, but I chased him and punched him without my parents finding out. But if they ever did, I would have to run away for sure.

I want to pinch myself in Elaine's room. I can't believe her bizarre behaviour. She's effectively blackmailing me.

'I could ask for money.'

'Alright, I'll give you anything. Just stop, please, you're doing ma head in.'

'Are you queer?'

'Nuh, I don't think so.'

She pushes me back on the bed and sits on top of me. I realise, suddenly, that she has just been teasing me about everything.

'Do you fancy me, like?' says Elaine.

'If a tell you, will you promise not to go mental?'

'Promise.'

'I do fancy you a bit.'

'How long fir?'

'For ages. More since the other day. I dunno.'

'Eurghhh, that's disgusting.'

'Please, don't go on about it to anyone. Please, Elaine, I'm begging you.'

She jumps up again.

'Can you get out ma house, please?' She stands by the door gesturing for me to leave.

'I don't understand what I've done. I'm sorry.'

'Ma sister's back soon. D'ae ye want me tae tell her what you've told me?'

'No, please.'

'Well, you better go.'

In a sad way, I actually think I'm getting somewhere. This is the least hysterical reaction to my declarations of love so far. She is disgusted, but there is no screaming and crying.

We both say 'see ya', which is strange, considering the conversation, and I head home.

The next day, she was back on the phone to me as though nothing had happened. We became friends and I got used to her strange nature. There were to be many more lying-on-top-of-each-other incidents, but they never amounted to anything.

It was always a sign of a family emergency when my mum took me to the freezer centre. This meant only one thing: my mum was going into hospital at short notice, and stocking up was needed. She had been waiting over the past few weeks for a bed at the Edinburgh Royal Infirmary, and her GP notified her to be on standby.

Mum had suffered from the skin disease psoriasis all of her adult life, a hereditary disease that her grandfather had suffered from, though no one knew what it was at the time. Mum used to tell me that when she was young she was treated like a leper – not allowed in public swimming baths and discouraged from trying on clothes in shops.

Although the treatment for this disease had progressed from when she was a young woman, by the time I was fourteen it was still pretty basic. Mum would get to a point in the year when her skin was so broken and itchy and painful she would be hospitalised for periods as long as two months. In hospital she would be bandaged from her neck down to her ankles. The bandages were thick, and she looked truly mummified. Every day the same ritual: she would be covered with tar, then talc over the tar, then the bandages. The treatment burnt her all over. Every few days she would be doused in warm oil, to help loosen the scales, then it would be rubbed off. Every other year she would receive blasts of ultra-violet treatment through a machine that would leave her face bright red and puffy.

When not in hospital, she would have to treat her skin herself every day at home. Smear it in tar. At its worst, her body and hair produced enormous scales, which would lie around the house and over the sofa. Mum would hoover at the start of every day, and one of my regular duties – as well as walking the dog after school and putting the potatoes on – was to hoover before mealtime. (Dinner was always perfectly timed, just for the start of *Crossroads*.) At night, Mum would rub oil into her hair, and pull it up so it stood on end for around an hour. With a comb, she would pull the scales to the surface, on to the ends of her hair, then pull them out and wipe them on a towel. She would then attach the rubber shower-head to the kitchen sink and lean over while I scrubbed her hair with medicated Polytar.

'Harder,' she commanded me. 'Really get into it!'

Sometimes in the evenings, before she went to bed, she would ask me to help apply creams to her back, where it was impossible for her to reach.

She would sleep with a special sheet and pillowslips that would be permanently stained with the oil, much to my gran's dislike. My gran didn't like my mum hanging out 'dirty sheets' to dry. In my gran's world, having dirty sheets was one of the worst crimes you could commit. It would make the neighbours think badly of you.

So off we went to the freezer centre for Findus pancakes, and frozen veg and pizza. Mum began preparing loads of homemade soup, ladling it into Tupperware boxes. She upped her labelling of everything in the freezer, so that Dad and I wouldn't get confused between human food and the dog meat.

She packed a small suitcase with toiletries and nightdresses, and made sure I understood where all her items of clothing were, in case, once in there, I'd need to bring stuff up for her.

Then, one morning that week, in the middle of October, she got the call saying treatment was available from that night.

She made me sit down and write a thank you to my American pen pal for the Levi's I'd received on my birthday, while she tied up some loose ends and made some calls. She showed Dad and me where her address book was, in case we had to contact anyone for any reason. She brought two chops and an apple pie out the freezer for our dinner that night, and told me to stick at my homework. Mum then cuddled Hector, who looked extremely sad, and left in the car with Dad to go to Ward 47 (Dermatology) at the Edinburgh Royal Infirmary.

eleven
november

heinz tinned soup always reminds me of my father's illness. By now it was practically all we ate, apart from the odd times my dear old gran was able to come down, taking time away from looking after her brother, my Uncle Hebbie, who was increasingly frail. When she did manage to visit us she'd bring with her a beef-steak pie from the butchers. I started coming home for lunch from school because Dad was getting visibly worse, and I wanted to keep an eye on him. He was increasingly moody and lethargic, doing virtually nothing except eating a little and going to bed. The doctors had been pleased with his progress, and he had been expected to return to work later that month, but I could see that wasn't going to happen. Soon after Mum left for hospital he went rapidly downhill.

In the first week of my mum's stay in hospital, Dad made nightly visits up to town to see her. I would join him when it wasn't a swim night. Other than that we both went at the weekends. When we couldn't make it, a rota was organised with my gran, my Auntie Rona, my dad's two brothers and my Auntie Kay and Uncle Jim.

In front of Mum, both Dad and I lied about how we were doing at home, with no reference to the tinned soup situation. Visiting was two-to-a-bed only, so I'd often wander off around the corridors of the infirmary so my mum could chat to people. I always remembered to take home her nightdresses to wash before the next visit; my grandmother and I did this between us.

By the second week in October, Dad was failing to make the evening visiting hours and swapped with my grandmother for the afternoon slot. He told my mum he was tired because he was getting better, and therefore doing more during the day, rendering him exhausted by night-time. But it was a lie, and a desperate bid to keep from my mother the fact that he was getting weaker all the time. I played a part in the lies to help everybody: I didn't even tell my gran, whom I could always turn to. I didn't know what to think about my father's condition, so I tried not to think at all. Instead, I continued to swim, and cried, while holding on to the dog.

Throughout this time, I never missed a swimming session. I would look forward to it even more than usual, viewing my time in the water, on the treadmill of laps with tumble-turns at either end, as a welcome break from the sad, ill atmosphere of home. Dad would drive me there when he could, leaning against the window with all the other parents, looking into the pool, watching us splashing around for an hour and a half. I would see him smoking the odd cigarette but I wouldn't bother asking him about it because I knew he would lie again. I felt beaten by his smoking and resigned myself to the fact he would never give up.

I had also begun to increase my own smoking. I would steal Dad's when he was asleep early in the evening. It wasn't something I enjoyed, I just did it. I would hide a Regal King Size in my pocket and take the dog down the railway. We'd walk as far as the railway went, then I'd climb the embankment to the highest point, where it was very windy, which made the cigarettes even less enjoyable. There I would puff away, with views over our estate, a miniature Musselburgh in the background, wondering why my father was permanently chained to such an odd addiction.

I started wearing different clothes to school. I had grown tired of my school uniform, which I'd worn and looked after meticulously since school began. I also gave in to my desire to wear trousers most of the time. This helped me feel less self-conscious when talking to the various girls I was infatuated with. Flat shoes also made it easier to race round the school corridors, tracking down Joan Carlisle.

I became particularly attached to a pair of fawn cords and an orange V-neck Shetland jumper, and spent most of this time in them. With age, and time moving on, it felt inappropriate to remain in my beloved tracksuit out of school hours. Instead, I would wear my one pair of jeans and an old discarded Levi's sweatshirt. I had fallen victim to fashion ignorance before, and got so severely slagged off for it at school, I didn't want to go through it again. I was officially the last girl of my age to move from knee-length socks to tights. Other girls, it seemed, couldn't wait to wear bras and tights, and experiment with make-up. I, on the other hand, felt bereft without my red Kays catalogue tracksuit with Union Jack flag sewn on the right breast.

Tights were a complete bastard. Although I appreciated them on other girls from a visual perspective, on me they only added to my perpetual resentment of being female. In the winter it was a struggle getting up and down to school – a 25-minute walk – wearing heels and nylons, the wind and rain belting your shins.

Finally I gave in to the cords. Then I eased in the school shirt with the cords, worn under a V-neck jumper and blazer. At long last, I was going to school dressed as a boy. I also opted for carrying my books by hand and discarded the school bag. This gave things a more American college feel.

But school wasn't getting any easier.

I used to hate travelling from class to class, but certain parts of the school were unavoidable. I would dread certain routes that would take me past grade-A nutters shouting, 'Fuckin' lemon!' Lemon being Scottish slang for lesbo.

I would stare ahead, not reacting, walking on until the shouts faded, or until I turned a corner.

There was a narrow staircase from D to A floor by the science labs. Whenever I walked down it, I had to duck a shower of gobs of spit coming from above. Mainly they missed, but sometimes I would end up entering my next class covered in it.

In English, we were reading a book called *Consider the Lilies* by Ian Crichton Smith. It was a story about a proud old Scottish woman living in the Highlands, struggling to keep her croft while getting a complete shafting by a bunch of English bastards. I became very quickly involved with any story or situation where someone was the victim of a terrible injustice.

One day, I walked into Joan Carlisle's biology class, pulled up a stool and joined everyone around her desk. She was looking at me oddly, something I'm used to, but she seemed a little nervous, or concerned. The class were muttering to one another, when Miss Carlisle stopped the lesson and looked at me.

'Rhona, I think you should go outside and clean your jacket.'

'Why? What is it?' I asked, assuming I'd failed to dodge the spit again.

'Just take five minutes to go and look at your jacket. I think you've got something written on it.'

Some of the class snigger. The more sensitive ones, like Susanne Flynn, look awkward and down at the floor.

I leave the class, dreading what I'll find. Outside, in the corridor, I remove my blazer, to find the word 'queer' chalked on the back. I have no idea how it had got there. But there it is. That word from the Jeremy Thorpe trials, that thing I knew I was but must hide from bad people as much as possible, until I was far away from this heartless town and all its occupants. I rub at the chalk frantically with my fist, stopping every time someone walks past, but it will not disappear. Finally, to add insult to injury, I have to go back into class, jacket over my arm, and ask Miss Carlisle for an 'excuse me' note – which I later add to my collection – so I can go to the school nurse. The nurse unlocks the girls' toilets so I can gain access to water and paper towels. After some intense scrubbing the 'queer' fades, and I return to my class, who mention nothing of the incident.

DATE: 11 November   *DAY: Wednesday*
Today is a day that I will remember for the rest of my life. My

Dad was taken ill and has been put in hospital 3 days ago, his condition was getting slowly worse.

My dad has been ill for a year, and yesterday my Mum broke down in tears for an unknown reason, today she told me that my own dad whom I love with great respect has lung cancer (due to smoking) and he's going to die in a while, he does not know it. But now I would give up everything for my dad to be well again for I love him more than I've ever done before, I told my mum today that she must promise never to cry again. My dad (said my mum) thought he was well and looking bright today. But now even though the odds are 100-1 he's going to die I am going to try everything to save him. I'm praying, sticking (?) in at school. And most of all hoping that he will live. I love my dad.

One afternoon, in the first few days of November, I arrived home at lunchtime to find that my father had completely changed colour. He was yellowish – Elastoplast colour. He was in his dressing gown and pyjamas, though that wasn't unusual. I found him hunched over, sweating and clearly feverish. His hair had fallen over his face and he no longer seemed my tall dad of six feet three inches. He seemed not much bigger than me. He had sick stains down the front of his dressing gown. I felt ill with fear looking at him. He was burning a pot of something. I could see a tin of Heinz sausages and beans on the kitchen top. I was angry.

'What are you doing?' I snap.

'You have to eat – you must keep your strength up.' He dishes me out the burnt meal.

I try to eat it. I have a lump in my throat, hoping my dad won't see the tears in my eyes, scared to blink in case they fall down my face. I can't swallow the food. My dad collapses in his chair, exhausted. I go upstairs to the toilet, to be as alone as I can, to cry. The bathroom walls and floor and sink are sprayed with sick.

Blank.

I go downstairs. I'm crying in front of him by now, but suppressing it as much as I can.

He points at me from his chair.

'You promise me you won't tell anyone about this? Promise?'

'You need to see a doctor.'

'I don't want anyone to know and I don't want your mum finding out. Do you promise me?'

'I promise.'

'Now off you go to school, and don't worry about me. OK?'

I nod and leave. I don't remember walking to school. I got there without thinking. I was just glad to leave the house and feel the wind on my face.

When I came home from school at the end of that day, Dad was in his bed asleep. He didn't get out of his bed for four days. I brought him up cups of tea, only to bring them down again, cold, hours later. He ate nothing and hardly spoke. When anybody phoned, I lied, and made excuses for him. I lived on more Heinz soup and macaroni cheese.

The dog was different; he seemed lethargic and his ears were down a lot. He sensed my sadness, and would sleep on the end of my bed at night. It's the only time he ever did it. When I cried he licked my face.

I made a decision at the end of the fourth day, having hardly spoken to my dad, to take the situation into my own hands.

Later that night, when Dad was asleep at around 9pm, I had a tin of Heinz tomato soup and left to visit my mum, to tell her the truth. I took two buses from Musselburgh to get to the hospital in the centre of Edinburgh. By the time I got there visiting hour was over and it was dark outside. I was in tears by the time I reached my mum's ward. I went to her bedside and confessed everything: how Dad had been in pain for weeks and in bed for days, how he'd hardly eaten, and how I was living on tinned soup. Mum cried, and told me to bring her clothes into the hospital the next day so she could come home. I felt as though I had betrayed my father and started something very big. I also felt guilty about my mum having to leave hospital before her treatment was over. A kind man, visiting a lady a few beds down from my mum, offered to run me back to Musselburgh, and I left the ward, still sobbing. The man steered me out, with his hand on my head. I looked back, and saw the wife of the man sitting by my mum's bedside, holding her hand while Mum sobbed into a tissue.

the next morning, I woke up and checked on Dad. The room smelt very bad, so I opened a window. Dad turned over, clutching his back.

'How's it going, kiddo?'

I could barely look at my dad these days without my leg shaking or nodding my head manically, while raising both my eyebrows to appear active and OK, avoiding tears.

'Alright. I'm off to school. See you at lunchtime.' I closed his bedroom door, knowing that by lunchtime everything was going to change. He was rarely compos mentis, and hadn't even noticed me sneaking into his room the night before, scrabbling about in Mum's wardrobe, grabbing some of her clothes.

I kissed the dog and headed straight for the school secretary's office.

Mrs Harley was a fairly surly woman who looked like Kenneth Williams. She knew me, through the visits I'd made to the headmaster for the odd incident or two.

'Yes, Rhona. How can I help you?'

'Miss, I can't be at school today. I've got to take these clothes up to the hospital for my mum, because she has to wear them so she can come home because my dad is really ...' (Complete outburst of tears.)

Blank.

Mum and I arrived home in a taxi. I stayed out of the house, while Mum attended to Dad. I walked the dog and hoped Dad wouldn't be mad with me.

Dad begged Mum to give him one more night to get better before she called for a doctor. She agreed.

The next morning he left in an ambulance again. This time lying down.

My father was admitted to the Eastern General Hospital, then, soon after, for reasons I was not told, he was moved to the Northern General where he had been earlier that year.

I found it hard to see him. He looked worse than ever, but somewhere inside of me, I believed he would recover. I had no reason to think otherwise because so far, as far as I knew, nobody knew what was wrong with him.

I would sit on his bed, in my school blazer, showing him my various schoolbooks, as my mum had instructed me to do. She said it would 'take his mind off things'.

I often took Hector and lifted him up to the window, holding his paw and waving it for my father to see. This made him laugh. He'd wave back to us, his hospital name tag wobbling around his tiny wrist. I would often meet my cousin Fraser and my Uncle Sandy at visiting time, and we would go out to the gardens and play, or walk to the hospital sweet shop. I hated the drive to the hospital, it was so far away, and after a while I grew agitated and resentful of the amount of time I was spending going there.

Most Tuesdays, for my entire life, my godmother, Rona McIntyre, had visited my mother. We all had dinner and chatted, then she would go home around 10.30. They never deviated from this routine. If one couldn't make it that particular Tuesday, for whatever reason, they would not suggest meeting another night that week; they would wait until the next Tuesday.

I loved my Auntie Rona coming. I loved hearing her ranting about her boss, and all the trials her job entailed.

This particular Tuesday, I'm sitting on my dad's chair, which is mine when he's away. *Butterflies* is on TV. I love *Butterflies*. I love it because it seems real and depressing, and people seem disappointed with their lot in life. Not only that, but they talk about it – and Wendy Craig has fantasy scenes about jacking it all in and running away with Leonard. I'm half watching the TV, but I'm also concentrating on the conversation coming from the kitchen. It's between Auntie Rona and Mum.

I sense something terrible again. So does the dog. He comes into the lounge from the kitchen with his ears down and sits beside me. I want to find out what's happening in there, but I'm too scared. Mum is crying. I definitely hear the words 'can't cope' from my mum.

The play-out theme tune starts. 'Love is like a butterfly ...'

Mum is crying louder, but I can't make out what she's saying.

'Soft and gentle as a ...' I must go through. I don't want to, but I have to find out. I can't stand sitting there any longer. Soon the tune will stop, and it will be obvious that I'm sitting there anyway, able to hear them. So I get up and walk through.

I have never seen my mum like this before. She's leaning back against the sink, her face a mess, all red and puffy. She has been crying a lot. Her hair is messed up and standing on end, which I know means she's been pulling it up, running her fingers through it in despair. My Auntie Rona has both her hands on my mother's shoulders. Next to my mum, on the kitchen top, is our decanter of whisky, half empty. I look down and see my mum has a glass in her hand. The lump comes back in my throat.

'What's wrong?' I ask, meekly.

Auntie Rona turns round. Mum doesn't acknowledge me.

'Your mum's just upset, that's all. She's just tired with everything. Go and watch the telly.'

I know that's all a lie, but wish I didn't. I go back into the lounge. I can't stop thinking about the whisky, and wonder about the significance of it. My mother is an occasional, social drinker. Tonight she looks like Sue Ellen.

I look at the dog. The dog looks back at me.

Blank.

It's three days later. It's evening. I'm crossing the landing from the bathroom to my bedroom when my mother calls me.

'Rhona! Come through here, will you?'

Fuck. Fuck. This is going to be very bad.

I have been avoiding closeness with my mother, because I just can't cope, and I don't think she can either.

I go into her bedroom. She pats her bed.

'Sit down, will you, dear.'

'I don't want to.' As if standing will make it go away, whatever it is.

'Please, I want to talk to you.'

We both sit down. She holds my hand, which I hate, because it makes me want to cry and I know she's about to tell me something earth-shattering. That's what sitting down is for.

'Your dad has cancer, and he's going to die.'

Shallow breathing, panic, heart racing, head spinning. I want to punch the wardrobe, the wood stained in the shape of a giant rabbit, which used to scare me when I was young. I would run into my mum and dad's bedroom and cuddle up between them, the sound of their electric clock making a comforting tick.

'When?'

'Doctors said any time. Could be in the next few weeks or months. At the very most, he will live six months.'

'No! Bloody doctors, what do they know? They're crap, they know nothing. He'll be OK. It's a mistake …'

'No, Rhona. Listen to me. This is very important. Dad is going to die, but he doesn't know it. He doesn't know he's got cancer, and you mustn't tell him.'

'Why not?' This seems like madness.

'Because if he finds out he'll give up completely. You mustn't tell him. Promise.'

'He'll get better. I'll start going to church again, and I'll pray, and be good, and stick in at school, and he'll be fine. He's not going to die! He'll be alright! It's not possible …'

'Darling, promise me to help your father. Don't tell him.'

'What will I do when I visit?'

'Just continue chatting about your swimming and how things are going at school.'

I nod, slowly, staring at the floor, thinking. Six months?

Blank.

the next time I visit it's harder than the other times, because I know he's going to die, and he doesn't. I find it difficult to look him in the eye. I want to cry and throw my arms around him, beg him to try and get better. I sit on the edge of his bed, looking at the wall opposite.

'Swimming's going well.'

'That's good, kiddo.'

'Tell your dad about your times.'

'Oh yeah, I got good times for breaststroke – beat my personal best.'

'Great stuff. How's school?'

'Yeah, I'm thinking about joining the debating group next year. My English teacher thinks I would be good at it.'

I feel sick at the mention of a next year and could punch myself for saying it.

'I'll get Hector.'

I leave to get the dog from the car to take to the window to wave at my father. My mother goes into her purse and gives my father change for the payphone. Through the pane of glass, I watch my mum and dad's lips move as they talk, unable to hear them. My father twists round in his bed to wave back, and my mother tries to muster a smile for all of us.

At the end of the afternoon, which was a Saturday, Dad walks us to the end of the corridor. He's wearing a blue dressing gown with darker blue piping. He holds on to the wooden handrail along the wall, provided for people having difficulty walking. It takes him a while to move. He shuffles, no longer seeming the giant that was my father. We kiss him goodbye and walk away. He stands until we reach the double doors. I turn around before I walk through them. We both wave at each other again even though we're not far away. He looks very yellow.

That's the last time I'll see my father.

A few days later he telephones from a payphone the nurses have wheeled over to his bed. He's had some tests; a gland from his neck is being looked at. I stand in the hall on the big red phone at the bottom of the stairs, listening to all the information. He sounds bright and cheerful; things feel better. The tests could be a breakthrough.

'You'd better put Mum on, my ten-pence pieces are running out.'

That's the last thing my father will say to me.

friday, lunchtime, I'm nearly home from school. I always arrive home at 12.50 and leave again, after lunch, at 1.25. I'm wearing my cords, with a shirt underneath my orange Shetland jumper and blazer. There's a chill in the air, but it's a bright day. I walk over the

Grassy Bit, having just left Amanda McDonald, my school walking partner at that time. As I turn the corner from the Court into the Drive where we live, I see my Uncle Joe's blue Triumph in the visitors' parking space in front of our house. I'm delighted. I love my Uncle Joe and Auntie Ella. They rarely visit unexpectedly, and work during the day in their jewellers shop in Edinburgh. I can't wait to get into the house and joke about with them – I'll use it as an opportunity to show off and be entertaining. I wonder if my Uncle Joe will have any new jokes. He, my dad and my Uncle Sandy always compete to see who tells the best one.

My key goes in the lock; it turns to the right. Before I'm fully inside and I've taken the key out the lock and put it back in my pocket, my mum is moving towards me. The house feels quiet; there's no Auntie Ella. I'm in the centre of the lounge. My mum grabs me and puts her arms around me. Close to my left ear she says, 'Rhona, your dad died at five past ten this morning.'

My body is limp. I want to throw up. I don't cry. My Uncle Joe stands in front of a set table with half-eaten lunches on two plates and a pot of tea.

'I'm sorry, Rhona.'

My Uncle Joe is crying a little.

'Come on, Rhona, you've got to eat something – we've got to keep our strength up.'

I stand in the kitchen, leaning on the Formica surface with one hand. Mum and Uncle Joe retake their places at the table and continue eating: sliced boiled ham, Heinz spaghetti hoops and a slice of bread and butter folded over. There are side plates. I find this annoying.

'Rhona, please eat, darling.'

'Don't want to eat. Bloody doctors, useless bloody crap doctors, bloody useless!'

I want all this fucking food thing to stop. My Uncle Joe's still got his jacket on. I pour myself a pint of milk and add some powdered Raspberry Nesquik to make a milkshake. I stir it, and drink it like a man drinks a pint.

I finish it and pick up the same schoolbooks I've just brought back, even though they don't match my next classes.

'You don't have to go to school, dear,' says my mum, as she half eats while sniffing and wiping away tears.

'I do. I want to be out the house.' And I leave, without looking back at the Triumph or saying goodbye to them.

I march to Amanda's house. She's not ready. I'm early. She invites me in, brushing her hair. Her mum is talking to me, but I don't know what she's saying.

'My dad's just died. Can we get going, please?' I announce.

Amanda and her mum become tearful. I'm moving from foot to foot. I don't want to stop. I can't stand still or look at them for fear of collapsing. I must hold it in. Must keep moving hands, and legs, keep my eyes wide open.

We walk to school. I don't know if Amanda's talking to me or not. It's the fastest we've ever walked to school.

We walk in to the science department on the ground floor.

'See ya,' I say, tersely, to Amanda. The corridor is filling up. I run into a classmate of mine, Julie Peterson.

'What's wrong?'

I must look pale or something, for I haven't told anyone else.

'My dad's died.' Just as Julie is making a big song and dance, Miss Carlisle walks down the stairwell, towards the lab doorway we're standing in.

'What's going on?'

'Miss! Rhona's dad's died.'

She touches my arm.

'Oh, goodness me, I'm sorry. Are you alright?'

I break down.

I spend the rest of the afternoon sitting with Miss Carlisle between the science labs in an adjoining room, where we sit across a desk and talk. Another science teacher, Mrs Malcolm, sits with me when Miss Carlisle has to go to classes. She offers me a Tic-Tac, which I accept. We sit for a while, finishing the box. She occasionally cries, telling me about the death of her own father.

My guidance teacher joins us for a while and asks me if I'm OK.

I don't feel anything, nor do I talk much. I'm just so glad to be at school with the teachers beside me.

Joan Carlisle has to go to a lecture theatre for a while to teach a class. She takes me with her, and I sit at the back. She explains to the class that I'm not very well and have to be there for a while.

It's 3.45. I'm exhausted, but I don't want to go home. I don't know what to expect, and I'm frightened to face any more, to see my mum upset. The house is claustrophobic. I want to stay the night in school.

Miss Carlisle stays as long as she can with me, along with Mrs Thomson from guidance. When the school empties and the cleaners arrive, just when it's getting dark, they tell me to go straight home and be with my mum.

I wander out into the playground. I'm the only one there. I think about all the other kids, going home from school to their various routines, watching television until their parents come home from work. I feel terribly guilty that I'd complained about visiting my dad at the Northern General.

I walked the longest way home, over the Roman Bridge, past the swans. I didn't care about Susanne Flynn being in the flat opposite. I felt empty and totally alone in the entire world, drifting.

The street lamps were on, and the air was all smoky and cold when I arrived outside my house. The curtains were pulled. I stood and watched for a while before going in. When I did, I don't remember anything for a while.

Upstairs in my room I began playing my tribute records to my father.

When he was in bed and my mum in hospital, I had moved the hi-fi into my bedroom and it remained there.

I began with Tony Bennett singing 'I Left My Heart In San Francisco', one of my dad's favourites. Then Perry Como, 'It's Impossible'.

I stood in the middle of my bedroom, with my headphones on, remembering my father promising to buy me a white double-doored wardrobe with mirrors for my eighteenth birthday.

The doorbell rang. I ran down to answer it before my mum. It was my gran. She had a small suitcase. A taxi drove off in the background.

'Gran, I'm still going swimmingstillgoingswimmingright?'

My gran sighed, and moved me to one side.

'Let me see your mother.'

She went into the lounge. I closed the front door and went back upstairs.

A few hours later, the car pulled up outside with all the swimmers in it. I let Mum answer the door to one of the parents. I heard her telling them. Then she called for me to come down.

I was going to the Royal Commonwealth Pool to watch my team-mate Heather Stewart compete for a place in the under eighteen Scottish team. Everybody in the car said they were sorry when I squeezed up next to Douglas and William. I didn't say anything.

In the pool I sat with Douglas, William and Heather's mum and dad, cheering Heather on as she swam to victory and made the team.

I stared into the pool – the pool where my Auntie Kay had taught me to swim – from high up in the spectators' area. I remembered how, a few summers ago, Valerie and I found 50 pence in the pool and handed it in to the janitor's office. The man accepting the money was rude to us. I went home and told my dad, who phoned up and complained that the man was a bad example to children who were trying to be honest, and I felt he was my hero once again.

When I returned home it was after ten o'clock. Twelve hours had passed since my father left the world.

In bed I wrote and wrote and wrote.

'The Event That Altered My Life'

8 am   *This morning I felt rather ill for no particular reason. I got up and got dressed at the usual time. Like every other normal day, I have the same for breakfast, and I went in for my friend Amanda at the usual time of 8.30 am.*

9.05 am   *I arrived at school, I never really thought about my dad today, only the fact that I was to go up town tomorrow for a jacket. I moaned about being out all day on Saturday, and not really letting on at that time that going to see my dad was taking up most of the time. I went to my first period class, Anatomy, and Miss Carlisle made an embarrassing remark by saying I've been following her recently. I took it seriously and went in the huff.*

9.45 am   *I left my class and went to English. I felt rather sick so I walked slowly along the corridor to English. When I arrived there, I got sent outside the door with my friend. Then I went in, and all through the period I set up cheek to my teacher. Then at the end, Mrs Reid announced that she was going to report me. (Like every other normal day.)*

10.25 am   *I left English and went to Arithmetic with Mrs Meldrum, I sat and did nothing because I didn't feel well.*

11.05 am   *I went out at break and stood about B floor (like every other normal day).*

11.20 am   *I went to French, and we had a great laugh with Mr Meldrum. I never thought about my Dad.*

12.00 pm   *I went to Biology and told Miss Carlisle that I wasn't following her. And she said that she knew and I take things too seriously.*

I then got a Biology test.

12.40pm   I went home with Amanda and I was in a good mood, relieved about Miss Carlisle. We had planned to go down the street after school.

1.00pm   I arrived home, outside I could see a blue Triumph. I knew it was my Dad's brother, Uncle Joe. And I thought Uncle Joe and Auntie Ella had come for dinner. But the moment I put my key in the lock, I knew that something was wrong. My Mum came into the living room, her eyes were blood-shot and my Uncle looked down at the ground when I came in.

'What's wrong?' I asked.

'Your Dad died at 10.05 this morning'. Immediately I felt sick and my eyes filled up with water. My Mum lent on my shoulder as she cried. It was reality but I couldn't believe it.

My Dad, William Campbell aged 55 died at 10.05 am, in Edinburgh Northern Infirmary, of cancer, not of the lungs, not of the throat, but of the whole body, the disease had eaten away his body, he relapsed at 9.45am, and as my Mum went up to the hospital she arrived to find the news that my Dad had died in a coma at 10.05 am.

The few seconds before I opened the front door, panic seized me, all week my Dad's life was like an egg timer, and now the sand had reached the bottom and the time ran out. On Friday 23rd November.

A date that when I grow up I shall never forget. But my Dad was not aware he had cancer, and he never suffered any pain. I'm thankful for that.

And now, as I sit in my room, when downstairs my Mum

and Gran are talking, when visitors come to the door to give their sympathy, and where the ringing of the phone is perpetual.

I remember all the things my Dad taught me, and I go over in my mind all the fun we had.

But all I can regret is the times I've shouted at him. If it wasn't for my Mum and Dad I may still be in a home.

Once my Dad was walking along the street with me, when I was 5 years old. And my Dad's friend passed us in the street and asked, 'what do you want your daughter to be when she grows up?'

And my Dad replied, 'HAPPY'.

Clipping from the *Edinburgh Evening News*

On Friday 23rd November at 10.05 am, at the Northern General Hospital, William Campbell, dearly beloved husband of Jean and devoted loving Dad of daughter Rhona, died peacefully in his sleep. Funeral to be held on Tuesday 27th at 10.15 am at Morton Hall, all friends welcome, please donate flowers to Ward 47 of The Edinburgh Royal Infirmary.

Mum had a lot of things to attend to between Dad's death and the funeral. My uncles drove her to and fro. She went to see lawyers and Dunbars, the funeral directors, near my gran's house in Edinburgh.

I had some things to attend to myself. Outside, as I was walking up the driveway, Valerie called out from her front door.

'Rhona! Come 'ere.'

I walked towards her. Her dad appeared at the door. He was a tall man, the same build as my father. He put his arms around me and hugged me. My head just above his waistline. He didn't say anything, and I appreciated that.

Valerie closed her bedroom door behind her and sat on the bed.

'My dad says I've t'ae cheer ye up, but ...' She burst into tears. I sat beside her with my arm around her, telling her it was alright.

'Man, I'm sorry, Rhona. I loved yer dad too. He was so nice to me when my granddad died.'

Last year, Valerie had appeared at our gate in tears as my dad was tinkering with his car. She was upset, having just heard about the news of her grandfather. My dad bent over the gate and held her while she cried.

'I'm alright. Look, I'll see you later, I've got to go to the library.'

And I walked off down the street, in the same trance I'd been in for days.

The librarian is very kind as I explain I know nothing about Shakespeare, because we haven't started it at English yet. I tell her I have to find this speech from one of Shakespeare's plays that goes:

'Let Me Play The Fool ... Then something about mirth and laughter and being peevish and ... wrinkles ...'

'It's OK, it's definitely Gratiano's speech from *The Merchant of Venice*,' she says, as I run out of words I think belong to the quote.

I feel choked up as I run my fingers over the text, excited at finding something associated with my father's teachings.

'Do you have a pen and a piece of paper, please?'

The librarian hands me one of those slips that gets stuck inside the sleeve of a book. I find a place at the table, and sit down to copy the relevant part:

'Let me play the fool: With mirth and laughter let old wrinkles come, And let my liver rather heat with wine, Than my heart cool with mortifying groans ...'

I don't understand what it means, but I know I've played the fool on so many occasions, and that my father felt very strongly about this speech because he recited it to me so often.

I took the speech as a celebration of life, with the 'rather have my liver heat with wine' part, although that totally confused me because he had mostly used it to demonstrate his disgust at my misbehaviour at school.

I was just glad I had it, and pressed it into the palm of my hand, where it stayed with me for days.

I began my collection of things before the funeral: my father project that no one knew about.

I was playing cassettes in my room when I came across a *Top of the Pops* recording marked 'April'. I wanted to re-use the tape, so I played a part of it to get an idea what was on it. 'Cavatina' by The Shadows played, but I noticed the recording was interrupted by odd pauses. Then, out of nowhere, in the middle of the recording, came my father's voice, telling me to shut up. I pressed rewind to make sure, and there it was again: The Shadows playing the theme from *The Deerhunter*, interspersed with my dad shouting at me during a row we had had while I was taping from the television some months previously. This was the only recording I had of my father's voice. I stood, playing it back and forth, for about an hour. I took it to bed with me with my headphones on, so as not to alert my mother to my bizarre find. I closed my eyes, picturing him sitting in his chair.

'Shut up' … guitar strings … pause … guitar strings … 'Shut Up!'

I lay in bed, staring at the ceiling, listening out for all the sounds in my mother's bedroom. I could hear her turning back and forth in her bed. She would often get up in the night and go downstairs for a while. The first few nights I could hear her vomiting. I did my best to avoid her. I couldn't cope. I was afraid to ask or know anything.

I stood in the study, in my school uniform, where my gran and mum couldn't see me, watching the road for the funeral car arriving. It was 9am on Tuesday 27 November. The funeral was at 10.15, at Morton Hall Crematorium where I'd been for my swimming coach a few months before.

I looked down at my shoes: they were well polished. I was wearing my dad's tie-pin on my school tie. In my top left pocket I arranged one of his handkerchiefs in the old-fashioned way he'd taught me, with two peaks and the initial showing. In the inside pocket I made sure I was carrying the speech from *The Merchant of Venice*, while clipped to the pocket was my dad's 'Serks Services' Parker pen that he got when he retired from the garage. I was also wearing his Tressa digital watch, which my mum had given me the night before. Upstairs, I could hear my mum's gold charm bracelet jangling around. She only ever wore it on special occasions, and added on a charm each year to commemorate a special event.

The house smelt of a mixture of my gran's and mum's perfume, which were powerful. My mum wore Figi, my gran wore Tweed.

I was flicking through a book called *Coping with Loss* that the minister had brought down for my mum that week. On the cover was a photograph of flowers and reeds. The first chapter was called 'Stage One, In The Beginning'.

I hear a car, and quickly return the book to its place in the bureau. At the end of the street, I see a big, black, old car with the bonnet up. Mr Elphinstone, a few doors along, is handing the chauffeur, in a grey uniform and peaked hat, a kettle, the contents of which he pours into the engine.

'That's him putting some water in the engine, Jean,' my gran calls upstairs.

'Rhona! Come up here, please, will you?' shouts my mum from her room.

My heart is thumping. I don't want to cry.

My mum is sitting on the edge of her bed, dressed in black. She looks elegant.

'I want you to have this for today. It was your father's. He got it from his father.'

She opens her hand to reveal a gold ring, a coiled snake with stones in its head for eyes.

I put it on my middle finger.

'These are diamonds, can you see them?'

'Uh huh.'

'It's a snake ring. He wore it on his pinkie, but only at special times.'

'It fits my big finger. Thanks, I love it.'

'Come here,' she whispers, holding my hand and leaning her forehead against mine.

'That's us, Jean!' Gran shouts, opening the front door.

The three of us sit in the back, Gran next to me. It all feels so unreal and floaty. The car drives very slowly because, as my grand-mother explains to me, it all must be timed perfectly. I see an old man on the street, as we drive through Niddrie, take off his flat cap and bow his head as a mark of respect. Some people cross themselves. We don't react. I feel special in the car, as though all the people outside know I've lost my father, and knew him personally.

As we drive into the grounds of Morton Hall, the car stops completely.

'Why are we stopping?' I ask.

No one answers.

A few seconds later, a longer car, carrying a coffin with deep red flowers placed on top, lurches around the corner to meet us.

'There it is,' says Gran. I want to scream at her.

Then it finally sinks in. That is my father's coffin. He is in there. It isn't right; it makes no sense whatsoever. I hate myself at that moment for being such a fantasist throughout my childhood, and wonder if that is why I have so much difficulty in understanding the moment when I first see his coffin. I wonder what he looks like inside there. I want to find out: I haven't seen him for eleven days. How has he changed in that time? I go over the last words he spoke to me in my life.

'You'd better put Mum on, my ten-pence pieces are running out.'

'Shut up' ... guitar arrangement of 'Cavatina' ... 'Shut up' ... 'Cavatina' ... pause... 'Shut up' ... 'Cavatina'.

I see him, waving to me from the end of the hospital corridor, in his dressing gown that has since been washed and I have been wearing.

I see him the day I came home from school with sick down his front. I see him rushing me to the hospital in his arms when I was a little girl after I fell through the glass front door. As my hand is stitched by a nurse, I watch him crying.

I see us, doubled over laughing, with a banana skin he is holding to his nose, a piece hanging down, like snot.

I see his Jimmy Cagney impression, his ridiculous dive off the board in the outdoor pool in Blackpool the week Elvis died. His teaching me to walk with my shoulders back and head upright, saying always, 'Walk Tall Look The World In The Eye.' His golf swing while I caddy for him. Him and Mum dancing around the floor at cousin William's wedding. His unveiling of his strange 'hand and a half sword' present for my mother's birthday. Us carrying a pail, each on the brow of a hill, full of soapy water on a caravan site, and we spilt it all because we couldn't stop laughing. Him and my Uncle Joe doing Al Jolson impressions while Uncle Sandy played the piano. His clicky-finger trick, his bounce-the-orange-off-the-inside-of-his-elbow routine. The sound of his bike engine entering the drive late at night. His drippy nose on winter nights. His big, huge hands stroking over my ear, sending me to sleep, and the last few weeks with him alone in the house, feeding him soup, guilty for not telling Mum sooner, but always loyal to him. But at what price?

Maybe I should have told people sooner? Perhaps he could have been helped?

Four undertakers lift the coffin on to the stand, in a packed crematorium. I watch them closely for any reaction, aware that the coffin contains the weight of my father's body.

There are hundreds of people, people I've forgotten about, people I have only met once, people from our estate, my Guide Captain, and cousins and second cousins I haven't seen since I was little.

'Sit in beside your mum,' orders my gran, ushering me forward to the empty row at the front put aside for us. But I can't.

'Leave me. I want to sit on my own.'

'Just leave her,' my mum says calmly.

I sit on my own, at the end of a long wooden pew, in the front row, with my mum and gran at the other end. I face the granite wall and begin tensing my jaw, pressing the Gratiano speech into my hand.

There are three ministers who each take a part of the service.

Firstly, my godfather, the Reverend Jim Mean, gives the talk about my father. He says my dad was known for his 'wry sense of humour'. Which I like. I remember nothing else about what was said. I do everything I can to avoid looking at the coffin again. I know what's coming next. I remember what's coming next, from Mr Collins' funeral. There is a hymn, during which 'IT' goes for good.

'The Lord's My Shepherd' begins, which increases everybody's crying. I still stay fixed on the wall, not singing, not picking up a hymn book.

Out of the corner of my eye I can see the coffin has begun to move slowly downwards. I turn and look at it, willing it to stay, strongly considering diving across and jumping on top of it, levering off the lid like they do in vampire films and pulling my dad out, just to see him one more time. Now the coffin is level with the surface it's resting on, and all that is showing is the small arrangement of red carnations from my mother and me.

I watch every last flower disappear underneath the building, to meet flames that will finish my father's body for good.

In all this time, in these miserable three or four weeks, this moment, of his coffin starting to move down, is the most painful for me.

Mum and I cry, holding each other, walking past the mourners.

I leave Mum at the door with Gran and my two uncles, as everybody files past them, paying their respects.

I'm sitting in the funeral car, staring ahead, activating the stopwatch facility at the bottom left-hand corner of my dad's digital watch, timing how long I can hold my breath for, when there's a knock on the side window. It's my Uncle Matt, my gran's cousin, a kind, warm and sensitive old man who lives with my Auntie Ruby, amidst a flat full of china ornaments and photographs of their many happy years together. He taps again. I press the button to make the automatic window go down. When it's fully down he leans in and touches my hand.

'I'm sorry,' he whispers, nodding a little as he squeezes my hand.

My eyes fill with tears as I press the button to make the automatic window go up, mouthing the words 'I've got to go' slowly and clearly.

Back at the house, Auntie Rona and Gran prepare two types of sandwiches for the guests: tinned salmon and ham and mustard. Everybody sips sherry or whisky. Uncle Sandy and Uncle Joe tell jokes my dad used to tell. I sit against the radiator, watching everybody.

After I have a cup of tea and a sandwich, I get my books from my room and announce I'm going to school.

'You dinnae have to go to school,' says my Uncle Joe.

'She wants to,' says my mum.

'I want to,' I say.

I don't remember school.

In the evening, I find myself going through Dad's coat pockets on the coat stand in the study. It's a big heavy waterproof he wore on his motorbike when he went to work at the university as a security guard. It had been lying there for weeks but I never thought to examine it, being so used to it always being there. I smelt it, opened it up and stood inside it, wrapping it around me. It smelt of Brylcreem, petrol and rubber. I went through his pockets and pulled out a packet of Benson and Hedges. I rushed out the back door to the bin, and tore the packet, and every cigarette individually, to pieces, before throwing them away.

'Fuckin' bastard killer cigarettes, fuckin' hate you, FUCK OFF!!!!"

I played Elvis, singing 'You Were Always On My Mind', on my headphones, and wondered what world my dad was in now.

I went to bed.

twelve
december

DATE: 25 December   **DAY: Sunday**

Today was Christmas day, it was very sad and lonely without my Dad but I got lots of presents and everyone was wonderful. All the family came down as usual and we had a meal, and the usual routine the only exception was my dad

Mr and Mrs Ritchie and their son Jamie were sorry, The Petersons, who ran the farm shop, were sorry, my teachers at school were sorry, everyone at church and Guides and swimming were sorry. People I ran into down the street were sorry. Even the mafia hoods that bothered me were sorry. Mrs Tate, across the road from us, wasn't sorry yet, because she'd been away for most of November. I ran into her on the corner of the Court and the Drive, while walking the dog. She put down her shopping.

'How's your dad, Rhona?'

Out of nowhere, I start giggling out of nerves, and have to stifle a smile.

'Oh, right, he's dead.'

'NNNOOO!'

Her face contorts with disbelief. This makes me want to laugh even more. I have to touch my mouth to talk to her more.

'When? Oh my goodness ...'

'23rd November.'

'No!'

'Yep, sorry you didn't know.'

'No, *I'm* sorry ...'

I put my hands in my pockets and dance, kicking about a stone on the pavement.

'I'll drop in later and see your mum, but will you tell her I'm sorry?'

'Yeah, I will. I'm sorry, I've got to go.'

It was actually very nice, the level of sorry surrounding us. Everybody at school was extra nice to me; it gave me a window into what it would be like being Carol Cowan. Somebody told me that when I was at my father's funeral, the teacher had told the class that I 'needed support' and to be nice to me from now on.

I was summoned to the school secretary's office.

Mrs Harley looks over her glasses at me.

'Now, then, how are you?'

'Alright, thanks.' I shrug my shoulders as I say it.

'Well, we're all very sorry to hear about your dad.'

'Thanks.'

'Now then ...' She takes her glasses off and puts them down on the desk. 'Now that you and your mum are technically a single-parent family, you are eligible for free school meals. That means you get a red ticket, not the usual green one. I know you do sometimes have school meals, and I just wanted to let you and your mum know about the benefits available to you now. OK, dear?'

'OK, thanks. I'll tell my mum.'

I close the door to the administration office and walk slowly along a quiet corridor in between classes. My head is reeling. I start crying. I lied. It wasn't OK. Far from it. It was awful. My mum must be hiding things from me: we were obviously now officially a poor, single-parent family. What would become of us? Perhaps we would lose the house and have to move in with my gran. Where would we all sleep? I'd have to sleep on the uncomfortable sofa in the living room, turned around against the wall, as I did when my granddad was alive, with my gran's odd neighbours filing in one after the other early in the morning to talk about the stair-cleaning rota and the traffic wardens. Would I have to move school? Or travel miles to this one? When was this all going to happen? When would we officially become poor? I'd have to sit at the special free-school-meals table, where everybody slags you off and no one talks to you. I'd have to sit beside the poor skinny girl with mad bushy hair and dirty socks that gets called 'Annie', and who wears a thin cagoule all year round, and the mad, hyper, shaven-haired boy whose father is in prison and who threatened to open a schoolteacher's face with a can opener. We might be poor but I didn't fit in there.

I'd have to get some more baby-sitting work and try and get a paper round that will pay for my meals, I thought. Meanwhile, I'd have to make my blazer last right through the winter. I pulled the sleeves down over my orange V-neck Shetland jumper. Were we losing my father's estate? (An expression I'd heard on *Crown Court* but didn't understand the meaning of.) On the way back to class I timed my journey by pressing the stopwatch button on my father's watch.

It was not unusual for me to roam around the corridors or further afield, and I had been issued, by my guidance teacher, a special note to show to a teacher in case I was caught. It read:

Please excuse Rhona from class. After the loss of her father, she has taken to wandering around the corridor, and often the graveyard nearby.

It was signed by Mrs Thomson.

Inveresk graveyard sat on the top of the hill next to the school. It was a beautiful graveyard, with views all over Musselburgh and across the Firth of Forth. I wished so much that my dad had been buried there: it would have enabled me to go and talk to him, sit on his grave and be near. But the way things stood, I knew his body was gone. I asked my mum where the ashes went.

'Sprinkled in the Garden of Heaven.'

'What's that?'

'It's a place at Morton Hall where all the ashes are scattered, called the Garden of Heaven.'

'Who scattered them?'

'The men that work there.'

'The ones that were at the service?'

'Perhaps, or the ones that are there to scatter them.'

My mum continued chopping, as I timed how long I could hold myself up by my hands between two kitchen surfaces.

'Do people work there whose only job it is to scatter ashes?'

'I don't suppose so. It would be whoever was there at the time.'

'I wish I could have seen them.'

'No, they're in the Garden of Heaven. That's where they go.'

What a lot of shite, I thought. Garden of Heaven, my arse. They were probably thrown in the bin or among a massive pile of other ashes accumulated that day. Besides, there was no heaven and no God. I was sick of God and the pointlessness of going to church. If there was a God he wouldn't have let my dad die. After all, I prayed during his illness but it didn't help. God could fuck right off as far as I was concerned, and all these pathetic weak, humble, weird people that fill the church every Sunday. I wasn't going to go any more.

I still liked our minister, though, the Richard Burton lookalike.

I walked among the gravestones reading various inscriptions.

'To live on in the hearts of those left behind is not to die …' was a popular choice for the families of the dead in Musselburgh, I noted.

I would have 'Let me play the fool …' inscribed on my tombstone, I decided.

I saw a lady tending to some flowers surrounding a grave, which made me feel jealous. I had nothing to do regarding my father, nowhere to visit. The house was still full of his things but I knew they wouldn't be there for ever. I still carried around with me, in my blazer pocket, the speech and the time-coded report of the day he died. But I needed a shrine of some kind. I heard the school bell ring in the distance and sat down on a bench with the wind howling around my ears. High up, looking down at the playground and the tiny Lowry-type children running around in it, I felt comforted by my surroundings.

I spend the entire day thinking about being poor. I think about it in class, in break time and on the walk home from school with Valerie.

I think I should prepare her for my imminent departure.

'Valerie, guess what?'

'What?'

'I have to get free school meals cos my mum and I are really poor.'

'God!'

'I know. My mum might have to go to court and fight for my father's estate, and I'll probably have to live with my gran.'

'Really?'

'Yep.'

'When?'

'Dunno. Soon, I suppose.'

'When did you find oot?'

'Just back there.'

'Oh no, I dinnae want ye tae go …'

'Me neither. I'm gonna to ask my mum about it when I go home just now.'

'A'right, see ye.'

'See ye.'

In the house, my mum is on the phone for four minutes and 42.3 seconds to Jimmy Sinclair, my dad's best friend, whom I saw cry at the funeral.

'I'd better go, Jimmy, that's Rhona home from school … Uh huh … OK … I will. Bye then.'

She will what? They're planning already. It must be about my father's estate … She had to change subject when I came in … She must be talking to everyone about how poor we are going to be while I'm not around. I thought about the film *Oliver* starring Mark Lester.

'Who was that?'

'Jimmy Sinclair.'

'What were you talking about?'

'I'll tell you later. I've got to rush down to the chemist for my prescription. I'll be back in a minute. Walk the dog, will you, dear?'

You see, I was right. She's avoiding telling me what they were talking about. She'll 'tell me later'. She has to go out and think about how to say to me that we are poor people.

As soon as Mum reverses out of the driveway I play my new game with my dog.

'Hector!'

He runs in from the garden.

'Hector! Where's Dad? Where is he?'

I make my voice happy and excited. The dog goes mad, running around from the gate to the front door, then up on the stool next to my dad's chair, with his front paws on the windowsill.

'Where is he? Where's Dad? Here he is!'

Hector starts barking and whimpering, running up to my mum and dad's bedroom and down again, jumping up on me.

'Let's get him! Let's get Dad.'

I run out to the garden with him, to the double gates that lead up the drive. He starts howling, like a wolf, looking back at me every so often, then up the drive again, sitting dutifully, waiting on my father.

'Good dog.' I say, patting him. 'Where is he? Eh?' Hector paws at the gate. 'He's dead.'

The game stops, and I leave Hector, waiting there, and walk away.

I go up to my dad's wardrobe, a closet big enough to stand in, and surround myself with his jackets and shirts. I drape handfuls of ties around my neck and slide my feet into a pair of his size 12 shoes. Everywhere it smells of him. I cuddle his sports jacket and close my eyes, imagining his voice. I begin rummaging at the back of the wardrobe and manage to find his hairbrush. It's an old-fashioned hand-brush, kept in a plastic slip held shut by a popper. My heart pounds as I open it, to find strands of my father's black and grey hair. I cup my hand around the brush and my nose and take a massive breath and inhale Brylcreem and Grecian 2000. I slide down the wall in the back of the wardrobe, hiding amidst the jackets and trousers, in brown shoes with a white tongue that are seven sizes too big, breathing in the brush as though it is an oxygen mask. Crying.

t he task of getting rid of my dad's possessions had begun. Mum gave quite a lot of stuff to Valerie's dad, because he was the same height, like a couple of suits. And his golf clubs. A lot of his other clothes went to my uncles. I begged Mum to keep the bike another two years for me but she said no, on the grounds that it could be sold for Christmas, and that she didn't like the idea of me riding around on a motorbike because it was too dangerous.

The car was a different matter. I couldn't let that go so easily. I begged, on a daily basis, for her to consider keeping it in the garage until I was seventeen.

'No way,' she replies. 'We have to sell it.'

'Is it because we're poor?' I start sobbing. 'It is, isn't it? Do I have to get free school dinners? Cos I don't want to, Mum.'

'You don't have to get free school meals if you don't want to, dear. And no, we're not poor. I'm going to have to watch things for a bit until I get another job, but we're not poor, and I would never let us lose this house, OK?'

Silence. More sniffling.

'OK, then when I'm seventeen I can get my provisional licence and you can take me out in it.'

'No, Rhona, it's a cumbersome, big thing. I'm not having it sitting there for years. We've got the Fiesta, and I really can't afford to run two cars, darling.'

I hated the lady Fiesta. I wanted the huge red Cortina that my father had promised me for years, after I'd nagged him about painting a Starsky and Hutch stripe down the side.

'Please!' I clasp my hands together.

'No, and that's final.' I can sense my mum is getting upset, so I call it a day.

I was gutted. I sat in the car in the garage fiddling with my dad's discarded Juicy Fruit wrappers, pulling the ashtray in and out. The garage was full of my father. Lots of old biscuit tins, full of screws and bolts and nails. At the end of the garage was a bench, and above it was a magnetic strip than ran from one wall to the other. Stuck to it were screwdrivers and files and spanners. Attached at the left-hand corner was an enormous vice – my father had let me saw bits of wood gripped in it. There was an old set of lockers that Dad had obtained after an office at my mum's work was cleared out. On the front he'd put a cartoon picture of a golfer with wobbly legs delivering a really bad swing. Inside, he kept his clubs and waterproof overalls. I didn't want any of it to go; it would make my father's departure from my life too final. On the other hand, I found it hard to live in a world surrounded by his possessions but without him. I went up to my bedroom for another fix of 'Cavatina'... 'shut up'...

he Musselburgh Grammar School drama group held its meetings in the school assembly hall immediately after school. We sat in a circle listening to the drama teacher, Mrs Taylor, who let us call her Julie. Julie was English and wore smocks and huge chunky wooden jewellery. She spoke rather quickly and excitedly and seemed wide-eyed, stressed and enthusiastic about everything anyone said.

'Right then, everybody, stand up.'

Everybody scraped their chairs along the floor and moved to a standing position.

'And just begin by having a good stretch.'

Most people giggled and started chattering, as we half-heartedly stretched and yawned.

'Come on! Really stretch.'

Now everybody began competing with one another as to who could stretch and yawn the loudest.

Gordon Bain, the boy in my class who mostly got the lead part in all the plays, yawned so loud it echoed around the hall.

'That's it, and shake it off.'

Everybody shook their hands by their sides as though they were freezing.

I loved all this. It was so different from anything else, and all the people in the group were really nice and friendly, straightforward and well spoken. And Julie Taylor smiled at us the entire time. We played a few warm-up games before Julie sat us down to tell us that there was only three weeks to put on the play, which was really no time at all. We gasped. Rehearsals would be four nights a week until then, so if anyone had other commitments they should say so now. I raised my hand and said I had swimming two nights a week, but could possibly miss a couple, it depended. Someone else had recorder practice. Gordon Bain made a joke that he played rugby, which he so obviously didn't because he wasn't sporty at all. Everybody laughed, and I was a bit jealous.

The play chosen by Julie for this year's Christmas production was called *Time Sneeze*, a play about time travel. It was going to be a short, uncomplicated play, and at our next meeting Julie and William Blaire – an eccentric, pipe-smoking, beardy older man who taught biology and got called David Bellamy because he was English – were going to cast us in the various parts. I immediately felt at home with everyone and it took my mind off home a bit.

Sitting next to me in the circle was a girl in the year below me that I'd seen Gordon talking to a fair bit at break times. Her name was Nicola Russell, a quietly spoken, mature girl for her age, with jet-black hair and the most striking blue eyes surrounded with thick black lashes. In the five-minute break, while Julie and David Bellamy looked at scripts, the two of us got talking.

'Hiya.'

'Hiya. Have you been in any of the other plays?'

'No. Have you?'

'No, this is my first one. Gordon persuaded me to come along. I've been thinking about it for a while though.'

'Me too ... My dad's just died.'

'I know, I'm sorry.' She touches my arm.

'How come you know?'

'Everybody knows, I suppose. You know how things get round this school.'

I am struck by her use of the words 'this school' and like her for saying that. As though she, like me, is in the school but outside and aware of all its goings-ons.

Julie claps her hands and pulls the group's focus.

'This is for you,' Mum says, sorting through mail in her dressing gown as I eat my cereal.

'What is it?'

'I don't know, dafty. Open it and see.' The letter is brown and official and addressed to me with my full name, including my middle one.

A year previous to this I had put my name down on the NHS waiting list to have a birthmark removed from the back of my neck. It turns out the hospital had a slot for me this month, at short notice, on 22 December, only three days before Christmas. I desperately wanted the birthmark taken off as I hated it. It was big and covered most of the back of my neck, and it was dark brown and raised. It had always been a considerable size, but had grown over the years. Mum had agreed with me that it was unsightly, especially if I was to 'wear dresses in the summer, where it might catch'. And so we visited our GP and had me added to the list.

Mum says nothing for a while, as I read out the letter. Then, staring out the window, she says quietly, 'It's just one bloody thing after another.'

'It's OK, Mum, it's only a silly birthmark. I may as well get it done, otherwise I'll never get round to it.'

She sighs deeply and looks exhausted. I can hear her most nights and know she's not sleeping, despite being given pills from the doctor.

'Well, it's up to you, if you think you can go through with it.'

'Do you think they'll let me use my stopwatch during the operation?'

'I shouldn't imagine so.'

nicola Russell examined my birthmark as I stood in the assembly hall, my head bent forward, my chin resting on my chest.

'Can you feel it?'

She ran her fingers over it gently.

'No. It's dead. It's coming off. I think it looks quite interesting.'

I was given a small part in the play, and was to star next to Gordon as Smith, the laboratory assistant, who was a man. We both had to wear lab coats, spectacles, with the glass taken out, and, joy of all joys, a shirt and tie. Nicola was cast as an Arabian princess in one of the lands visited by Jake the time traveller, played by a handsome blond boy called Stephen. I had very few lines, but it didn't matter. I was just glad to be able to extend my school days into the evenings, and to be in the company of so many normal people and the lovely

Nicola, who made me feel peaceful. Plus, I had landed a part where I could be a boy and nobody batted an eyelid.

'Do you know,' said Julie, clutching her clipboard, 'that in the early days of performing Shakespeare, the parts of men were often played by women?'

I had begun to dread teatime at home, and loved it when the drama group ran on. I would have a bag of chips from the chippy on the way home so I wouldn't have to take my place at the table with my mum. Teatime was very sad, because we no longer had to extend the table leaf to make it enough for three to sit round. Instead, Mum and I assumed a new position, opposite each other, without mentioning it. When I set the table, which had always been my job, I would have to remember to forget to bring out my father's tablemat. The pictures on the mats were of a glass of wine and various accompaniments: I had cheese on my mat; Mum had grapes; Dad used to have the bread. Every time I wiped the mats and placed them back in the drawer I wondered how long things would go on like this. The careful and secret managing of the loss of my father.

I kept my dad's Hawaiian shirts and two jumpers that my mum had knitted him, his toolbox, which I emptied and filled with my drawing equipment, a blue baseball hat he wore for golf and a black tie to wear in the school play. I continued slipping into his wardrobe for a fix of the hairbrush, and to check it was still there.

The dress rehearsal took place on the afternoon of the first night. Julie Taylor was even more stressed than usual.

'You know what they say, bad dress rehearsal, good first performance!' bellowed Julie, running across the stage picking up bits of fabric off the floor that had come loose from the set.

I was pleased, so far, with my performance, and had learnt all my lines word perfect.

'OK!' She clapped her hands. 'I want everyone IN COSTUME, ready and made up, word perfect, and sitting in the music room two hours before we open. That's five o'clock.' She clapped again. 'Now go and eat your packed lunch, or whatever you must do, but get out of my sight for the next hour. I must be undisturbed. Any questions, ask William.'

She looked over at William and smiled, and he put his unlit trademark pipe in his mouth and made a jokey face back at her, as though he didn't know what she meant. We all laughed and disbanded.

I sat in the music room with Nicola, Gordon and most of the cast members, eating our various sandwiches out of Tupperware and tin foil.

I was sad that tonight would be the first school thing that my mum would have to come to on her own, and wondered if any of the other actors were from single-parent families. I did try to look on the up side and remember that Tucker Jenkins only had a mum, and he was one of my television heroes, by far by the coolest pupil at Grange Hill.

I finished my cheese roll and stared out into space. I was still in costume.

'Are you alright?' asks Nicola, top half a school jumper, bottom half an Arabian skirt.

'This was my dad's tie,' I tell her, pulling it out of my lab coat.

'It's nice you kept it.'

Then Nicola slips her hand in mine.

Nobody seems to notice, and Gordon certainly doesn't care. She keeps it there for a good five minutes, and squeezes it before she lets it go. In the whole time she holds it, I don't say a word.

the play opened to rapturous applause and an out-of-tune school orchestra. Some pupils in the audience giggled. Gordon and I were on in the first scene in the laboratory. Our dialogue was divided up so we had to finish each other's sentences.

Smith: If only we could utilise our database to …

Jones: Create time travel …

The hall lights went up to create a lightning effect. I could see lots of members of staff, including Miss Carlisle, and my mum, sitting, looking teary-eyed. I felt a lump in my throat again.

During the interval, backstage in the music room, everybody was manic. Gordon had more make-up applied, even though he didn't really need any, and the wardrobe mistress attended to a queue of pupils who had torn costumes and buttons missing.

'So far, so good. Well done, everyone!' shouted Julie Taylor, who'd worn a special flowing dress for the evening and pink lipstick I'd never seen her in before.

Backstage, before the second half, Nicola takes my hand again as we are queuing for the toilet.

'Are you alright?'

'Yeah.' I think, for her own good, I'd better warn her.

'You'd better watch, you'll get a bad name.'

'Look, I've heard things about you, that folk say you're a lesbian an' all that. But I don't care what they say, it doesn't bother me.'

And with that she squeezes my hand again and smiles.

the curtain opens and closes twice, and we all line up on stage holding hands, bowing to cheering and some wolf-whistling. We all chant for Julie to come on stage.

She stands in the wings, shaking her head, until we increase the level of noise and stamp our feet.

'JULIE! JULIE!!'

She runs on and everyone cheers some more.

She thanks all the actors for their hard work, the art department, the orchestra, the costume people, and lighting and sound, and the audience for coming. Then we all applaud again and the curtain closes for the last time.

In the dining hall, parents, pupils and teachers mingle. Everybody has tea, juice, crisps and cakes that various people have brought in. I'd brought in some coconut sponge that my mum had baked. That was one of the first things to go. I drag my mum around to meet everyone. She asks me to take her to my guidance teacher and Miss Carlisle, who, I had told her, looked after me the day Dad died. My mum shakes Mrs Thomson's hand, which makes her neck and cleavage wobble slightly.

'Thank you for seeing she is OK. It's been a terrible …' Her voice fades as I move away to talk to Miss Carlisle.

I find her, surrounded by a group of excited first years who are making her laugh.

'Miss! Miss! Come and meet my mum – she wants to say thanks for looking after me.'

I drag her over to where my mum is still chatting to Mrs Thomson, and walk in at the end of the report about my dad:

'... and he never woke up.'

'I'm very sorry, it's an awful thing.'

'Mum! This is Miss Carlisle, my biology teacher.'

My mum thanks her, and Miss Carlisle says she hopes she's OK, and that I'm not too much trouble, and jokes that I am in biology classes, and we laugh. Mum ruffles my hair.

On the way out I say goodbye to Nicola and tell her I won't be at school for the last day tomorrow, or be able to attend the Christmas disco, because I'm having my neck operation.

'That's a shame,' she says, and gives me a hug goodbye.

When we arrive home I see that my dad's car has gone from the garage and I feel sick again.

'Where is it?'

'Tam Cruikshank in The Grove bought it. He said he would tow us and the caravan if we needed him to. That's why I sold it to him, so we can still have the use of it.'

I stand alone in the vast garage staring at the space where my dad's car had lived. I know I will never sit in that car again. A few weeks later he sold it on, and I was to see it from time to time, passing quickly in the town with a different family in it. I stared at it, willing the car to stop because it knew me.

I sit in the bath for ages, till long after 11pm, soaping up the tiles and scrubbing them with the nailbrush, over and over. Then I wipe them down with the facecloth, only to repeat it all over again.

Suddenly, two men appear.

HOOD 1:   So they got you doing this now.

HOOD 2:   Yeah. Looks kinda cute.

ME: What d'ya want, guys? I've got work to do.

HOOD 1:   You tell us what you want. Boss says you've had a change of heart.

HOOD 2:   Yeah, says you might reconsider your plans.

ME: If the money's right, I might.

HOOD 1:   What brought this on? A good honest living got too much for you, did it?

ME: Let's just say, my circumstances have changed.

HOOD 2:   We knew you couldn't stick it out. Once you're rotten you're always …

ME: Shut up! *(I look up from my scrubbing.)* You supply the car and I'll do it. Then I'm out of here. D'ya hear?

I'm out of here, and far away from you guys, d'ya understand?

HOOD 1:   Sure, we hear ya.

ME: So, when do we move?

HOOD 2:   Tomorrow. You'll get a call.

ME: Tomorrow it is, then. Now if you'll excuse me I have work to finish.

The hospital was an old hospital that I'd never heard of before. It lay in its own grounds, miles across the other side of Edinburgh. It was freezing inside and smelt of disinfectant. Mum wiped some tears away as the nurse escorted me off.

'I'll be fine!' I shouted from along the corridor, as my mum waved. I didn't want to let on to her that I was terrified, and that all hospitals made me feel faint and sick now.

I was given a long green surgical gown and told to remove my clothes, except for my pants and socks. It was so cold in the operating room I found it hard to tie the strings on the gown.

I sat on the edge of the operating table, listening to the doctor explaining what he was about to do.

'Now then ...' He looked at my file. 'Rhona. Today we are going to be removing your birthmark.'

Stating the fucking obvious there, then, I thought, exercising my newfound disdain for all doctors.

'We'll start by freezing the area with a couple of injections, then when that's done we'll work at taking it off, OK?'

'How long will it take?'

'Not too long, maybe an hour.'

'Can I time myself?' I point to my father's digital watch.

'No, I'm afraid not. You shouldn't really have any watch on during the operation, but we can time it for you if you want.'

'Doesn't matter,' I say, taking off the watch, but smelling the strap before I tuck it in my cord pockets, hanging on a peg on the back of the door.

Three nurses stand around me. I lie face down on a table, covered in a long, continuous paper towel. My face sticks through a hole at the end, my head surrounded by a towel.

'Now this might sting a little, like a nettle.' As they inject it into me I let out the most enormous scream.

'Now, now, try to stay calm, it'll only hurt for a short while.'

Then he does another five or six like that. I start sweating and trembling and feel as though I'm going to vomit.

'That's it, now keep still. I'm going to begin the removal … Nice and still for me.'

The nurse stands in front of me and places her hand on my head to keep me still as I'm wriggling around. I am starting to have grave misgivings about this whole thing.

The drill starts making as much noise as a lawnmower and blood splashes over the apron of the nurse standing in front of me. I'm really panicking by now, and the more I do, the more I panic them, and the more they do to restrain me.

'Aaaah! No, please stop, I've changed my mind.'

I don't want to call for my mum, because I don't want her to see me like this, even though there's every chance she can hear me screeching from down the corridor.

'Please!' I am sobbing by now, and there's blood everywhere, even on the floor.

'Come on now, you're making this difficult for yourself.' The doctor begins to sound like a Nazi interrogator in a war film. I want to get up and punch him, but one nurse has both my arms outstretched in front of me, rendering me unable to move, and another is holding my feet. I keep shouting that I can feel everything, but they just ignore me and continue. Eventually, I use the nurse's hands to squeeze and give in to the whole thing, sobbing through to the end, wishing Nicola Russell was the nurse.

I sat, slumped against the passenger-seat window, with my mum crying most of the way home.

'I'll never forgive myself.'

'It's not your fault,' I mumbled, totally drained.

I went straight to bed.

In the middle of the night I awake, boiling hot, sweating, with an immense pain in my neck. I feel my glands, which are swollen.

The next morning my mum sends for the doctor, who is becoming a regular feature of our lives by now. He removes the dressing issued by the hospital.

'Oh, my dear,' he says, peeling it off.

'Can I see?'

'No. It's not a pretty sight. I think we should change this and get you on some antibiotics, young lady.'

I feel very sorry for myself.

'Am I going to die, Dr George?'

He laughs, then looks at me sincerely.

'No. You're not going to die, although you might not be having a very lively Christmas.'

He leaves my room, and I feel spiritually uplifted by his attention.

As my mum leads him down the stairs I can hear her say, 'It's just one bloody thing after another.'

'Life does feel like that at times, Jean,' says the doctor.

Christmas morning arrived. I didn't want to get out of bed. I knew my mum was lying next door, feeling the same. Usually, by now, we would all be up, opening our presents. I'd be making my dad his strong cup of tea with two and a half sugars. Mum and I would have coffee, made with hot milk. It was the only day in the year we ever had it. Every Christmas throughout my life, Mum looked out my two Santa sacks – big red sacks with white embroidery. I had had them since I was a child. My mum would fill them with my presents the night before and place them under the tree. Hector would sit all evening guarding them, before going to bed.

We sat with our coffees, surrounded in wrapping paper. I got some new headphones for my stereo, a red and white striped top, some cuddly toys and a paperweight pen. The best gift of all was a racing bike, which I knew I was getting but pretended to forget about. I gave Mum a bottle of Figi perfume and a headscarf I bought at the airport when I was in Italy with the school. I'd kept it safe all this time. Mum and I gave each other a hug and tried not to cry.

Gran, Uncle Hebbie, Auntie Kay and Uncle Jim arrived at lunchtime, and we all tried to stick to our old Christmas routine as much as possible: there was sherry when they arrived; Christmas dinner, with far too many courses, that my mum cooked; the Queen's speech on television that my auntie liked to listen to. My uncles nodded off in their chairs afterwards, the four of us left to do the dishes, which had been my dad's job that one day a year. Then we all sat down to watch *The Two Ronnies*. I passed around the Milk Tray and After Eights, then we had tea and Christmas cake and everyone left around 11pm.

We didn't mention him. Not that day, not that evening, not that week.

With the use of two mirrors, I strain to see the back of my neck, peeling some of the dressing off to look. It's puffy and red with yellow bits full of pus. I stick the dressing back down, wondering whether the woman who gave birth to me knew I had a birthmark.

'What are you wearing?' my mum calls through from her bedroom, her charm bracelet jangling.

'Just a jumper and a pair of trousers.'

'Mmm. I'll just do the same, I think.'

My mum had transferred most of her clothes by now into Dad's wardrobe, and mostly kept bedding in what used to be hers. The brush remained, however, and I checked whenever I could.

'Do you want Dad's ring?'

'Yes, please.'

Mum comes through to my room, opens up the box and gives me it. I put it on.

She looks around my room. 'Would you like to start looking in the Kays catalogue for a new wardrobe?'

'Yeah, please.'

'OK, then.' She looks at her watch. 'Och damn, look at the time! We'd better be going. What will I take? What do you think? Whisky?'

'Yeah, everyone likes whisky, I suppose.'

'I'll put in some black bun as well. I don't think Edith makes it.'

It's ten minutes to midnight, 1979. I'm sitting on the Armstrongs' sofa, with my mum and Valerie. Her mum and dad are in opposite chairs. The television is on, and the Alexander Brothers are singing 'Jeanie McCall'.

'Let's see your neck?'

'Valerie, don't be daft, she can't take the plaster off, that's stupid.'

'She's been picking at it, haven't you?'

'Mum!'

Valerie and I giggle at the way our mums speak to us.

'Right, then, who wants a top-up before the bells?'

A round of 'I'll have one' begins.

Valerie and I are allowed Martini and lemonade, seeing as it's New Year's Eve.

'Five minutes left.'

'Do you want one, Jon?' Valerie's dad shouts upstairs to his son. He calls back,

'Aye, I'll take a half.' The bell rings. 'Will you get that?' he shouts down again. My mum and his mum roll their eyes and laugh a little.

I hear the voice of Jamie Ritchie in the hall, greeting Mr Armstrong.

He walks into the lounge. He's wearing a leather jacket and a V-neck jumper.

'Evening.'

We all say hello, or evening, back.

'Can I get you a shandy, Jamie?' asks Mrs Armstrong.

'Please, that would be gid.'

He pulls a chair from the dining-room table and turns it round, facing us.

'A'right?' he says, winking at me like a grown man.

'A'right,' I say, fiddling with my hair that looks bad. Because of my neck plasters I've been unable to wash it for days.

'How are you, Mrs Campbell?'

'Not bad, thanks, Jamie.'

There's a drum roll on TV.

Valerie's mum shouts up the stairs. 'Jon! THE BELLS!'

Jamie smells of Old Spice, my father's aftershave. Mr Armstrong rushes around with everybody's drinks.

The clock chimes and the fireworks explode down the walls of Edinburgh Castle on STV, forming a sparkly waterfall. Everybody shakes, hugs or kisses on the cheeks. We chink glasses. Jonathan bursts in.

Everyone on Scottish television sings 'Auld Lang Syne'.

Mum hugs me first. I'm swallowing too much. She whispers in my ear as she holds me tight.

'I love you, darling.'

'Well, it's a new decade!' exclaims Mr Armstrong, raising his glass, 'Here's to our good health'.

I look down at my father's watch. It reads 00.00.

1980 flashes on the screen. We sit back down. I make no promises.

epilogue

about three Christmases ago I was at my mum's when, out of the blue, I decided to phone Jamie Ritchie. We arranged to meet. He didn't have much time, as he was looking after his two daughters for the weekend. I learned he was going through a divorce and working hard to buy a new house for himself. We met at his uncle's house nearby, where he was staying temporarily. We were alone in the house, and being Christmas he offered me a Drambuie from the mini-bar. I declined; it was a bit early for me that particular day.

He hadn't changed much at all. He had retained his good looks, remained slim – perhaps lost a little muscle – and still had all his own hair, which is a bonus if you're a Musselburgh man. I felt nervous and a little apprehensive about meeting this man who, without even knowing, had been one of the biggest influences of my teenage years.

We begin talking about the past. He initiates the subject by telling me he has something he needs to say.

'You see, Rhona ...' he begins. 'I have two wee girls now, and I love them with my life, my heart and soul. If anyone was to treat them, when they're older, like I treated you, I would fucking kill them.'

I feel choked up at this point. He continues.

'I treated you like an absolute cunt, and I'm sorry. I was just a young boy. I was a dick.'

I ask him why he never wanted to go out with me properly, and romance me like the other girls. Or dance with me, or hold my fucking hand. At this point I decide to take a drink. He answers my question.

'You were always off-limits, Rhona. We all knew you were gay, and we could n'ae go out with you. To us you were one of the boys, but we all tried to shag you – it's just what we did.'

I remind him about the gang hut and all the other stuff. And he remembers it all.

He takes a long drag on his cigarette.

'Nobody really touched you, though, did they? I mean, really gave you a proper kicking?'

'No, I suppose not,' I say, trying to take something good from it.

'Ken why that is?'

'Why?'

'Cos I wouldn'ae let them.'

Am I to take it that he protected me in some way, that he did care, that I was in some way his sister, or secret girlfriend?

He begins unloading washing from the machine. I notice that his underwear is Armani.

'Nope, at the end of the day, if anyone really touched you they had me to answer to.'

I'm genuinely touched.

'I am truly sorry, though, Rhona. I am. I often think about it, and I cannae believe half the things I did.'

We finish our drinks. He's got to be going, to pick up his girls. As I put on my coat, I tell him how much he, and everything that has happened, has affected my life, and that one day I may write a book or make a film about some of it. He laughs, and tells me that all us media types are neurotic. Which I know already, but it makes me laugh that he knows it.

'Rhona. I've got to say this.'

Oh my God. What? I think.

'It wis that you were gay. It was that you were gay in a small town.'

And this knocks me out. His awareness of it. And he's so right.

As we walk across the lounge to the front door we hug, and I'm remembering his charm. I can't help but ask if he did shag Carol Cowan. Of course he did.

As we are about to leave the house and step out into the grey December morning that smells of sea, he turns and looks at me intensely.

'And I'll tell you another thing, Rhona. After all this time …'

And I have a lump in my throat.

'You've still got the best tits I've ever seen.'

I'm sitting in the conservatory, on a deckchair, at my mum's, writing this book. I'm watching my mother practise her Tai Chi in front of me in the garden of my childhood – a pursuit of hers since her second heart attack and bypass operation. I'm listening to music. It feels like spring has arrived today. My mother moves gracefully between the white sheets on the line, gently blowing in the breeze, going through the 'Snake'. She is concentrating hard and looks peaceful. Things have changed so much in both our lives; almost everybody has gone, but we remain ever-evolving. I watch her carefully. She is unaware. And I think about all she's been through in her life, and me in mine, sometimes together. This woman who brought me up. My mother.